Grammar Rules!

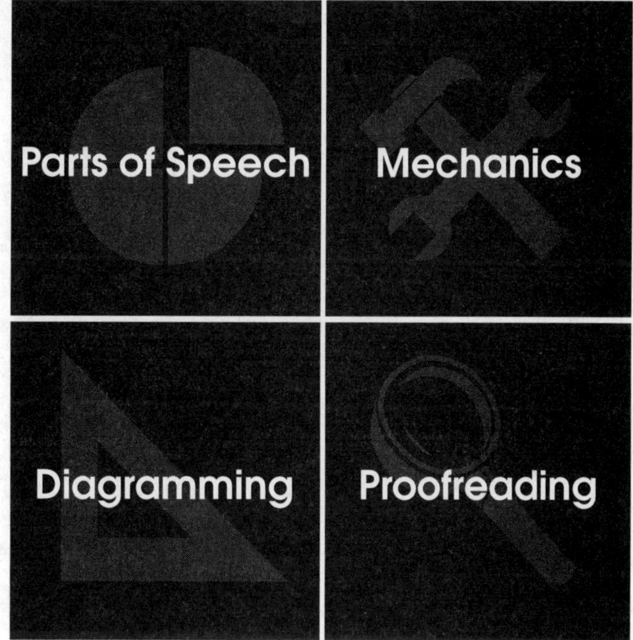

For students, parents, & teachers:
A straightforward approach to
basic English Grammar and Writing Skills

Mary S. Schatz

Published by
Garlic Press
605 Powers St.
Eugene, OR 97401

ISBN 1-930820-02-X
Order Number GP-102

www.garlicpress.com

To the Teacher

This set of exercises grew out of my frustration with correcting college students' philosophy papers. Their papers were full of grammar errors. When I pointed out that a sentence was a fragment because it lacked a verb, the usual response was "What's a verb?" These exercises are designed to teach basic grammar concepts and to show how those concepts are used in correct writing.

The first section of each unit (A) introduces the **Parts of Speech** and teaches the student to recognize them. In a classroom situation where writing is analyzed, students need to understand the vocabulary of grammar. When a teacher points out a dangling participle, the student needs to understand what a participle is.

The second section of each unit (B), **Mechanics**, explains some rule or common error associated with the part of speech just learned. The issues are chosen to reinforce the understanding of the Parts of Speech section and to address the errors commonly found in student writing and the SAT II writing test.

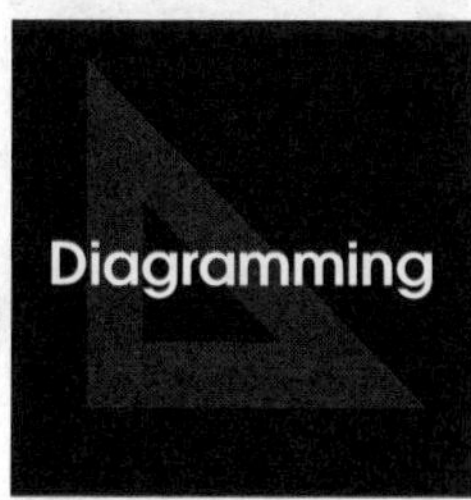

The third section (C), **Diagramming**, teaches the student the structure of our language. Sentence diagrams provide on-going review of all the parts of speech as well as pictorial explanations of relationships of words and phrases.

The final section (D), **Proofreading**, reviews all the skills learned in the previous sections. It teaches students to examine their work carefully for errors. Correct writing and effective proofreading are the ultimate goals of these grammar exercises.

Table of Contents

Lessons 1-10

Table of Contents

Lessons 11-20

Table of Contents

Lessons 21-30

Table of Contents

Lessons 31-40

Table of Contents

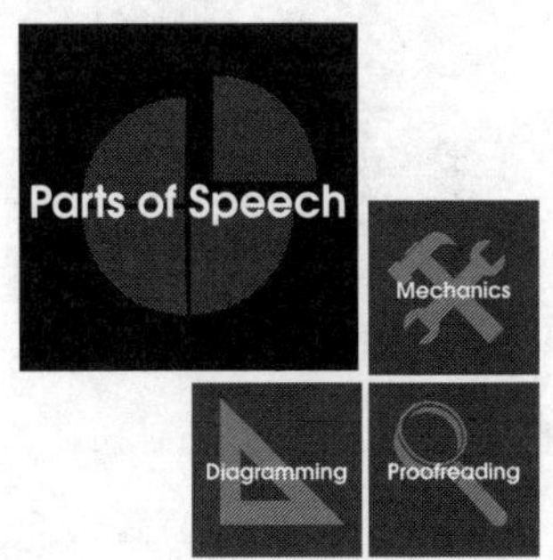

Know Your Building Materials!

A **noun** is a word that names a person, place, or thing (John, barn, hat).

Draw a line under each noun.

1. A nasty dragon ate the teacher. (2)
2. Desserts should be eaten before vegetables. (2)
3. Barbie and Skipper are annoying. (2)
4. Ask Joe and Jim to come. (2)
5. The Beatles were a singing group. (2)
6. Rich hit the ball and then ran around the bases. (3)

Fill in the blanks.

A **noun** is a word that names a ________________, ________________,
or ________________.

Good Mechanics Are Hard to Find

In formal writing, avoid expressions used in speech such as **well**,... or **like**. Instead of slang, choose words that express your meaning exactly.

Cross out slang expressions and replace them with better word choices.

Example: Tarzan was ~~like~~ the ~~coolest dude~~ in the ~~flick~~.

Tarzan was the most exciting character in the movie.

1. Well, he hung out with the monkeys.
2. His lifestyle was totally awesome.
3. His hood was like a jungle.
4. Like, the world is a jungle out there.
5. His buds were animals.

Fill in the blank.

A ________________ is a word that names a person, place or thing.

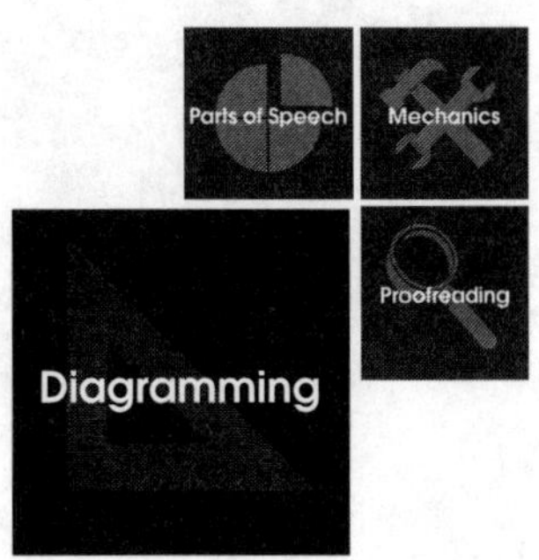

Understand the Structure

Sentence Subjects

Every sentence must have a **subject** and a **predicate**. The **subject** is usually a **noun**. The **subject** is what or who is being talked about. The predicate tells what the subject is doing.

*The **boy** hit the ball.*

In a **question**, the subject often is in the middle or at the end.

*Where is the **hamster** going?*

In a **command**, the subject is understood but not stated.

***(You)** Go to bed!*

In sentences starting with **There is (are)**, and **Here is (are)**, the subject follows **is** or **are**.

*There are the **girls**.*

Underline the subject in each sentence. If the subject is understood, write it in parentheses.

1. The cat ran away with the hat.
2. Where is the cat going with the hat?
3. The man with the funny hair is going to find that silly cat.
4. Watch out for that cat's claws!
5. Those claws are sharp.
6. Under the pine tree, he lurks.
7. Why am I reading about this stupid cat?

Careless Mistakes Can Cause Big Problems!

Careless mistakes can make the difference between a great paper and a poor paper. Proofreading errors can make a paper difficult to read. Sometimes they can unexpectedly change the author's meaning entirely.

Correct the mistakes in the sentences below. Each line contains one mistake.

My little brother john likes to make a snack when he gets
home from schol. He spreads peanut butter on a slice of
bread. Then, he puts broccoli in the blender and mashes it too
a slimy green pulp. Next, he spreads the disgusting green slime
on another piece of bread and makes like a sandwich. Yuck!
Does that sound good to you.

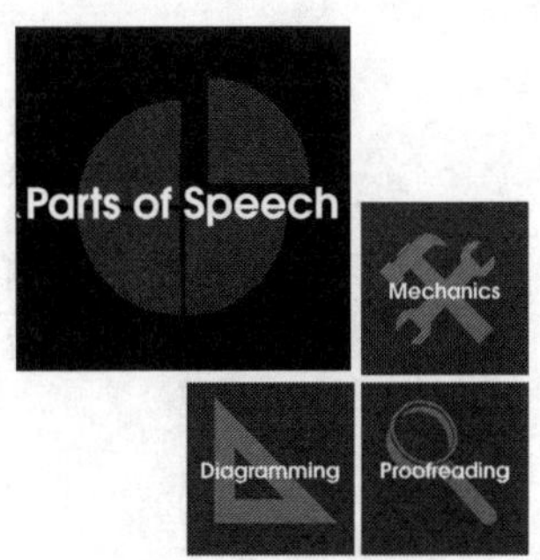

Know Your Building Materials!

A **verb** is usually an action word.

Sometimes action verbs work alone. (The bird **flies.**) Sometimes action verbs need helpers. (It **will** **fly**.) Some common **helping** verbs are the following: **is, am, are, was, were, did, do, could, might, can, may.**

---

*Identify the word in **boldface** as an action verb **(AV)** or a helping verb **(HV)**.*

1. The girl **jumped** in the lake.
2. She **was** swimming to cool off.
3. The lake **may** be freezing cold at this time of year.
4. Tomorrow, we **might** go to an amusement park.
5. I **dislike** roller coasters intensely.
6. My brother and I will **avoid** them if we can.

Fill in the blanks.

A **noun** is a word that names a ________________, ________________, or ________________.

Good Mechanics Are Hard to Find

A **singular** noun names one person, place, or thing (**hat**). A **plural** noun names more than one person, place, or thing (**hats**).

Rules: To change most nouns from singular to plural, just add **s** (bat, bats).

To nouns ending in **sh, ch, s, x,** add **es** (fish, fishes).

To nouns ending in **y after a vowel**, add **s** (monkey, monkeys).

To nouns ending in **y after a consonant**, drop the y and add **ies** (sky, skies).

To nouns ending in **o after a vowel**, add **s** (ratio, ratios).

To nouns ending in **o after a consonant**, add **es** (hero, heroes).

Words that refer to music are exceptions (solo, solos).

To nouns ending in **f** or **fe,** change the f or fe to **ves** (half, halves).

Some nouns completely change spelling (tooth, teeth).

Change these singular nouns to plural nouns.

1. fox ________________
2. woman ________________
3. fly ________________
4. tomato ________________
5. knife ________________
6. child ________________
7. piano ________________
8. rodeo ________________
9. ball ________________
10. key ________________

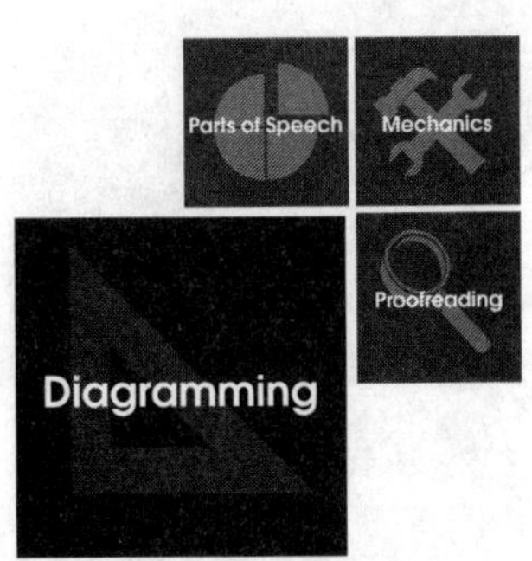

Understand the Structure

The subject of a sentence is what or who is being talked about.

My **nose** is upset.

In a **question**, the subject often follows the verb.

What is that awful **odor**?

In a **command**, the subject is understood but not stated.

(You) Find that rotten food!

In sentences starting with **There is (are)** and **Here is (are)**, the subject follows the verb.

Here is the **cause** of the stench.

Don't be fooled by possessive words describing the subject.

Tom's **sneakers** are the guilty ones.

Underline the subject in each sentence. If it is understood, write it in parentheses.

1. The tiger ate the elephant.
2. After his huge meal, the tiger's stomach began to ache.
3. What was the tiger thinking when he ate that?
4. There is a limit to what the stomach can take.
5. Most tigers know better than to overeat.
6. From now on, don't eat so much!

Fill in the blank

A ______________ is a word that names a person, place, or thing.

Careless Mistakes Can Cause Big Problems!

Correct the mistakes in the sentences below. Each line contains one mistake.

My friend Julie and i like to visit the candy store at the mall.
I like chocolate candys best, but Julie prefers the jellybeans. Of
course, we both like the fried potatos even more, and
sometimes after the candy stor, we visit the food court. Then
we have upset stomachs for the rest of the day

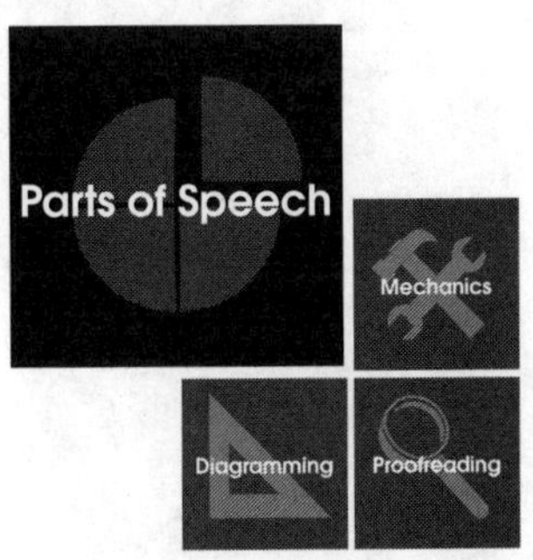

Know Your Building Materials!

A **common noun** names a person, place, or thing like **boy, bathroom,** and **car**.

A **proper noun** is the name of a specific person, place, or thing like **Jesse, California,** and **Toyota**. **Hint:** Proper nouns are capitalized.

Draw one line under each common noun and two lines under each proper noun.

1. The kids on the school bus were making loud noises. (3)
2. Jenny was using bad language too. (2)
3. The poor driver was unhappy. (1)
4. The kids were going to Skyline School. (2)
5. The teachers were waiting in the parking lot. (2)
6. With all the noise, Betty, the driver, was distracted. (3)

Fill in the blanks.

A ____________________ is usually an action word.

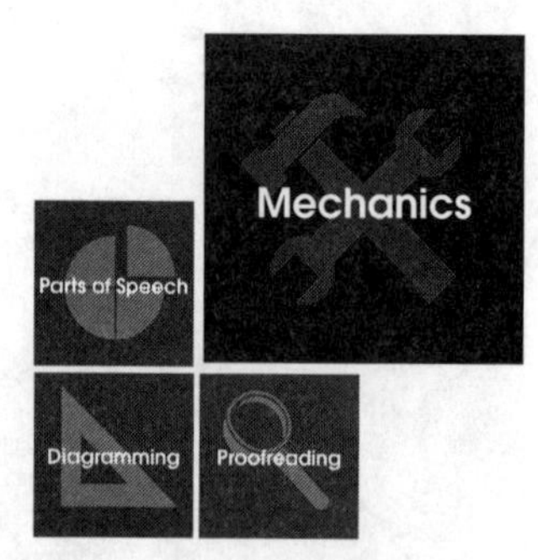

Good Mechanics Are Hard to Find

The verb "to be" can be a main verb or a helping verb. Verbs have different forms depending on whether the subject is singular or plural or whether the tense is past, present, or future.

Choose the correct verb form.

1. Roger (**is, are**) at least ten feet tall.
2. He (**is, are**) growing very fast.
3. He (**was, were**) huge when he (**was, were**) born.
4. His brothers (**is, are**) all very tall also.
5. His sisters (**is, are**) all going to be very tiny.
6. There (**is, are**) seven kids in the family.
7. Unfortunately, the boys (**is, are**) not very fond of basketball.

Fill in the blanks.

Singular Present, Past Tense	**Plural Present, Past Tense**
I am , was	we ____________
you ____________	you are, were
he, she, it ____________	they ____________

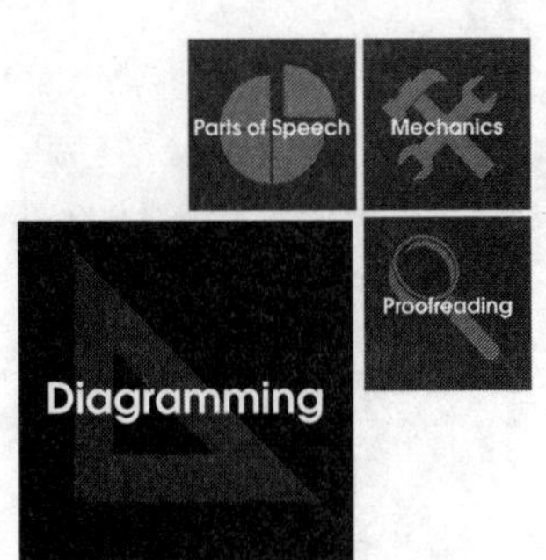

Understand the Structure

Sentence diagrams show the structure of a sentence.

The subject of a sentence is placed on a horizontal line. The verb follows and is separated from the subject by a vertical line.

Articles (the, a, an) are placed on a diagonal line below the word they modify.

Frogs croak.

Frogs | croak

The boy is running.

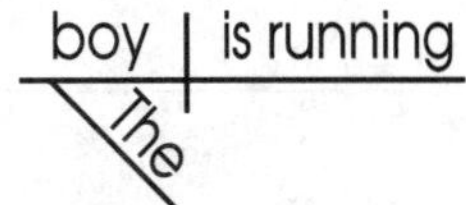

Diagram the following sentences.

1. Trees sway.
2. Bears growl.
3. A wave will crash.

Careless Mistakes Can Cause Big Problems!

Nouns can be **singular** (cat) or **plural** (cats).

Verbs are also either singular (A cat **runs**), or plural (Cats **run**). A singular subject must **agree** with a singular verb.

In parentheses, write the form of the verb that agrees with the noun.

1. A dog (eat)________________________
2. Parachutes (fall)____________________
3. Children (swim)____________________
4. A coyote (sneak)____________________

Circle the subject and underline the verb in each sentence. If they agree, write ***Agree****. If they don't agree, write* ***Don't Agree.***

1. The enormous wave loom over the surfer. ________________
2. The sand on the beach feels hot. ______________________
3. The hot dog taste great. ____________________________
4. Frisbees flies everywhere. ____________________________

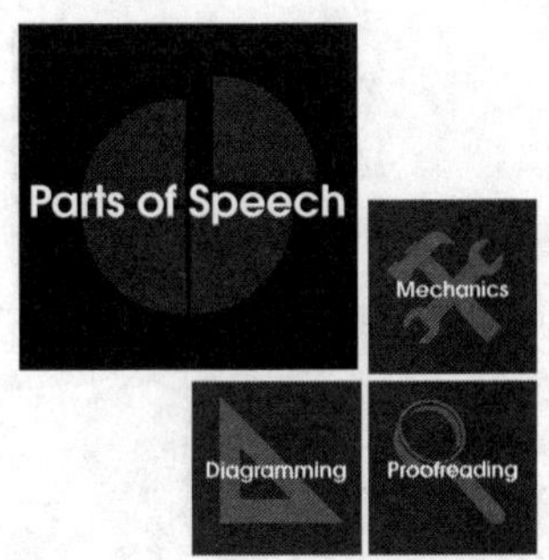

Know Your Building Materials!

Some verbs are action words. Other verbs show the appearance or condition of something. These are called **linking verbs.** Some common linking verbs are the following: **am, is, look, seem, feel, remain, become**. Linking verbs sometimes need helpers like action verbs.

---

*Identify the word in boldface as an action verb (**AV**), a linking verb (**LV**), or a helping verb (**HV**).*

1. I **am** going to buy some donuts now.
2. "You **look** ill," **said** Mother.
3. I **feel** fine, but I will **rest** in case I **am** getting a cold.
4. Maybe I **should** eat some donuts to keep up my strength.
5. The cinnamon crumb donuts **are** the best.

Fill in the blanks.

Run, give, and **go** are ________________ verbs.

Seem, look, and **become** are usually ________________ verbs.

Should, will, and **can** are ____________________ verbs.

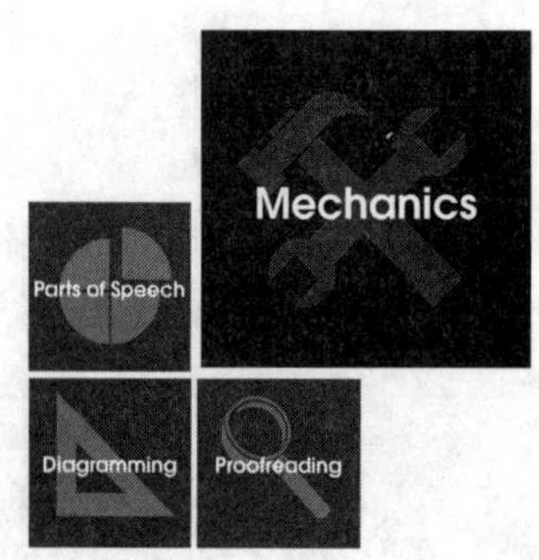

Good Mechanics Are Hard to Find

Contractions are two words (a verb and another word) that are combined into one with a letter or letters left out. Use an **apostrophe** where the letters are left out.

Fill in the blanks.

cannot	can't
I am	______
______	we've
had not	______
______	shouldn't
where is	______
it is	______
______	she'll
you are	______
are not	______

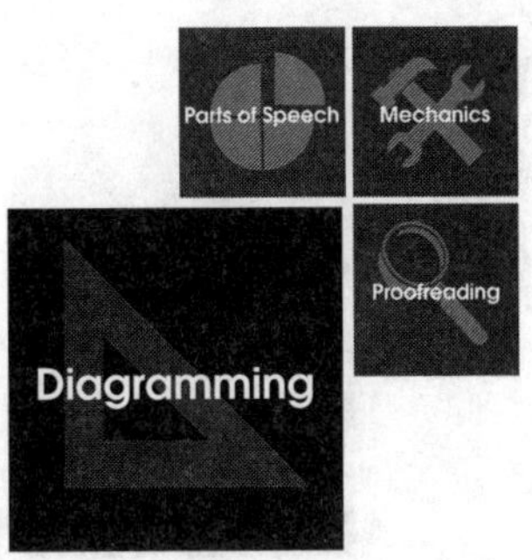

Understand the Structure

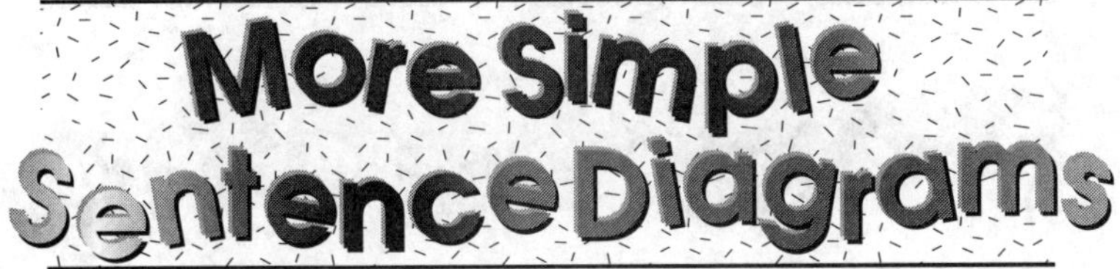

Diagram the following sentences.

1. The ball is rolling.
2. You should come.
3. A beast snarls.
4. Frogs can jump.

Fill in the blank.

A **verb** is a word that names an ________________.

Careless Mistakes Can Cause Big Problems!

Correct the mistakes in the sentences below. Each line contains one mistake.

Jack and Jill is good sports. They lugged that bucket of water
all the way up the hill without complaining. There is many
people who whine about doing anything dificult. When Jack
fell down, he didn't cry even though he broke his crown. Dont
you think it is a bit silly to wear a crown to climb a hill. Still, Jack
and Jill are my heros.

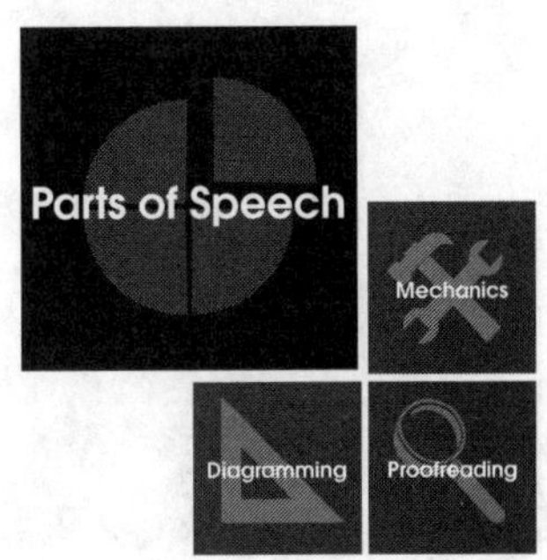

Know Your Building Materials!

Nouns and Verbs

*Underline each **noun** and **proper noun**. Label each verb as an action verb (**AV**), a linking verb (**LV**), or a helping verb (**HV**).*

1. Patty and Jill are going to the mall. (3N, 2V)
2. Jill hopes she will find a new dress for school. (3N, 3V)
3. Jill will look great in a bright colored dress. (2N, 2V)
4. Patty hates dresses. (2N, 1V)
5. Both girls adore the pizza at the Fashion Valley Mall. (3N, 1V)
6. The girls will eat too much pizza and become ill. (2N, 3V)

Fill in the blanks.

A ____________________ shows the appearance of something.

A ________________ is a word that names a person, place, or thing.

A _______________ verb can team up with either an action verb or a linking verb.

An ____________________ shows an action.

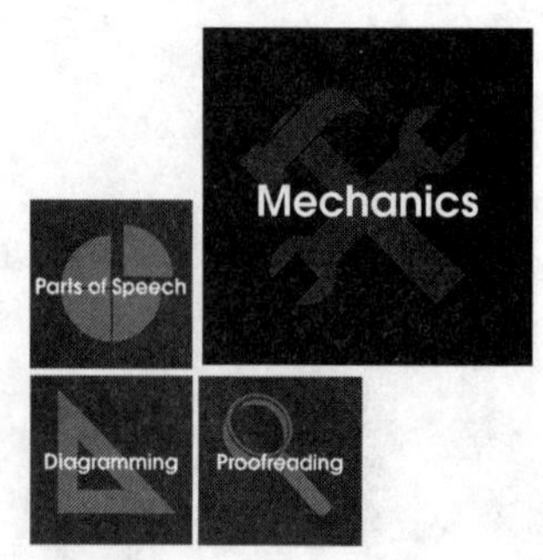

Good Mechanics Are Hard to Find

Fill in the blanks to complete the rules about forming plurals.

1. To nouns ending in **o after a consonant,** like tomato, add ________.
2. Nouns like **piano** that refer to ____________ are exceptions.
3. To nouns ending in **sh, ch, s, x,** like **crutch,** add _________.
4. To nouns ending in **y after a vowel,** like **key,** add __________.
5. To nouns ending in **y after a consonant,** like **fairy,** change_________ and add____________.
6. To nouns ending in **o after a vowel,** like **patio**, add _________.
7. To nouns ending in **f** or **fe,** like **half**, change____________ and add ________.

Change these singular nouns to plural nouns.

1. potato ______________
2. calf ________________
3. cello________________
4. berry ______________
5. match ______________
6. loaf ______________
7. hex ______________
8. sheep ______________
9. house ______________
10. radio ______________

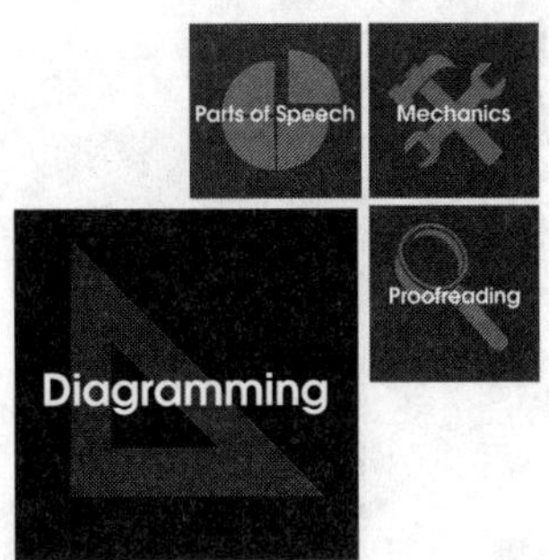

Understand the Structure

Compound Subjects

Some sentences have two subjects joined by **and**, **or**, or **but**. Diagram compound subjects like this.

The frogs and rabbits jump.

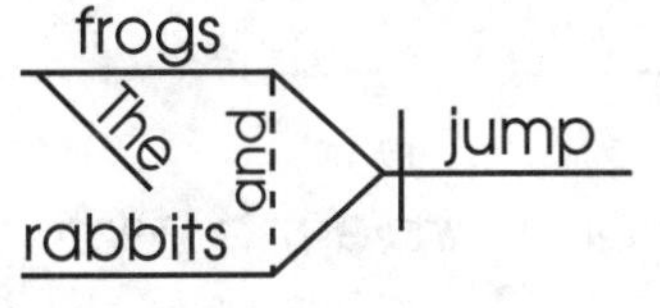

Diagram the following sentences.

1. John and Joe were running.
2. Bess and the giraffe raced.
3. Bob or I will go.

Fill in the blank.

A ____________ is a word that shows an action.

Careless Mistakes Can Cause Big Problems!

Rule: A compound subject connected by **and** always takes a plural verb.

Rule: If a compound subject is joined by **or** then the verb agrees with the subject closest to the verb.

Underline the subject(s) once and circle the verb that agrees.

1. The beast (howls, howl) throughout the night.
2. The flowers or the dust (is, are) causing my allergies.
3. My brothers and I (am, are) sometimes very noisy.
4. The whole team (was, were) unhappy.
5. Either my sisters or my brother (is, are) in big trouble tonight.
6. On April Fool's Day, my mother (likes, like) to short sheet my bed.
7. My snakes and my iguana (loves, love) to lie in the sun.

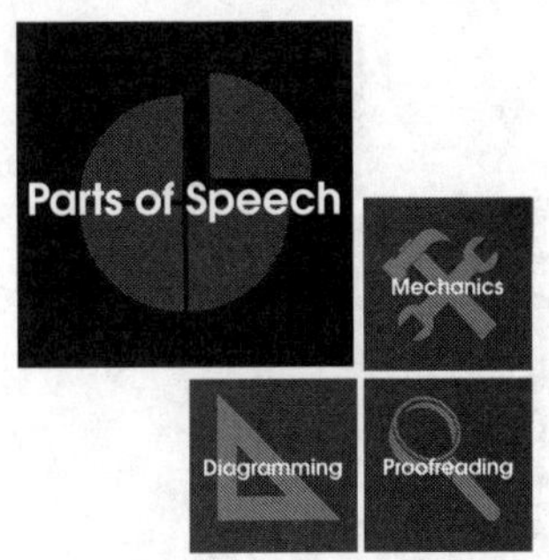

Know Your Building Materials!

Circle the nouns. Draw one line under linking or action verbs and two lines under helping verbs.

1. Fruit can be eaten in a variety of forms. (3N, 3V)
2. My favorite dessert is a pie. (2N, 1V)
3. Because of his sweet tooth, Pat adores snacks. (3N, 1 V)
4. This apple looks rotten.
5. Although Travis prefers ice cream, fruit is another favorite.
6. Tyler can spit watermelon seeds farther than Josh.

Fill in the blanks.

A ________________ is a word that shows an action or an appearance of something.

A ________________ is a word that names a person, place, or thing.

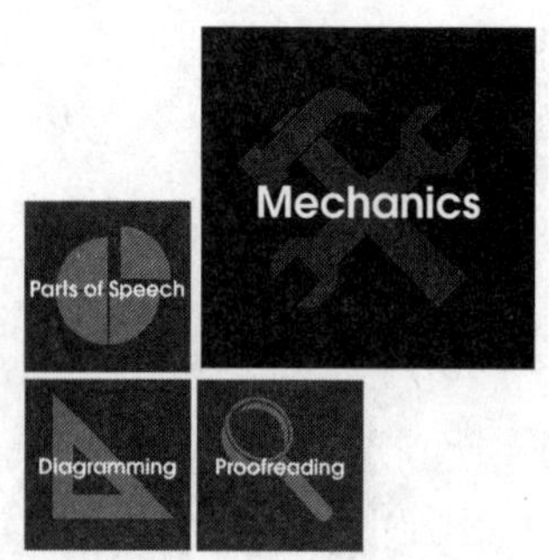

Good Mechanics Are Hard to Find

Possessive Nouns

To show possession or ownership add **'s** (dog, **dog's**).

For singular nouns ending in **s,** add **'s** if the noun is one syllable (boss, **boss's**).

For two-syllable singular nouns ending in **s,** check the dictionary because no one rule works (Texas's, righteousness').

For **plural** nouns ending in **s,** add the apostrophe alone (dogs, **dogs'**).

Add apostrophes to show possession.

1. The dogs bone was in Mothers garden.
2. Both boys minds were on the weekend.
3. Mrs. Jones car was dirty.
4. The fighters noses were broken.
5. The two ribbons colors were a match.
6. The childrens coats were on the mens hooks.

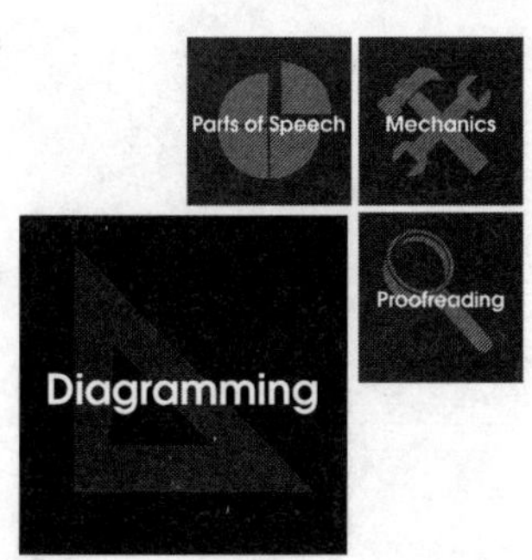

Understand the Structure

Some sentences have two verbs joined by **and, or,** or **but**. Diagram compound verbs like this.

The rabbits jump and run.

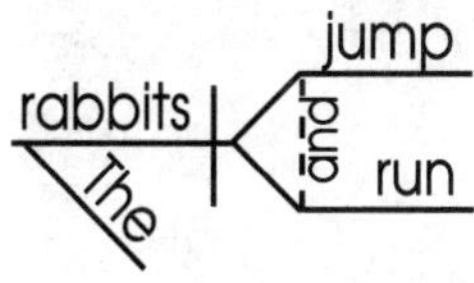

The class will either pass or fail.

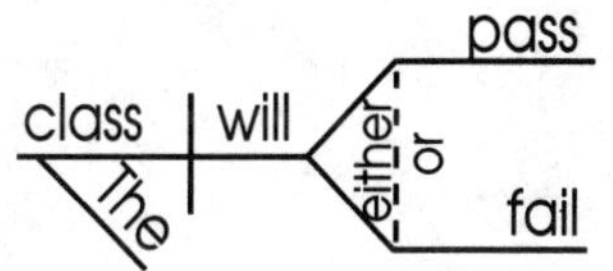

Diagram the following sentences.

1. Toddlers stumble and fall.
2. The Doberman may growl and bite.
3. Lions and tigers prowl and hide.
4. The crowd watched and waited.

Careless Mistakes Can Cause Big Problems!

Someone forgot to add the punctuation to the sentences. You will need the following:

2 question marks
1 set of quotation marks
3 periods
5 apostrophes
1 exclamation point
3 commas

1. Lets go to the mall right now
2. Unfortunately many of the dogs licenses are unreadable
3. John yelled Can you help me
4. The bosss father was born in Paris France
5. Why cant you hurry up
6. The two dresses colors were identical

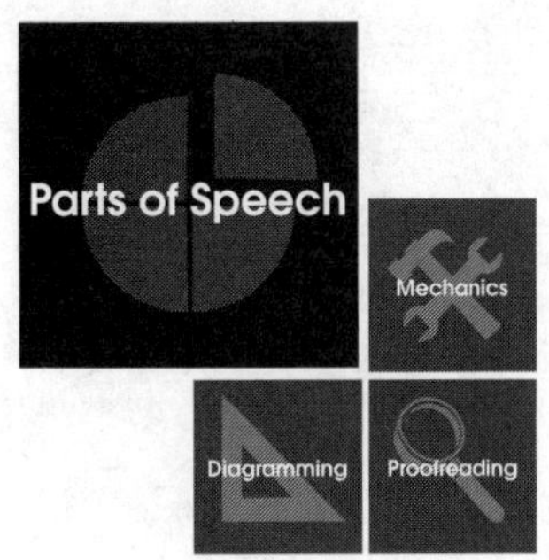

Know Your Building Materials!

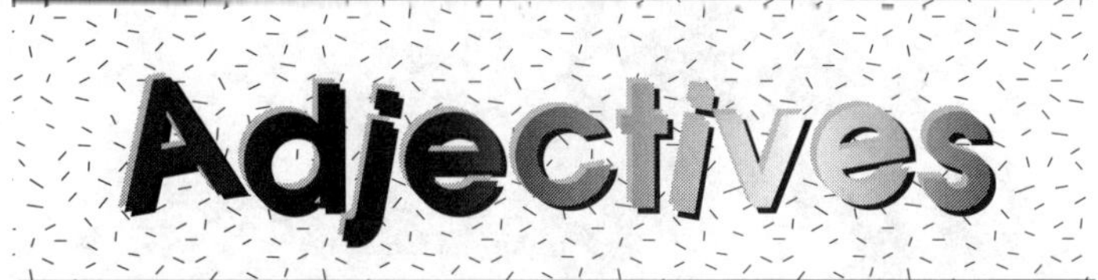

An **adjective** describes or modifies a noun or a pronoun. (A pronoun is a word that stands for a noun, like **he, it, them, or me.**)

An adjective describes **which one**, **what kind**, or **how many**.

That cat ran away.

The **black** cat ran away.

Many cats ran away.

---

*Underline each adjective and draw an arrow to the word being described. (Don't forget the articles **the, an,** and **a**.)*

1. The enormous boulder rolled down the hill. (3)
2. The huge rock squashed several tiny bugs. (4)
3. Flattened bugs are invisible. (2)
4. At the bottom of the hill, it stopped. (2)
5. The squashed bugs missed the gorgeous sunset that day. (5)
6. The huge boulder doesn't care if the sunset is ugly or pretty. (5)

Fill in the blanks.

An **adjective** is a word that modifies a ______________ or a ____________________.

Good Mechanics Are Hard to Find

Choose words from the parts-of-speech list below and fill in the blanks of the story.

Adjectives	**Nouns**	**Verbs**
smelly	tail	trampled
enormous	rhinoceros	ran
hilarious	clown	scared
green	nose	stomped
fuzzy	teeth	caressed
purple	superhero	patted
worried	crook	amused
scary	slug	danced
angry	rifle	leaped
kind	flower	screamed
happy	mud ball	covered
noisy	worm	devoured

One day at school, I saw a (adj)____________, (adj)___________(noun)_____________. It (verb) ______________ the entire class with its (adj)______________ (noun) ____________. The (adj)_____________ teacher (verb)________________ quickly. I was really (adj) ________________. The principal said, "Get that (adj) ________________ (noun) ______________ out of here!" He was very (adj) ___________________.

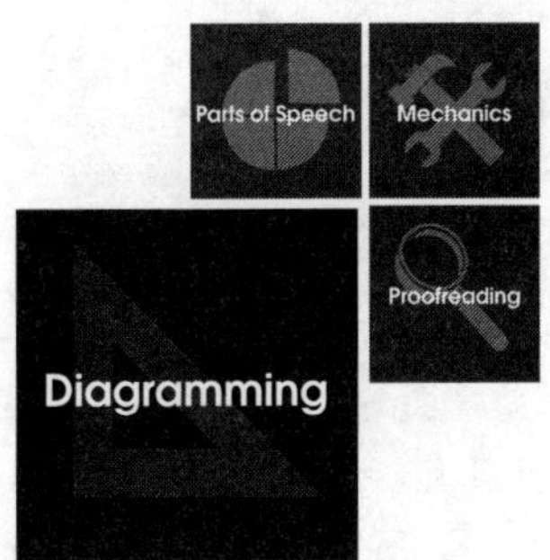

Understand the Structure

Place an adjective on a slanted line under the word it modifies.

The foolish clown smiled.

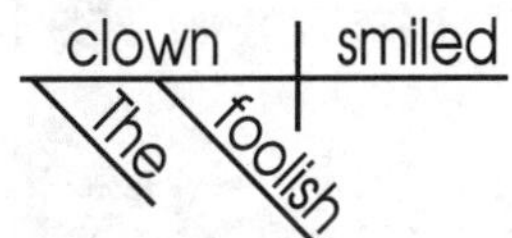

Diagram the following sentences.

1. The red balloon floated.
2. An impossible mission failed.
3. A large bear and a small bear charged.
4. An ugly red vase fell and smashed.

Careless Mistakes Can Cause Big Problems!

Capitalize each proper noun and add punctuation.

1. At least thirty soldiers mess kits were lost
2. Pick me up on time please mother
3. Babe ruths baseball mitt has holes in it

Write the contraction for each word pair.

1. would not ______________
2. it is ________________ (Note: The word **its** shows possession.)
3. they are __________________

Write the plural of each noun.

1. tomato ______________
2. dish ______________
3. monkey ______________

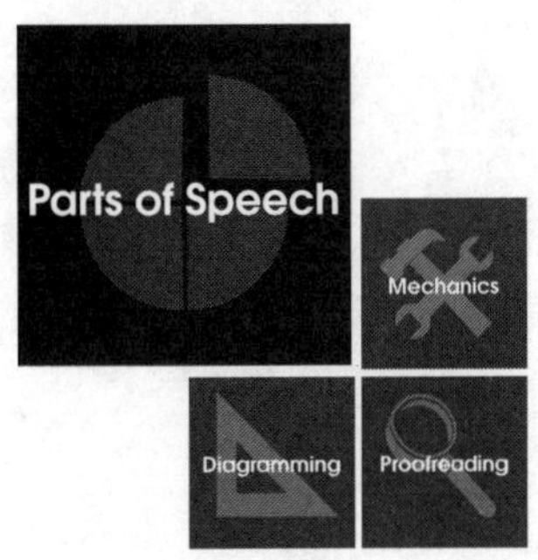

Know Your Building Materials!

The words **the**, **an**, and **a** are adjectives called articles.

Rule: Use **a** before words beginning with a **consonant sound** and **an** before words beginning with a **vowel sound: An** apple but **a** watermelon.

Sometimes consonants sound like vowels: **An h**onor, but **a h**orse.

Rule: Don't use **a** or **an** after expressions ending with **of**.

Wrong: What sort of **a** candy bar is it?
Right: What sort of candy bar is it?

Choose the correct expression.

1. Find (a, an) old, smelly shoe.
2. That was some sort (of, of a) large greyhound.
3. Wait for (a, an) hour before you go swimming.
4. (A, an) hard-boiled egg tastes delicious with lots of salt.

Underline each adjective and draw an arrow to the word being described.
Hint: *An adjective modifies a person, place, or thing. It cannot modify another adjective.*

1. A large, smelly dragon lives in the tremendously dank cave.
2. He is very kind and gentle, but he has really putrid breath.

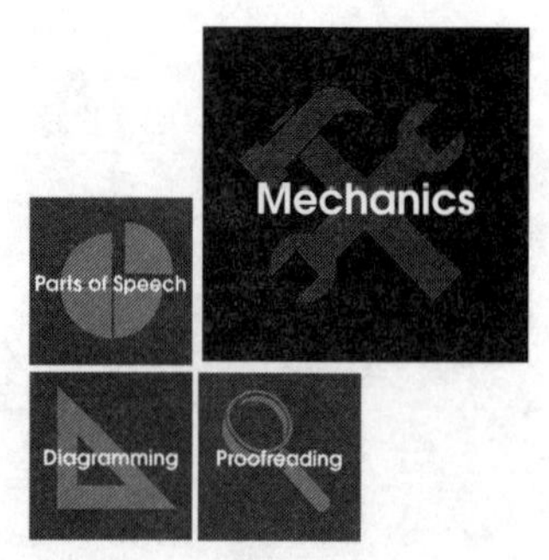

Good Mechanics Are Hard to Find

Adjectives can be used to compare two or more things.

A small dog

A small**er** dog (two dogs are compared)

The small**est** dog (more than two dogs are compared)

A vicious dog

A **less** vicious dog (two dogs are being compared)

The **least** vicious dog (more than two dogs are compared)

With some adjectives of two syllables and all adjectives of three or more syllables, use **more, most, less,** or **least.**

A **more** exciting movie, or a **less** exciting movie

The **most** exciting movie, or the **least** exciting movie

Write a correct form of the adjective in parentheses.

1. One of the (unusual)____________________ animals is the platypus.
2. My (fast)____________________ teammate is Jean.
3. A tiger is (frightening)____________________ than a house cat.
4. A bush is (tall)____________________ than a tree.
5. Cherry pie is (delicious)____________________than eggplant.
6. Reading is (fun)____________________than doing the dishes.
7. Math is my (difficult)____________________subject.

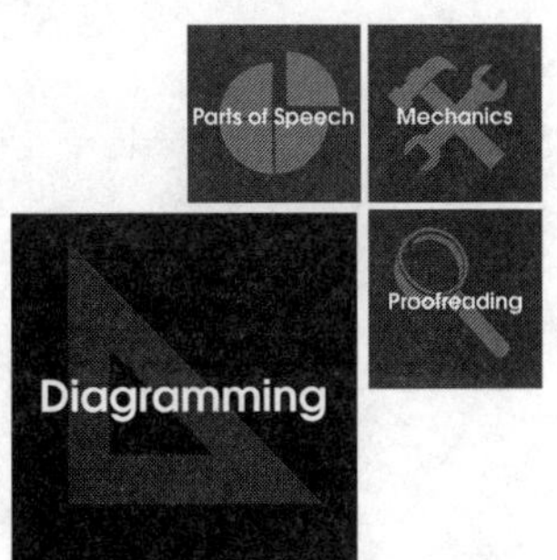

Understand the Structure

More Diagramming Adjectives

Diagram the following sentences.

1. A red ribbon flew.
2. A purple shirt and green pants clashed.
3. A lively dolphin jumped and splashed.
4. The wily fox either ran or hid.

Fill in the blank.

An **adjective** is a word that modifies either a ______________ or a ________________.

Careless Mistakes Can Cause Big Problems!

Correct the mistakes in the sentences below. Each line contains one mistake.

Humpty dumpty was awfully stupid to sit on that huge wall.
What did he expect? A egg is exceedingly fragile. Humpty's
balance wasn't that great anyway. Everyone knows that eggs
shells are very thin. Next time Humpty wants to act realy hot,
he should jump into a frying pan

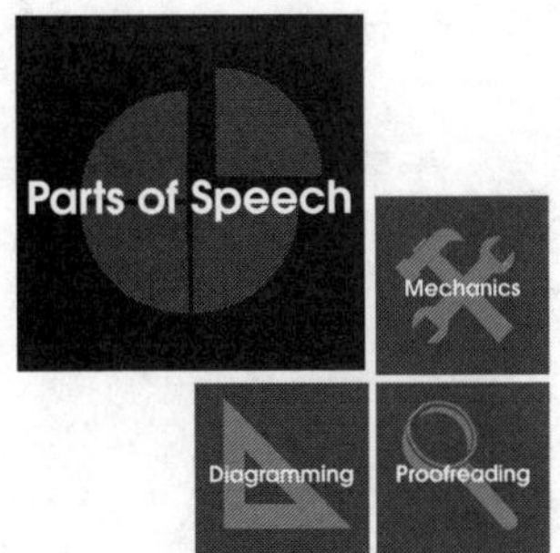

Know Your Building Materials!

An **adverb** describes or modifies a verb, an adverb, or an adjective. It answers the questions **when, where, how,** or **how often.** Adverbs often end in **ly**.

The dog will come **soon**.
The dog will come **here**.
The dog will come **slowly**.
The dog will come **frequently**.

Underline each adverb and draw an arrow to the word it modifies.

1. The alarm clock rings early. (1)
2. I get up slowly. (2)
3. Often, I eat breakfast too quickly. (3)
4. Sometimes, the car pool is really late. (2)
5. Tomorrow, I will get to school earlier. (2)

Fill in the blanks.

An **adverb** is a word that modifies a ________________, or an________________, or an ________________.

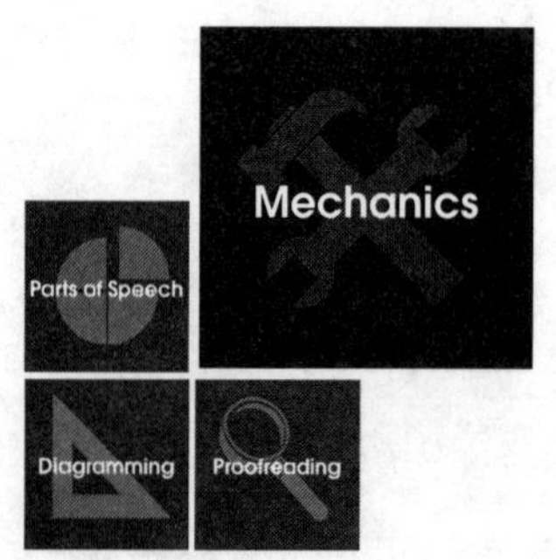

Good Mechanics Are Hard to Find

Underline each adjective and cross out each adverb.

1. The hungry beast gobbled furiously.
2. Without any thought, the hero climbed quickly.
3. The photo of the two children was very beautiful.
4. The hasty work seemed quite sloppy.

Draw an arrow from the boldface word to the word modified. Then identify the part of speech of the modified word.

1. ________________ The **enormous** hat looked silly on the man.
2. ________________ The huge hat looked **very** silly on the man.
3. ________________ The man looked **carefully** at the hat.
4. ________________ The man was exceedingly **careful**.
5. ________________ Then he walked away **very** quickly.

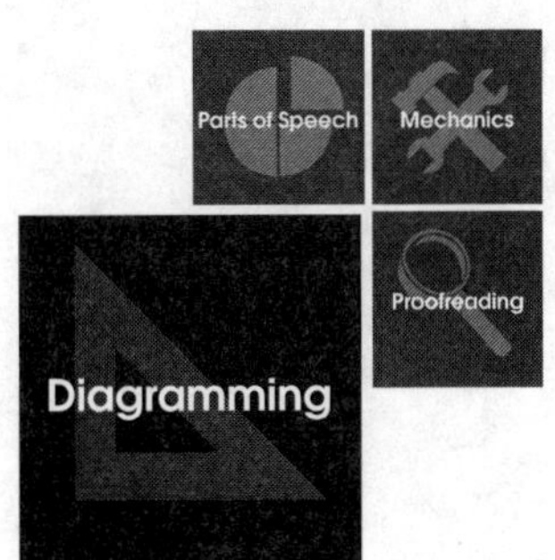

Understand the Structure

Place an adverb on a slanted line under the verb it modifies. An adverb that modifies another adverb or an adjective is placed on a line parallel to the word it modifies and connected to it.

The seal swam gracefully.

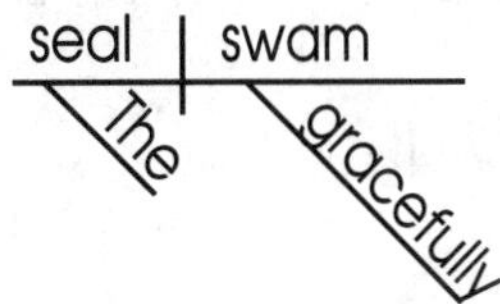

The seal swam very gracefully.

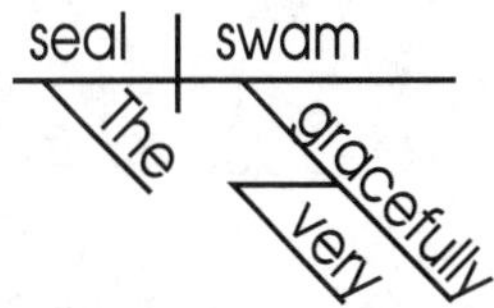

Diagram the following sentences.

1. Finally, the guests arrived.
2. The athlete cycled smoothly and ran fast.
3. Gazelles can leap very well.
4. The baby cried all night.

Careless Mistakes Can Cause Big Problems!

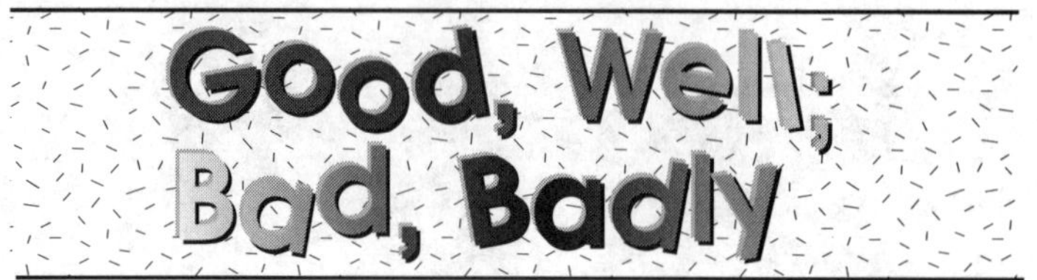

Good and **bad** are **adjectives** that modify nouns and pronouns. **Well** and **badly** are **adverbs** that modify verbs.

Choose the correct word in parentheses and underline the word it modifies.

1. The third baseman hits the ball (good, well).
2. He is a (good, well) player.
3. Unfortunately, he runs the bases (bad, badly).
4. In fact, his base running is very (bad, badly).
5. He steals bases (bad, badly).

Write the correct adjective or adverb (good, well, bad, badly).

1. A ________________ try (positive)
2. ________________ drawn (negative)
3. performs ________________ (positive)
4. A ________________ decision (negative)

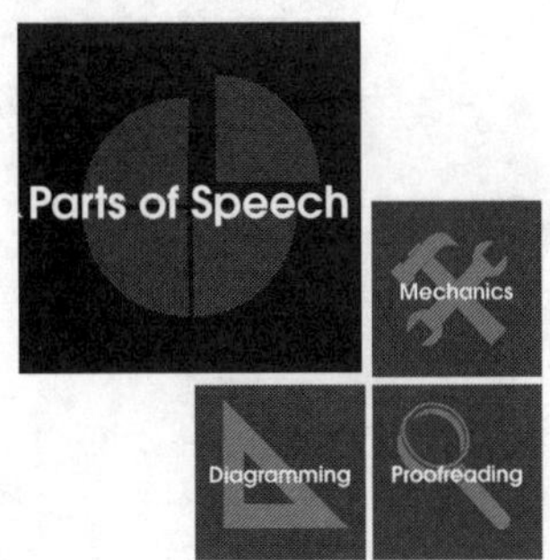

Know Your Building Materials!

An **adverb** describes or modifies a verb, an adverb or an adjective. It answers the questions **when, where, how,** or **how often.** Adverbs often end in **ly**.

Hint: To decide whether a describing word is an adverb, determine the part of speech of the word modified.

Underline each adverb and draw an arrow to the word it modifies.

1. Charles and Josh dashed quickly away.
2. Unfortunately, they were caught.
3. The big bear ate them greedily.
4. Then the bear barfed* loudly.
5. Charles and Josh emerged very happily.

Fill in the blanks.

An adverb answers the questions ____________, ______________, ________________, or ___________________.

**Editor's note: OK Ok...That word is slang and slang is not acceptable.*

Good Mechanics Are Hard to Find

Creating Adverbs

Often adjectives can be changed to adverbs by adding **ly**. If the adjective ends in **y** preceeded by a consonant, change the **y** to **i** and add **ly**.

Change the adjective in parentheses to an adverb.

1. I ran (quick)__________________ to save my buddy.
2. I would (glad)_______________help someone in need.
3. He lashed out (angry)_________________.
4. The octopus moved (easy)_______________ in the water.
5. The fox stared (wary)_________________ at the raw meat.
6. She was (complete)________________ happy for once.

Fill in the blanks.

An **adverb** modifies a ______________, an _______________, or an _________________.

An **adjective** modifies a _____________, or a _________________.

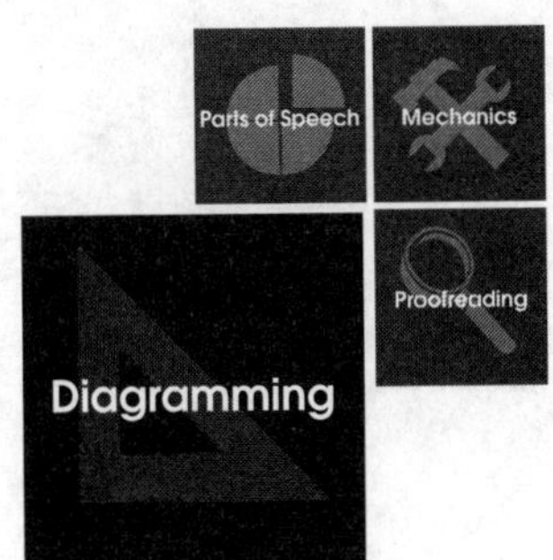

Understand the Structure

Diagram the following sentences.

1. The odd green stain washed out.
2. James and Rick worked very hard.
3. The dark green balloon popped loudly.
4. The quarterback runs well but throws poorly.

Fill in the blanks.

An **adverb** is a word that modifies a ________________, or an ________________, or an ________________.

Careless Mistakes Can Cause Big Problems!

Correct the mistakes in the sentences below. Each line contains one mistake.

Little Bo Peep didn't take care of her sheep very good. It was
silly to assume they would just stand around an not run off when
she wasnt paying attention. Sheep are about the least
intelligentest of all the farmyard animals. Of course, Bo Peep
wasn't so smart either. She must have searched bad for her
shep since she never found them.

Lessons 1-10

Connect each part of speech to its partners.

Adverb	A person, place, or thing
	It describes "what kind," "which one," or "how many"
Adjective	An action word
	It describes a verb, an adjective, or an adverb
Noun	It describes a noun
	Some are common, and some are proper
Verb	It describes "how," "when," "where," or "how often"
	It sometimes has helpers

Write the plural form.

church ________________ army________________ knife_______________

Write the possessive form.

mother_______________ spiders________________ children_____________

Fill in the blanks.

Adjective	Adverb
glad	_______________
_______________	completely
good	_______________

Diagram the sentence.

John and big Joe ate hungrily.

Lessons 1-10

Identify the part of speech.

Ex. Hat <u>noun</u>

will be ______________________ idea ________________
swift ______________________ destroy ______________
bad ______________________ quickly ______________
good ______________________ well ________________

Write the plural form.

Ex. hat <u>hats</u>

half ______________________ duty________________
lunch ______________________ key ________________

Write the possessive form.

Ex. cat <u>cat's</u>

boys ______________________ bird ________________
children ______________________ church ______________

Fill in the chart.

Adjective	Adverb
good	__________
light	__________
__________	slowly
noisy	__________

Diagram the sentence.

The agile player ran gracefully.

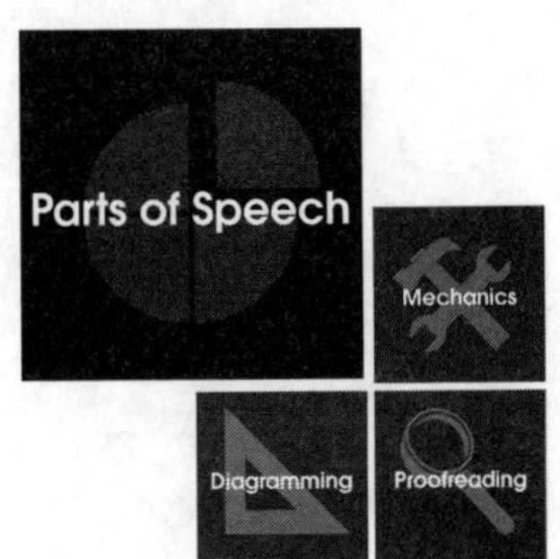

A Good Mechanic Is Hard to Find

A **conjunction** is a joining word. The most common conjunctions, **and, or, for, so,** and **but,** are called **coordinating conjunctions** because they join equal partners. They may join single subjects, adjectives, verbs, or even whole sentences.

Underline the conjunction(s) in each sentence.

1. For dinner, I plan to have a hamburger, some fries, and a shake.
2. My mother says I should have some vegetables and some milk, but I don't believe her.
3. Dinner without grease or fats is like living on bread and water.
4. Either I eat junk food, or I eat nothing, for junk food is the staff of life.

Fill in the blanks.

An adverb modifies a ______________, an ______________, or an ______________.

Good Mechanics Are Hard to Find

A sentence that consists of two independent sentences connected by a coordinating conjunction is called a **compound sentence**.

In compound sentences, a comma is always required before the conjunction. Sometimes, the conjunction is replaced by a semicolon (;).

Hint: Don't confuse a compound subject or verb with a compound sentence.

---

*Label each compound verb (**CV**), compound subject (**CS**), and compound sentence (**Csen**). Insert punctuation where required. Write OK after the sentences that do not need punctuation changes.*

1. John and Jim will go to the movies.
2. Jamie will also go to the movies but I will stay home.
3. I will stay home and do my homework.
4. I will write my essay first next I will finish my math.
5. I have homework to do because I didn't finish it on time.
6. Next time, I will avoid procrastinating and finish my work early and then I can go to the movies with my friends.

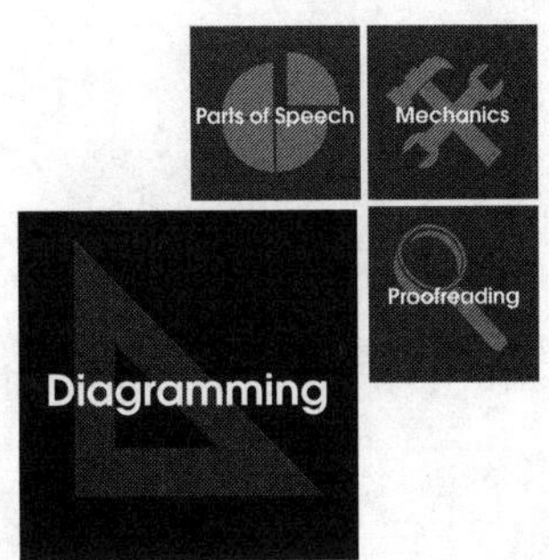

Understand the Structure

Diagram each sentence separately. Then join the two with a stepped line on which the conjunction or semicolon is written.

The monster ran fast, but the hero ran faster.

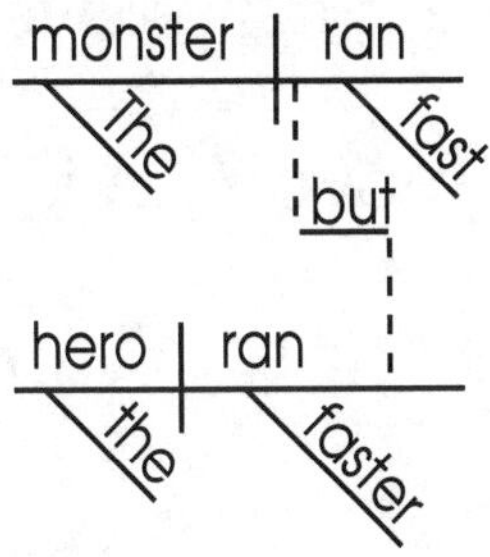

Diagram the following sentences.

1. I ran, but he followed.
2. The lightning flashed, and the thunder crashed.
3. The building collapsed suddenly; everything exploded.

Careless Mistakes Can Cause Big Problems!

Correct the mistakes in the sentences below. ***There are seven mistakes.***

Michael Jordan was a great player. The Bulls' realy missed him when he retired. He moved on the court really good and his shooting was completely amazing. I have a bet with my parent's that he will not come out of retirment again. I will be happy weather I win or lose the bet.

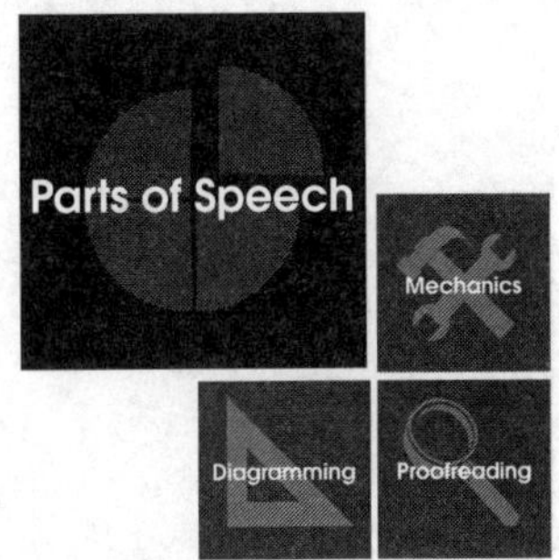

Know Your Building Materials!

Prepositions are always used with nouns or pronouns (pronouns stand for nouns). They show a relationship between the noun or pronoun and some other idea in the sentence. A preposition can be a single word or two or more words. Some very common prepositions are **in, to, of, into, over, under, above, by, like, behind, beside, because of, due to, inside, around.** There are many prepositions. (**Hint**: The **to** used before a verb—**to swim**—is not a preposition.)

Underline the preposition(s) in each sentence.

1. Under my hat is a snarl of curls.
2. After the storm, we are going to assess the damage near the barn.
3. Go into your room and find the laundry under your bed!
4. When we arrive at school, run to your classroom and apologize to your teacher.
5. Due to the traffic, we just couldn't get there on time.

Fill in the blanks.

Some coordinating conjunctions are ____________, ____________, and ________________.

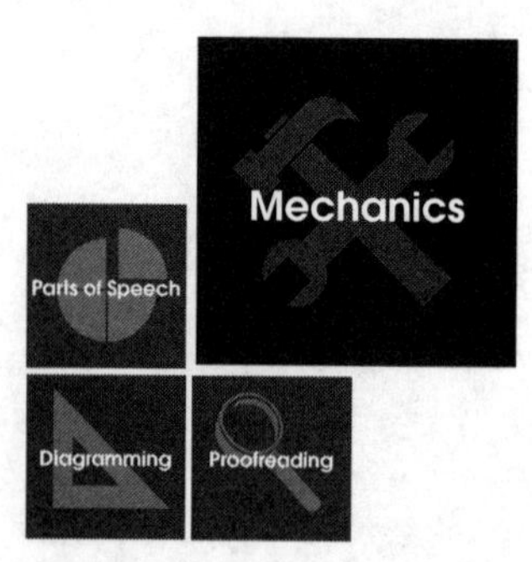

Good Mechanics Are Hard to Find

Write prepositions on index cards so that each one has a match. Shuffle and deal five cards to each player and place the remaining cards in a central pile. The first player may ask any other player for a specific preposition that the asker holds in his hand. If the other player has the card, he must surrender it to the asker. If not, then he tells the asker to "Go fish." When a player gets a match, he puts it on the table. His turn continues until he is told to "Go fish," and he fails to draw a match from the pile.

Common Prepositions

After	Of	On	With
At	Below	To	Off
Between	Behind	Inside	Within
By	Across	Concerning	Onto
Through	Over	Outside	About
Above	Against	Along	Under
Because of	Due to	Before	Amid
Around	Among	Since	Past
Except	Toward	Near	Out

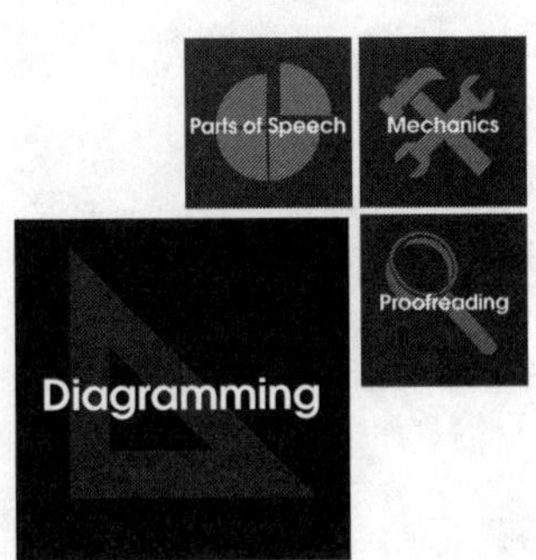

Understand the Structure

Write sentences to fit the diagrams below. Then fill in the words on the diagrams.

1.

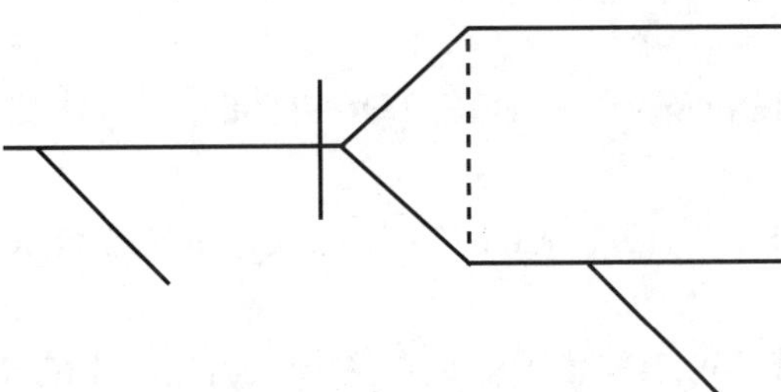

2.

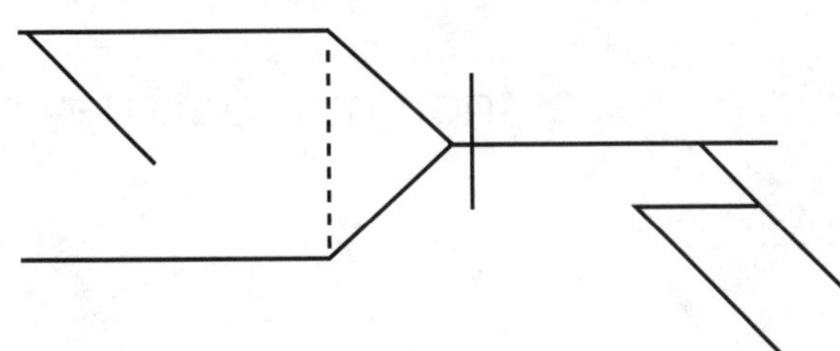

3.

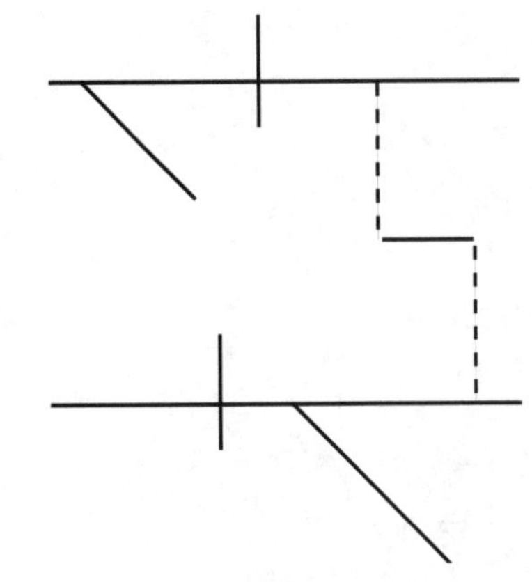

Careless Mistakes Can Cause Big Problems!

Correct the mistakes in the sentences below. ***There are nine mistakes.***

The Cubs are my favorite underdogs Even when they play good, it is a surprise to see them win. The team is full of players who is rejects from other teams. Even Sammy Sosa does'nt get the respect he deserve since his team so rarely wins. He hits plenty of homers but his homers aren't game winners. The Cubs may disappoint the fans oftener then not, but they are loveable even when they loose.

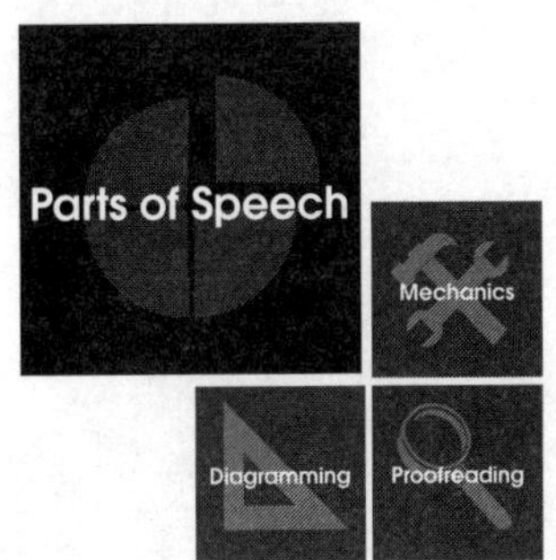

Know Your Building Materials!

A **prepositional phrase** starts with a preposition and ends with an object that is usually a noun or a pronoun.

The cat is hiding **behind the door.**

Come to the concert **with me.**

Climb **into the car in the driveway.**

Draw one line under the prepositional phrase(s) and two lines under the preposition(s) in each sentence.

1. The teenager in the red jacket ran past the door.
2. Under the tree in the back of the lawn is a wrecked car.
3. Among young men, suits and ties are not the fashion.
4. I would love to dance in *The Nutcracker* like you.
5. Between you and me, I think this exercise is too easy.

List six prepositions not used in the exercise above.

1. ____________ 2. ____________

3. ____________ 4. ____________

5. ____________ 6. ____________

Good Mechanics Are Hard to Find

People often misuse **of, off,** and **have.**

Of is a preposition that means "belonging to something," "containing something," or "about something."

Off is a preposition meaning "away from something." Do not use "off of" or "off" instead of "from."

Have is a verb or a helping verb used with "should," "must," "might," or "could."

Choose the correct word.

1. Mom should (of, have) gotten some milk at the store.
2. I got the answers (off, off of, from) my friend.
3. Please get (off, off of) my bed.
4. Beth ought to (of, have) gone to bed earlier.
5. The box (of, off) chocolates disappeared fast.
6. The girl must (of, have) been diving (off, off of) the cliff.

Fill in the blanks

The parts of a compound sentence can be connected by either a coordinate ____________________ or a punctuation mark called a ______________.

Understand the Structure

Some prepositional phrases function as adjectives. They are diagrammed below the noun or pronoun they modify.

The girl **in the red dress** dances well.

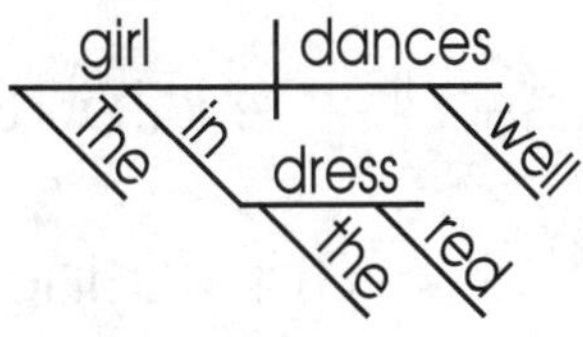

Diagram the following sentences.

1. The author of the book writes very skillfully.
2. The bird with the blue feathers flew overhead.
3. The black truck with the dent in the side was speeding.

Careless Mistakes Can Cause Big Problems!

Correct the mistakes in the sentences below. ***There are eight mistakes.***

Rasputin was one of the most great villains in history. He was a advisor to the czar of Russia in the late 1800s. His enemies tried to assassinate him but he kept refusing to die. First, they feed him poisoned wine and cake but he didn't die. Then they shot him in the back and left him to bleed to death. You would of thought that was enough, but Rasputin still didnt die. In desperation, they shot him six more times. The hole story sounds like a *Three Stooges* movie.

Know Your Building Materials!

A prepositional phrase starts with a preposition and ends with an object that is usually a noun or a pronoun. Sometimes the object has modifiers.

In the following sentences, draw one line under the preposition and two lines under its object. Cross out any modifiers of the object.

Example: **Under** ~~the spreading chestnut~~ **tree**, the child sat quietly.

1. Without his mother's permission, the teen took the family car to the beach.
2. The repulsive creature waggled his tongue over his enormous teeth.
3. His drool slid over his fuzzy chin and dropped into a puddle on the sand.
4. The teen drove the car directly into the gaping mouth of the horrifying monster.
5. He smashed it like a piece of hard candy.

Good Mechanics are Hard to Find

Whenever two or more words or phrases are connected, the elements must be expressed in similar forms.

Incorrect: He likes to swim, to read, and ice cream.

Correct: He likes **to swim, to read,** and **to eat** ice cream.

Incorrect: She likes strawberries, the salad, and the meat.

Correct: She likes **the** strawberries, **the** salad, and **the** meat.

Incorrect: Use this knife to chop or if you want to slice fruits.

Correct: Use this knife **to** chop or **to** slice fruits.

Rewrite the following sentences to make the structure parallel.

1. I love sun, the sand, and the water.
2. Writing is easy; to write well is difficult.
3. The teacher explained the problem, the method, and how to solve it.
4. We want a teammate who is skillful, reliable, and never gets tired.
5. Is it our ideas or how we write that matters for our grade?
6. The teacher hopes to improve test scores, and students will develop a better understanding of the issues.

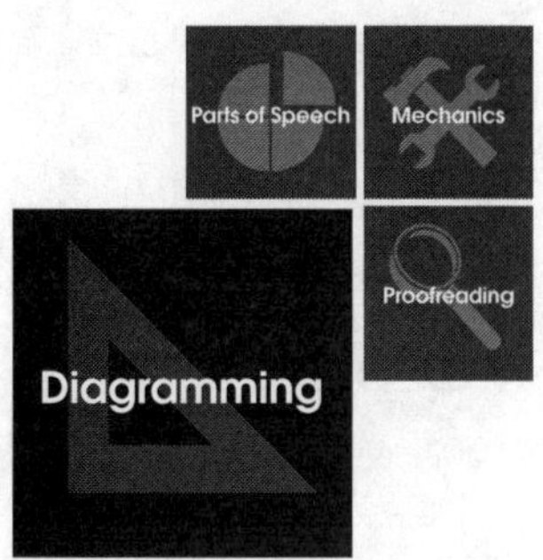

Understand the Structure

Some prepositional phrases function as adverbs. They are diagrammed below the verb, adverb, or adjective they modify.

The goldfish swam in the bowl.

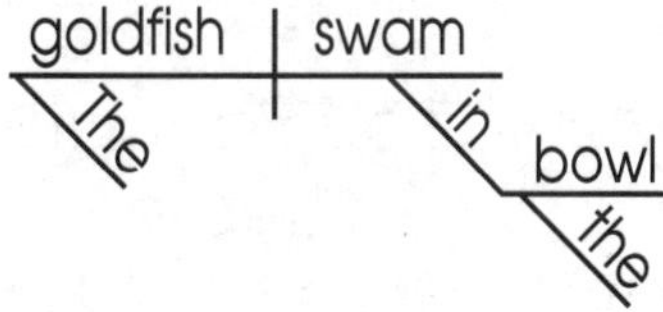

Diagram the following sentences.

1. The giant oak was struck by lightning.
2. My math book fell into the tub.
3. I jumped from the tree and fell to the ground.

Careless Mistakes Can Cause Big Problems!

Correct the mistakes in the sentences below. ***There are eight mistakes.***

The story about how everyone accept Columbus though the world was flat is plain false. Educated people during Columbus' time new the world was round. They just didn't know how big the world was Many mathematicians thought that the world was much smaller then it was. So When Columbus and his crew wanted to sail around the world, see new lands, and to find the Indies, they didn't realize what a long voyage they were planning.

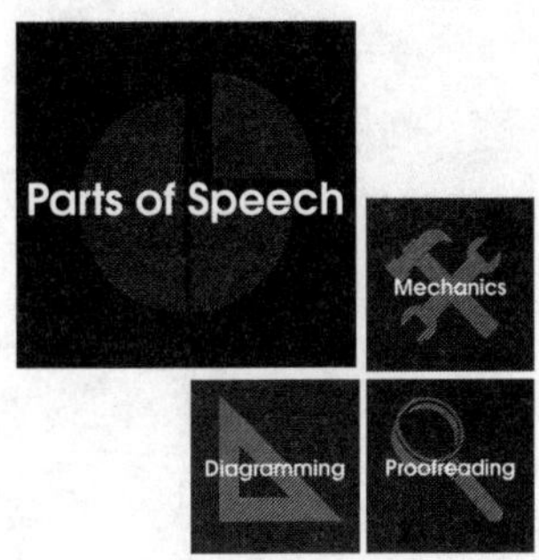

Know Your Building Materials!

A **direct object** is a noun or a pronoun that is acted on by the verb. It answers the question **"What?"** or **"Whom?"**

The boy kicked the **ball.** (The boy kicked **what**?)

Draw one line under the verb and two lines under the direct object.

1. My brother hit me.
2. I am arranging a trip to Borneo.
3. The red Mustang hit the little Toyota and the dump truck.
4. Babe Ruth got more hits than anyone on the team.
5. My friend swiped a candy bar from me.
6. Please give a bath to that dog soon!

Fill in the blank.

The most common coordinating ________________ are **and, or,** and **but.**

Good Mechanics Are Hard to Find

There is an adverb meaning "at that place" or "in that place."

Their is a word that shows possession.

They're is a contraction of "they are."

*Fill in the blanks with **there, their,** or **they're.***

1. ____________ are sixteen students in the class.
2. All the students have ______________ own projects.
3. _______________ expected to finish the work independently.
4. As a reward, ____________ going on a field trip to Sea World.
5. ______________, ______________ going to be allowed to

   feed_________ lunch to Shamu.
6. Unfortunately, Shamu may choose to bite off ____________ hands.
7. If ________________ maimed, the students will have to brush

   ______________ teeth with ________________ feet.

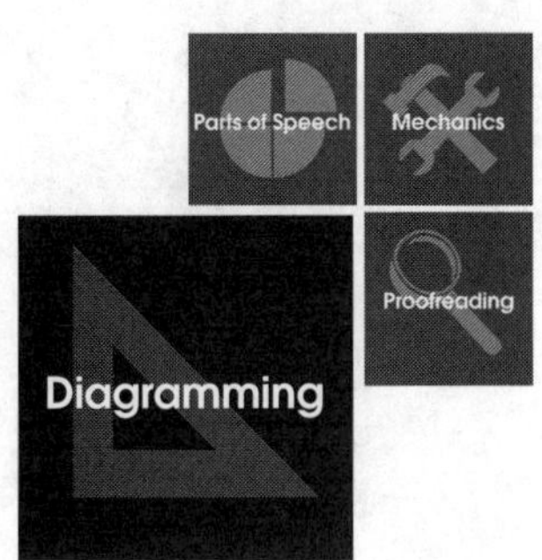

Understand the Structure

A direct object is placed on the main horizontal line. It is separated from the verb by a vertical line that does not cross the horizontal line.

The dog ate the bone.

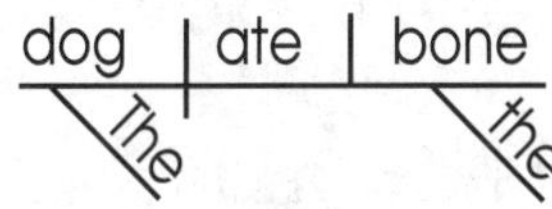

Diagram the following sentences.

1. The baseball player hit the ball into the bleachers.
2. Angrily, the teacher threw the papers down.
3. My mother baked a cake and frosted it with whipped cream.

Careless Mistakes Can Cause Big Problems!

Correct the mistakes in the sentences below. ***There are eight mistakes.***

Goldilocks would of been in big trouble if the police had catched her. Think of how many illegal acts she committed! First of all, she broked into the three bear's house without an invitation. Then, she smashed there furniture and stole all there dinner. She committed crimes like breaking and entering, destroying property, and she stole things. What kind of lesson is this story teaching little kids.

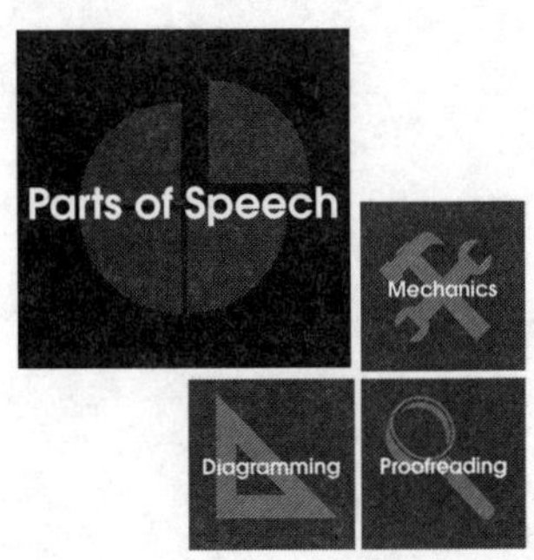

Know Your Building Materials!

An **indirect object** tells **to whom** or **for whom** something is done. It is always paired with a direct object.

Bessie gave me a cookie.

Cookie is the direct object. A **cookie** is what was given.

Me is the indirect object. **Me** indicates to whom it was given.

Draw one line under the direct object and two lines under the indirect object in the following sentences.

1. I wrote my buddy a long letter.
2. Jean told Jill an embarrassing secret.
3. My dad gave my brother and his friend two tickets to the hockey game.
4. She made Ben chocolate chip cookies and caramel popcorn.
5. I showed William my sister's surprise.
6. On her birthday, I sent my friend a large bouquet of balloons.

Good Mechanics Are Hard to Find

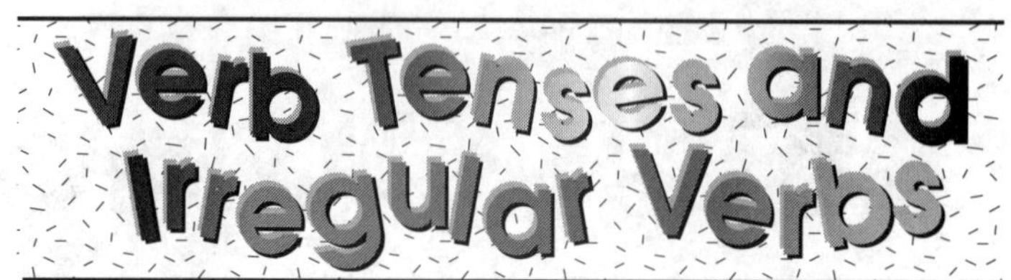

Tense means time. A verb tells us not only what action is occurring but also when it is occurring. The form and spelling of the verb change to tell us when an action is taking place.

Most verbs are regular and use the –ed ending to indicate past tense. Some verbs, called irregular, have different spellings to indicate past tense.

Fill in the chart.

Present tense	Future Tense	Past Tense	Past tense with helpers (Past Participle)
paint	will paint	painted	has, have painted
work		worked	
speak		spoke	
	will ring		
			has, have ridden
		ate	
	will draw		
do			
		knew	
			has, have driven
		took	
begin			
	will see		
move			
	will be		
		held	

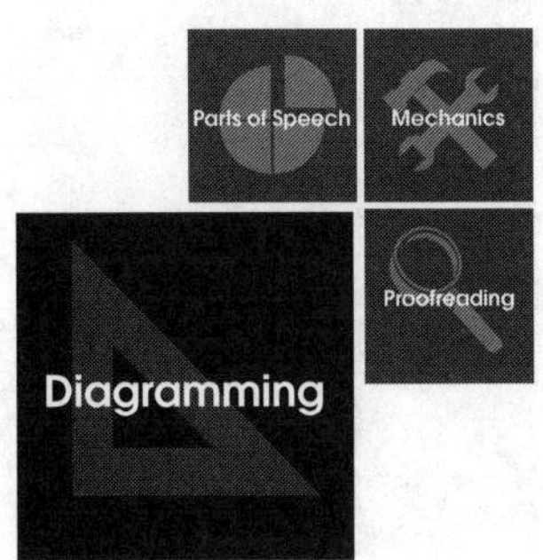

Understand the Structure

An indirect object is treated like a prepositional phrase modifying the verb. However, the slanted line has no preposition since **to** or **for** are understood and not stated. Mom sent **(to)** me a letter.

Dad gave silly John a scolding.

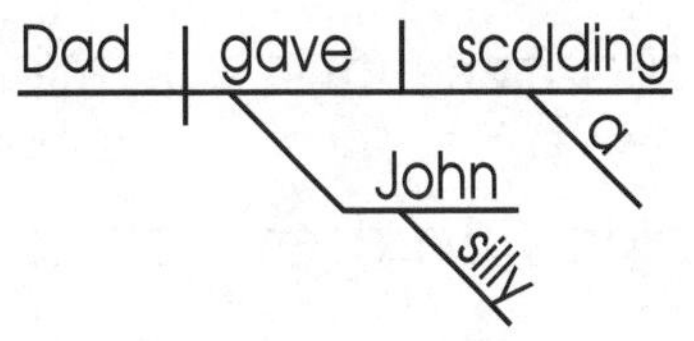

Diagram the following sentences. (Hint: Understood subjects are placed in parentheses on the subject line.)

1. José sent me a letter on the first day of camp.
2. Sadly, Lee told Jenny the story about the accident in school.
3. Bring him the large purple canister from the kitchen.

Careless Mistakes Can Cause Big Problems!

Correct the mistakes in the sentences below. ***There are eight mistakes.***

Rember all those pictures of the Pilgrims at the first Thanksgiving? There hats and clothes were black and white and they had buckles on they're shoes. Original letters from the period tell us thats not how the Pilgrims dressed. They weared colorful clothes, not just black and white. Buckles on shoes and wearing only black and white didn't come into fashion untill years later.

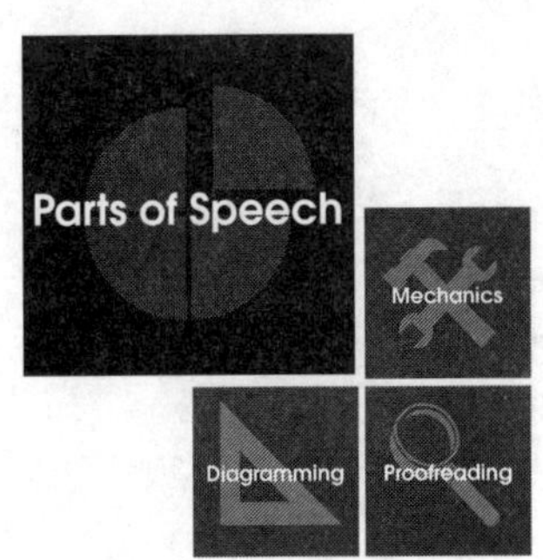

Know Your Building Materials!

A **pronoun** is a word that stands for a noun.

Some common pronouns are **I, you, he, she, it, we, they, me, her, him, us,** and **them.** Some point out things like **this** and **that.**

Some pronouns indicate possession (possessive pronouns) like **my, mine, your, yours, his, her, hers, their, theirs, our, ours.** Some are used to ask questions (interrogative pronouns) like **who, what, which,** or **whom.** Some reflect back on the subject (reflexive pronouns) like **myself, himself, ourselves.** Some refer to indefinite groups (indefinite pronouns) like **anybody, everybody, nobody.**

Underline the pronouns in the following sentences.

1. My friend and I got tickets to the concert that is at the Sports Arena. (3)
2. I would have earned the money myself, but my parents gave it to me. (5)
3. Everybody at school is jealous that we have tickets. (3)
4. I don't know who is performing before the main act, but I bet it is a band that is going to be good. (5)
5. Nobody who sits near the back can see anything because everyone else stands up through it all. (5)

Good Mechanics Are Hard to Find

It is easy to confuse some pronouns and possessive adjectives with contractions because they sound alike.

A contraction is a combination of two words, one of which is a verb. The apostrophe indicates a contraction, not a possessive pronoun. Some pronouns and possessive adjectives that sound like contractions are the following: **theirs, there's; your, you're; whose, who's; its, it's.**

Choose the correct word in the following sentences.

1. (Your, You're) a lucky snake!
2. (Its, It's) skin is scaly.
3. (Theirs, There's) the python in the cage.
4. (Whose, Who's) going to feed that creature?
5. Look at the size of the lump in (its, it's) stomach.
6. (Its, It's) likely to be full now.
7. Don't stick (your, you're) hand in the cage.
8. (Whose, Who's) food is that?

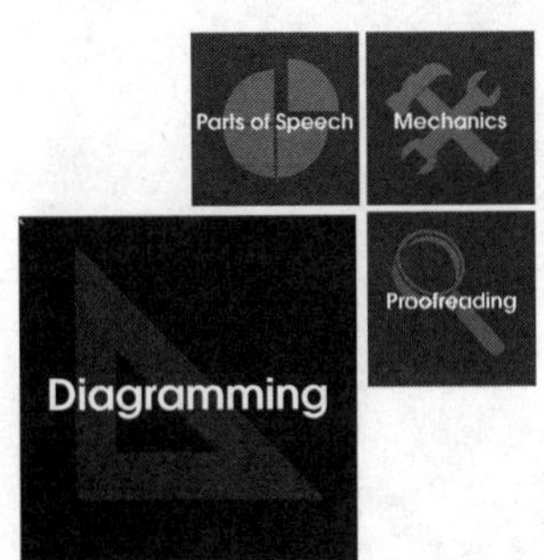

Understand the Structure

Diagram the following sentences.

1. Juan bought a record and gave me the change.
2. Lee sent Bill the tickets, and he tossed me the parking pass.
3. Either I will buy you a present, or I will take you to dinner.

Careless Mistakes Can Cause Big Problems!

Correct the mistakes in the sentences below. ***There are nine mistakes.***

I often have the same nightmare. My alarm doesn't go off and its late when I wake up. I miss the carpool, so I am late for school. I cant get my locker open. Then I am late for a test and I can't find the classroom but more often, I can't get my books and homework out off my locker. The bells are ringing wild, and the teachers are yelling at me, and all my class-mates laugh at me. If I had known how bad my dreams would be, I would not of had that last piece of anchovy, olive, and sausage pizza.

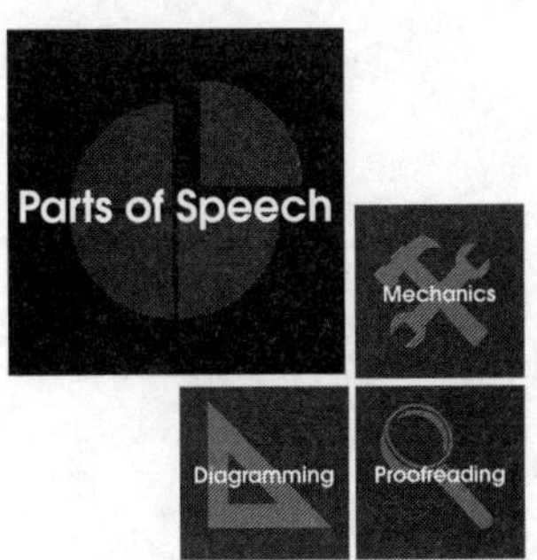

Know Your Building Materials!

A pronoun takes the place of a noun. Pronouns used as subjects and objects often have different forms.

The object form is used when the pronoun is a direct object, an indirect object or an object of a preposition.

I hit the ball (subject form).

The ball hit **me** (object form).

---

*Identify the form of pronoun in boldface as subject (**S**) or object (**O**).*

1. ______ Unfortunately, **I** missed the party.
2. ______ My brother gave **me** the chicken pox.
3. ______ My parents let **us** watch videos day and night.
4. ______ Then we gave **them** the chicken pox too.

Fill in the chart.

Subject form Singular	Object form Singular	Subject form Plural	Object form Plural
I		we	
you		you	
he, she, it		they	

Good Mechanics Are Hard to Find

The subject form of a pronoun is used when the pronoun is the subject of a clause or a sentence.

The object form of a pronoun is used when the pronoun is a direct object or indirect object of a clause or sentence or an object of a preposition.

Choose the correct pronoun in the sentences below.

1. Frank likes to play monopoly with Brad, Kayla, and (I, me).
2. (He, Him) often gives (we, us) a run for our money.
3. You and (I, me) will be on one team.
4. Frank and I sometimes gang up on (they, them).
5. Brad sits next to (he, him) and (I, me).
6. Please give (I, me) and (she, her) some cash.
7. When he wants to, Frank always beats (we, us).

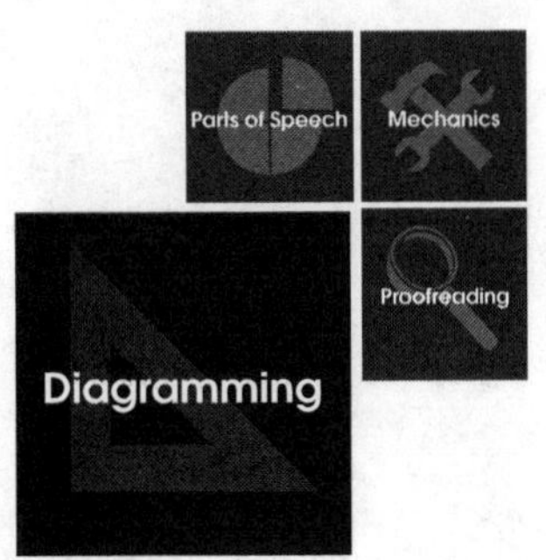

Understand the Structure

Diagram the following sentences.

1. John will roll the newspapers and ads and deliver them.
2. Give him and me the best positions on the team.
3. Mark baked the pizza and served it to his friends.

Careless Mistakes Can Cause Big Problems!

Correct the mistakes in the sentences below. ***There are eight mistakes.***

Sometimes, you just can't win. The other day, me and my friends were at a pizza place. My buddys spilled an entire pitcher of soda. I thought, " Either my friends or I are going to have to tell the waitress." I knew the waitres would be annoyed at the mess but she would be more angrier if we left without telling her. I wish my friends would of not foolled around so much.

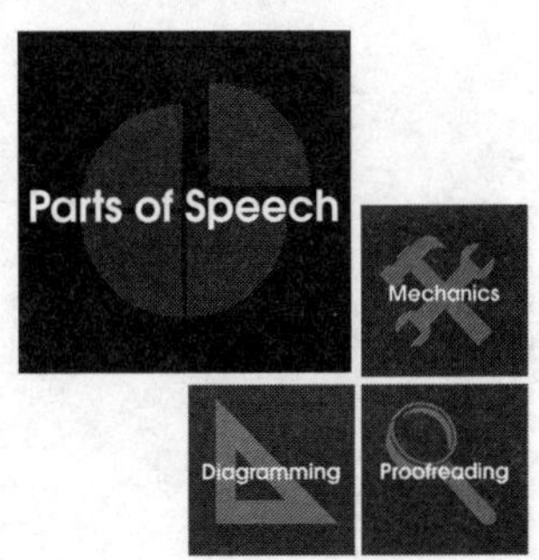

Know Your Building Materials!

Who and Whom

The pronoun **who** is a subject form, and the pronoun **whom** is an object form.

Who is going with me? (subject form—subject of sentence)

With **whom** is he going? (object form—object of preposition **to**)

Choose the correct form of the pronoun in the sentences below.

1. (Who, Whom) did he choose?
2. (Who, Whom) is going with you?
3. To (who, whom) did you send the letter?
4. She is the one (who, whom) is blonde.
5. Dave can go with (whoever, whomever) he wants.
6. (Who, Whom) did you tell the news to?
7. Jack is the unfortunate person (who, whom) the car hit.

Good Mechanics Are Hard to Find

Scrambled Pronouns

Someone threw all the pronouns into a pot and the letters were scrambled. See how quickly you can unscramble them.

Subject Pronouns

yeht ____________ ouy ____________ ew ____________

Object Pronouns

su ____________ hetm ____________ reh ____________

Reflexive Pronouns

veselmeths _____ ylfsme ____________ mlfhise ____________

Interrogative Pronouns

tawh ____________ hiwhc ____________ owh ____________

Indefinite Pronouns

smeo ____________ neoyna ____________ bdyoan ____________

Possessive Pronouns

nemi ____________ rsou ____________ rsyuo ____________

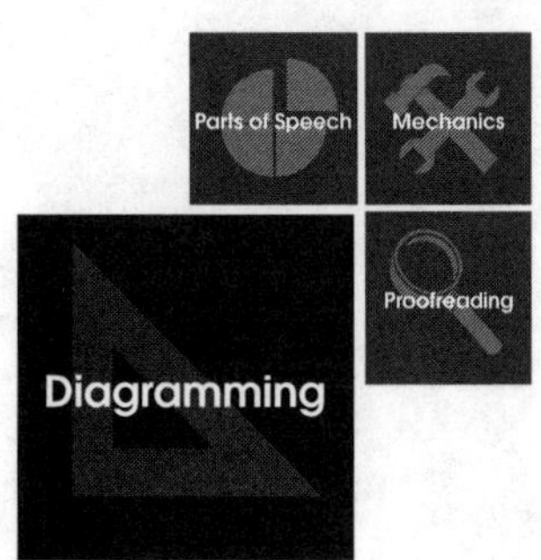

Understand the Structure

Diagram the sentences and choose the correct form of ***who*** *or* ***whom*** *depending on its placement in the diagram.*

1. (Who, Whom) did you tell the secret to?
2. (Who, Whom) will play the lead role?
3. With (who, whom) did you see the horror movie?

Careless Mistakes Can Cause Big Problems!

Correct the mistakes in the sentences below. ***There are nine mistakes.***

A myth is a story that reflect the values of a culture. It may or may not be true The importance of the story is based on the lesson and not because of the history. The story about George washington cutting down the cherry tree and than admitting it—"I cannot tell a lie"—is an example of a myth. Weather or not George realy did chop down a tree to try out his new ax doesnt matter. What matters is that American's value honesty.

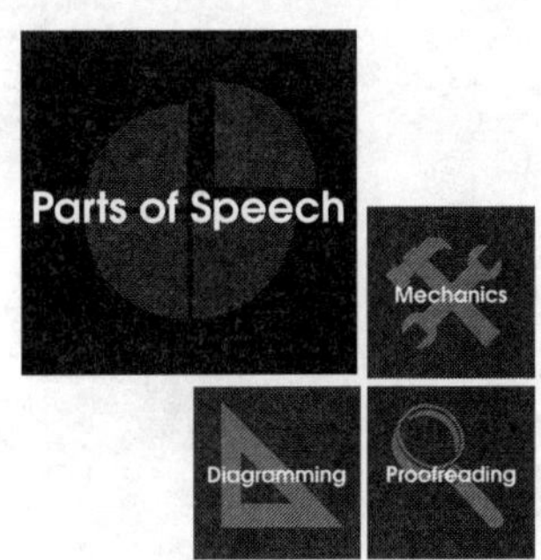

Know Your Building Materials!

Possessive Pronouns

Pronouns used to show possession are called **possessive pronouns.** Sometimes possessive pronouns act like nouns, and sometimes they act like adjectives.

Mine is in the closet. (**Mine** acts like a noun and is the subject.)

This is **my** jacket. (**My** acts like an adjective modifying **jacket**.)

---

*Identify each pronoun as a subject pronoun (**SP**), an object pronoun (**OP**), or a possessive pronoun (**PP**).*

1. Between you and me, I just don't like her attitude.
2. Her chip on her shoulder is bigger than mine is.
3. Your hat is sillier looking than his.
4. Don't make fun of me because of my hat.

Fill in the chart.

Subject Pronoun	Object Pronoun	Possessive Pronoun
I	me	my, mine
you		
he, she, it		
we		
you		
they		

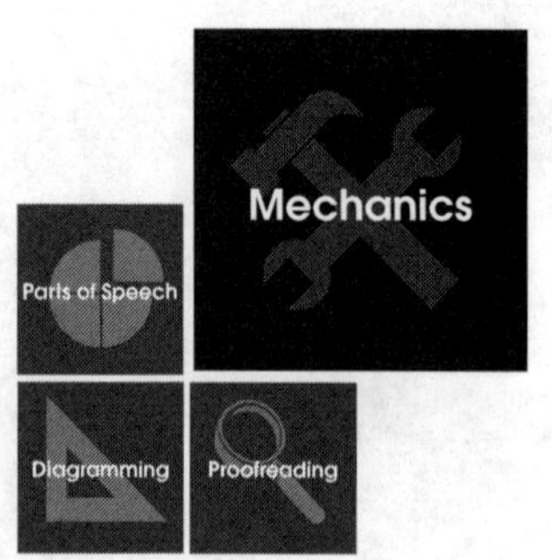

Good Mechanics Are Hard to Find

A **pronoun** takes the place of a noun. The noun that the pronoun stands for is called its **antecedent.**

The pronoun must agree with its antecedent. If the antecedent is singular, then the pronoun must be singular. If the antecedent is plural, then the pronoun must be plural.

My **dog** was gnawing on **his** bone.

The five **dogs** were gnawing on **their** bones.

Circle the pronoun and underline its antecedent.

1. The girls lost their homework.
2. The toddler wants to make dinner himself.
3. Barbara is combing her hair.
4. My dog likes to scratch behind his ear.
5. Jack and Joe will be late for their ride.
6. Jack and Joe hope Bob's brother will give them a ride.

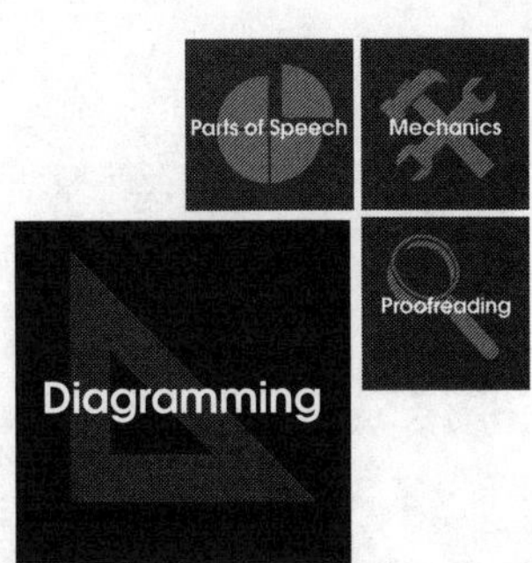

Understand the Structure

Write sentences to fit the diagrams below and then put the words on the lines.

1. 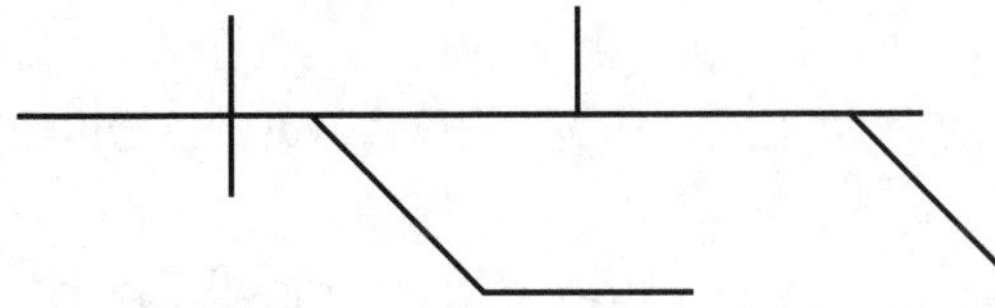

2. 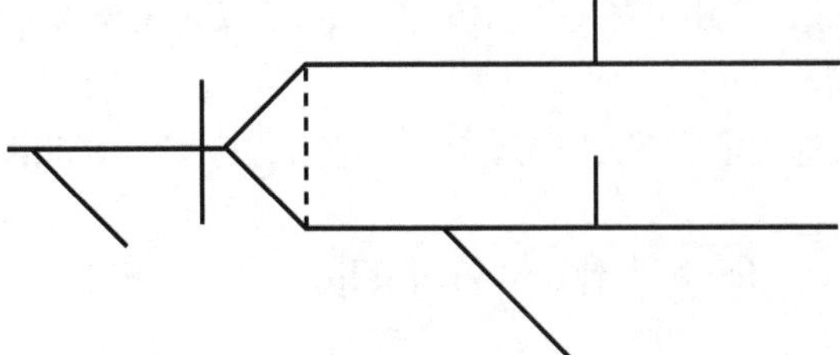

3. 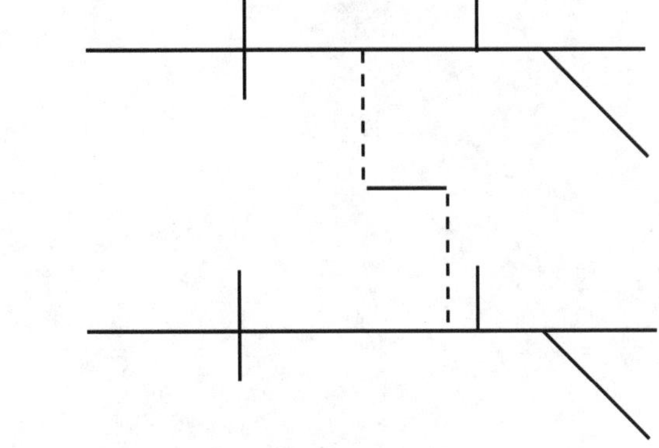

Careless Mistakes Can Cause Big Problems!

Correct the mistakes in the sentences below. ***There are nine mistakes.***

Fashions can be very odd. Why do women ware spike-heeled shoes that squash there toes and make it impossible to walk quick? Who's idea was it to design shoes that can cripple you. Do you like the silly fad of wearing you're baggy pants so far below the waist that it is always on the verge of falling of? How can that be comfortable? I think its silly!

Lessons 11-20

Connect each part of speech to its partners.

Conjunction	A word that stands for a noun
	"In," "over," "by"
Pronoun	"And," "or," "but"
	"Them" is an object form
Preposition	It is always followed by an object
	It connects two or more sentence parts

Write the plural form. Example. I we

he_______________ you_________________ me_________________

Write the object form. Eample. I me

we_________ he___________________ you_________________

Fill in the verbs in the correct form.

Present	**Past**	**Past with helpers**
____________	____________	have, has wanted
do	____________	____________
____________	was	____________
know	____________	____________
____________	drove	____________

Diagram the sentence.

I finally sent my mother a long letter from camp.

Lessons 11-20

Identify the part of speech. Example he pronoun

and ____________________ am ____________________

near ____________________ them ____________________

silly ____________________ by ____________________

but ____________________ sinfully ____________________

Underline the correct answer.

Always use the **subject, object** form of a pronoun following a preposition.

Always use the **subject, object** form of a pronoun as an indirect object.

Always use an **adverb, adjective** to modify a verb.

Always use an **adverb, adjective** to modify an adjective.

Fill in the correct forms.

Subject Singular	Subject Plural	Object Singular	Object Plural
____________	we	____________	us
____________	you	you	____________
he, she, it	____________	____________	them

Correct the following paragraph.

Jack and me love to hide from my sister and her friends. They think there so clever and can catch us, but we hide good. Sometimes we let them find us, but we could of got away. I love playing hide an' seek and to celebrate afterward with ice cream.

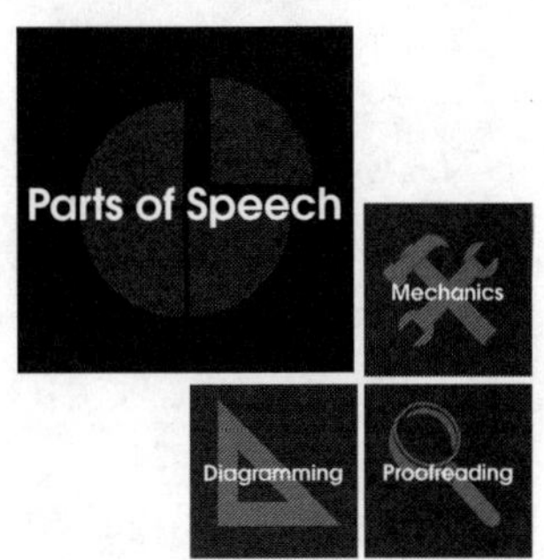

A Good Mechanic Is Hard to Find

Barbie's Sleepover

Fill in the blanks with the parts of speech. Then enter them into the story below in order. (Hint: To make a silly story, choose outrageous words.)

1. adjective ______________
2. prepositional phrase (place) ______________
3. adverb ______________
4. adjective ______________
5. proper nouns (names) ______________ ______________
6. adjective ______________
7. adjective ______________
8. prepositional phrase (place) ______________
9. adjective ______________
10. noun ______________
11. adjective ______________

After a ______________ (1) day ______________ (2), Barbie decided to invite some friends over to spend the night. ______________ (3), she called up her ______________ (4) friend, Skipper, and her other friends, ______________ (5) and ______________ (5). She rented a ______________ (6) video and got out ______________ (7) CDs. ______________ (8), she bought ______________ (9) snacks, chips and soda. Then she ordered a pizza with ______________ (10) on it. It was going to be a ______________ (11) party!

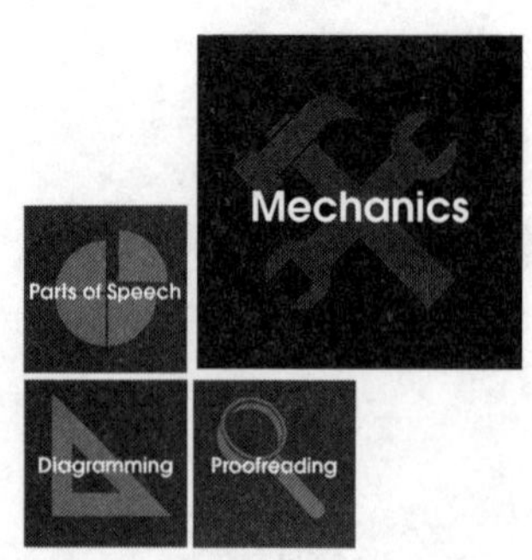

Good Mechanics Are Hard to Find

Pronoun Agreement

A pronoun must agree with its antecedent. If its antecedent is singular, then the pronoun must be singular. If the antecedent is plural, then the pronoun must be plural.

The words **everybody, nobody, anyone, everyone, each,** and **every** are always singular. Any pronoun referring to them must also be singular.

Choose the correct pronoun and underline its antecedent.

1. Everyone who is ready will be allowed to choose (her, their) new cheerleader uniform.
2. The cheerleaders wanted to choose (her, their) new coach.
3. Every guy wanted to have (his, their) say in the matter.
4. Nobody will wear plaid socks with (her, their) striped skirt.
5. The girls may have (her, their) showers first.
6. The locker storing the sweaty practice uniforms is famous for (its, their) odor.
7. Each of the players needs to bring (his, their) football helmet.
8. If everybody on the team would do (his, their) homework ahead of the game, the teachers would complain less about athletics.
9. Anyone who wants to make (himself, themselves) eligible for football needs to get his doctor's exam in the spring.

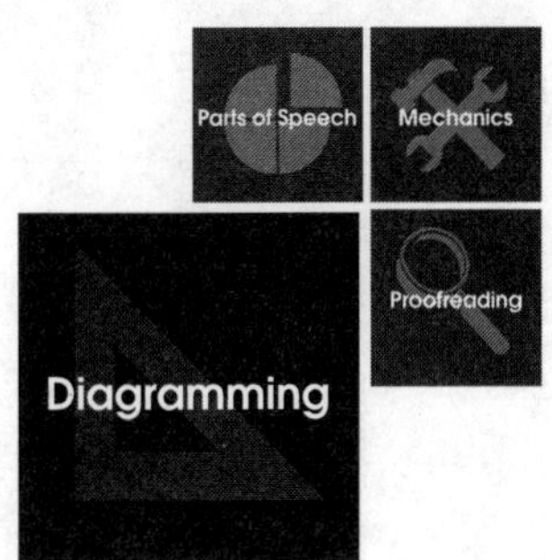

Understand the Structure

Sentence Patterns

Sentences follow a variety of patterns. Some sentences have a subject followed by a verb. Others have a subject, verb, indirect object, and direct object or any number of other variations.

Identify the sentence pattern: subject-verb, ***S-V;*** *subject-verb-direct object,* ***S-V-DO;*** *subject-verb-indirect object-direct object,* ***S-V-IO-DO;*** *compound subject-verb,* ***S-S-V,*** *compound sentence with the first clause subject-verb and the second, subject-verb-direct object,* ***cmpd—S-V; S-V-DO,*** *and so forth.*

1. _______________ The student studied.
2. _______________ The ambitious student studied his grammar lesson.
3. _______________ The student and the instructor ate ice cream and fudge sauce.
4. _______________ Either the ice cream or the grammar was tainted.
5. _______________ The student got sick and fainted.
6. _______________ From then on, no one ever studied grammar again.
7. _______________________ The student failed the test, but the instructor gave him credit anyway.
8. _______________________ All the students cheered, and all the instructors lost their jobs.

Adverbs answer the questions _______________, __________________, __________________, ____________________.

Careless Mistakes Can Cause Big Problems!

Rewrite the instructions to make each one parallel with the others.

Do you want to convince your classmates that you have special psychic powers? Try this trick.

1. Get approximately six identical envelopes and six plain pieces of white paper.
2. You should fold the paper over twice.
3. Inside one piece of paper, the psychic writes a word.
4. Then he refolds the paper and inserts it in the envelope and seals it.
5. Mark this envelope lightly so you can tell which it is.
6. Next, you ask five of your classmates to write a word on one of the squares of paper and refold it and seal it in an envelope.
7. Collect the envelopes and tell your classmates that you have psychic abilities. They must concentrate on the word they wrote, and you will read their thoughts. No talking is allowed during the psychic event because talking upsets the energy.
8. Take the first envelope and after concentrating with great drama, announce the word you wrote originally.
9. Open the envelope and the psychic looks at the word.
10. Then he places it back in the envelope without showing the class.
11. Take the next envelope and announce the word you read from the previous envelope.
12. Continue in this manner, making sure you open your own envelope last.
13. Finally, unfold each word one at a time and show the class how powerful a psychic you are.

Know Your Building Materials!

Subject complements follow linking verbs and describe the subject. A subject complement that is a noun or a pronoun is called a predicate nominative. A subject complement that is an adjective is called a **predicate adjective**.

Circle any linking verbs and draw one line under a predicate nominative and two lines under a predicate adjective. Cross out action verbs and their direct objects.

1. Bethany looked embarrassed after the compliment.
2. After the game, the coach seemed relieved.
3. My dog is an Australian Shepherd.
4. My dog bites men in uniform.
5. During the concert, I became enthralled by the music.
6. My parents prefer folk music to heavy metal.
7. The best shortstop on my team is I.
8. She feels incredibly sad about the incident.

List five linking verbs.

_______________, _______________, _______________,

_______________, _______________.

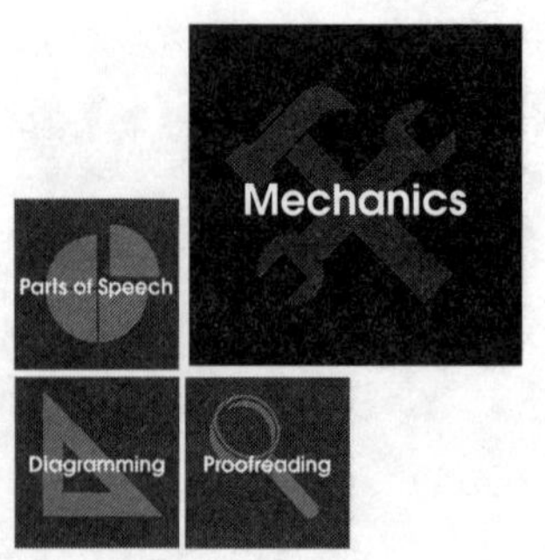

Good Mechanics Are Hard to Find

Rule: After a linking verb, use a subject pronoun. Use an object pronoun as a direct object, indirect object, or an object of a preposition.

In the following sentences, circle the pronoun(s). In the space, write ***S*** *if it is a subject pronoun used as a predicate nominative; write* ***D.O.*** *or* ***I.O.*** *if it is an object pronoun used as a direct object or indirect object; write* ***O.P.*** *if it is an object pronoun used as an object of a preposition.*

1. _______ The ball hit him in the face.
2. _______ The waves washed over me.
3. _______ The craziest one in the class is I.
4. _______ The teacher sent him and me to the office.
5. _______ It is I who did the evil deed.
6. _______ The next lucky person will be she.
7. _______ The dragon will eat you and him in one gulp.
8. _______ My mother brought me my lunch.

What Do You Think?

Do the subject pronouns sound funny after the linking verbs? People commonly make the mistake of using the object form instead.

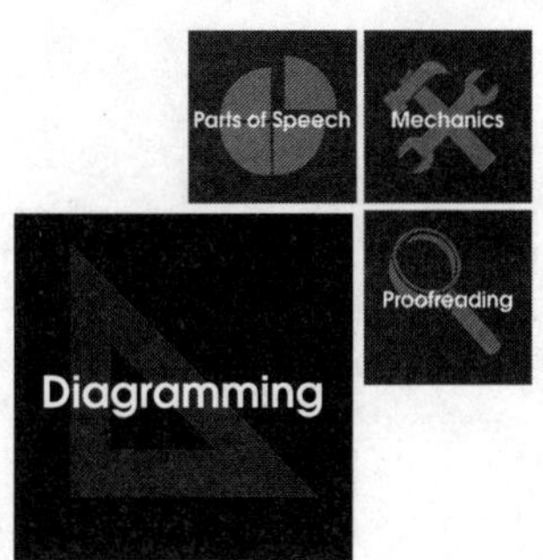

Understand the Structure

A subject complement is placed on the main line with the subject and verb. It is separated from the verb by a line slanted left.

My mother feels sick.

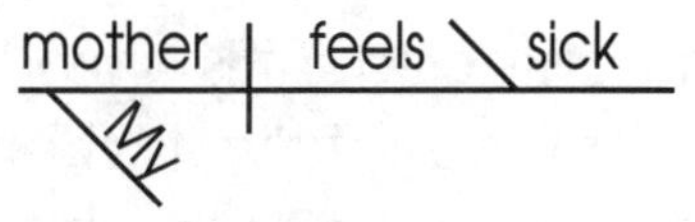

Diagram the following sentences paying special attention to subject complements.

1. The error was incredibly foolish.
2. My heartthrob looks gorgeous in his new outfit.
3. This painting is the best example of expressionism in the museum.

Careless Mistakes Can Cause Big Problems!

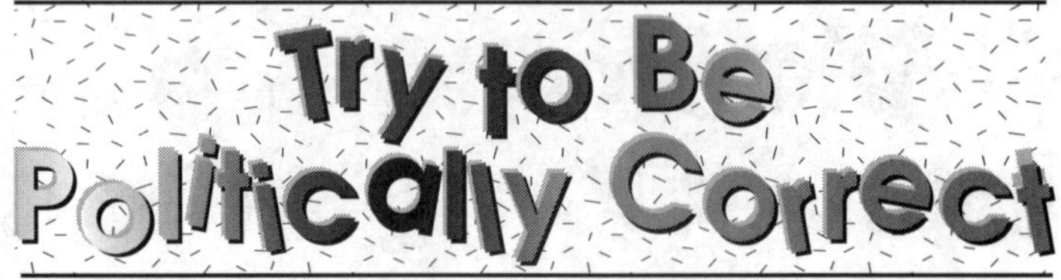

(without sounding awkward)

A pronoun must agree with its antecedent:

Each **shopper** must give **his or her** credit card number.

Sometimes the gender of the antecedent is unknown so the politically correct expression **his or her** is used. Unfortunately, that expression is awkward and wordy. A better choice is to reword the sentence so that **his or her** is not necessary:

Shoppers must give **their** credit card number.

This problem with agreement occurs with the indefinite pronouns **each, everyone, neither, anyone,** and **nobody** because they are treated as singular. The plural possessive pronoun **their** does not change gender.

Rewrite the following to get rid of the awkward expression.

1. Everyone loses his or her umbrella from time to time.
2. Nobody likes to be embarrassed in front of his or her friends.
3. Neither of the players remembered his or her uniform.
4. Each of us has his or her own plans.
5. Anyone with sense would bring his or her jacket.

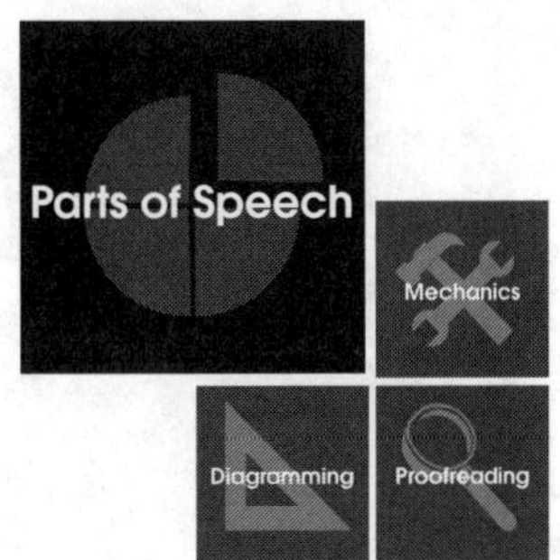

Know Your Building Materials!

Hint: Sometimes it is hard to tell whether a verb is a linking verb or an action verb. If you can replace the verb with **is, am, are, was,** or **were** without changing the meaning of the sentence, then it is a linking verb.

---

*Underline the verb. Write **A** on the line if it is an action verb or **L** if it is a linking verb.*

1. ______ The floor became sticky.
2. ______ The food tastes repulsive.
3. ______ The monster stared at me with glassy eyes.
4. ______ My sister looks sick.
5. ______ The locker room smelled bad.
6. ______ My voice sounded hoarse after all the yelling.
7. ______ Jack looks at the baseball cards with interest.
8. ______ The students smelled a wonderful aroma in the kitchen.

Did You Notice?

Did you notice how some words are linking verbs at some times and action verbs at other times?

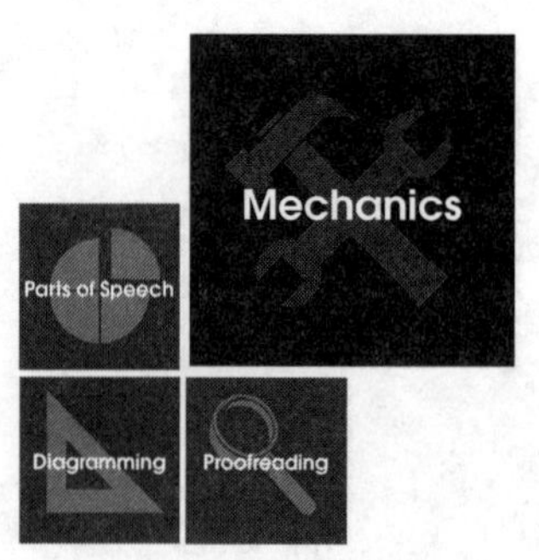

Good Mechanics Are Hard to Find

Rule: After a linking verb, use a subject pronoun as a predicate nominative. Use an object pronoun as a direct object, indirect object, or an object of a preposition.

Underline the correct pronoun in the following sentences.

1. The sweetest one is (she, her).
2. The lion crept softly behind (he, him).
3. We found (she, her) behind the sofa.
4. The most skillful in the class was (she, her).
5. The only possible suspect seemed to be (I, me).
6. The first to attack the pizza will be (he, him).
7. With (I, me) in charge, everything will get done.
8. The ones who adore peanut butter are (they, them).
9. Go with (we, us) to the movies tonight!
10. It is (I, me) in that picture.

What Do You Think?

Do the subject pronouns sound funny after the linking verbs? People commonly make the mistake of using the object form instead.

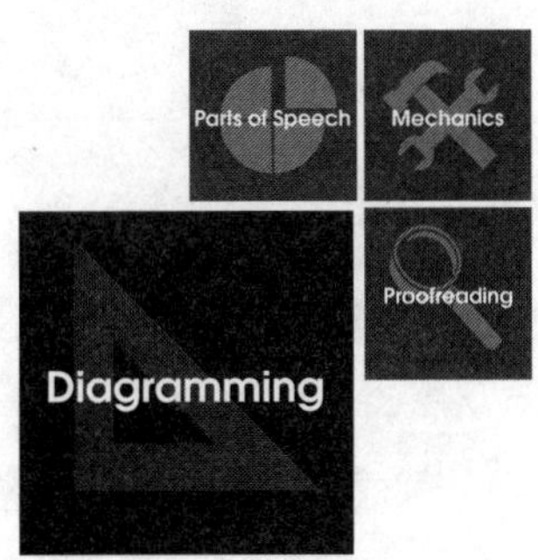

Understand the Structure

Diagram the following, paying special attention to whether the verb is a linking verb or an action verb.

1. Bulldogs with those smashed noses smell badly.

2. After a day in the swamp, my dog smells bad.

3. My dog hears the can opener and comes quickly to the door.

4. My dog may be full, but he still wants more doggy chow.

Careless Mistakes Can Cause Big Problems!

Correct the mistakes in the sentences below. ***There are eight mistakes.***

If someone offered to sell you the Brooklyn Bridge, would you write them a check? Amazingly, the Eiffel Tower, the famous Paris landmark, was sold not once but twice. Soon after World War I, the Eifel Tower was badly in need of repairing and paint. A con artist saw a news story about the huge cost of upkeep for the tower. Posing as a city official, he invited three businessmen to a secret meeting. He told them that the city had decided to sell the tower for scrap and that would be allowed to bid for the job. The con artist collected the deposit of a sucker who seemed real insecure. The crook then left to live the high life in Switzerland, hoping to avoid arrest. The sucker was so embarrassed about being swindled that they never reported the fraud. Two years later, the con man returned to Paris and sells the tower again. He then escaped to the U.S. where he was arrested quick for another fraud. He died in Alcatraz. On his death certificate, his profession was listed as "salesman."

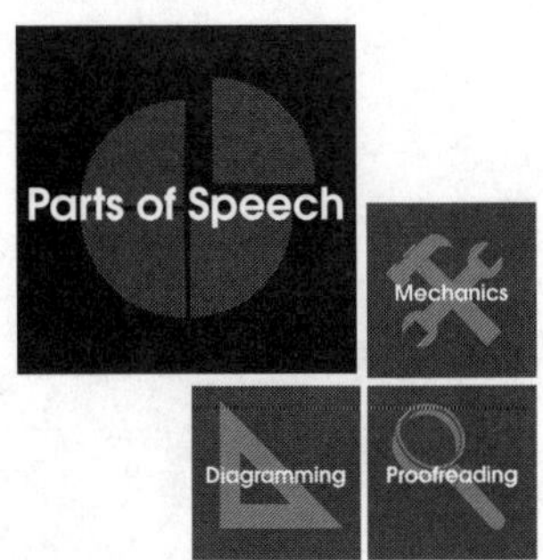

Know Your Building Materials!

Predicate Adjectives

Predicate adjectives follow a linking verb and describe the subject. Adverbs describe verbs, adverbs or adjectives.

Choose the correct form.

1. He was hitting the ball (good, well).
2. The receiver became (angry, angrily) after the late hit.
3. He ran very (quick, quickly).
4. My drives were fine, but I putted (bad, badly).
5. His attitude seemed (good, well), but inside he felt (sad, sadly).
6. He ran the bases (good, well) until the incident with the umpire.
7. Without any hesitation, the goalie sprinted (quick, quickly) for the ball.
8. Ruben runs (good, well), but he hits (bad, badly).

Next Time

Sportscasters are often guilty of using adjectives and adverbs incorrectly. Next time you listen to a sportscaster on television or the radio, count the number of mistakes made in two minutes.

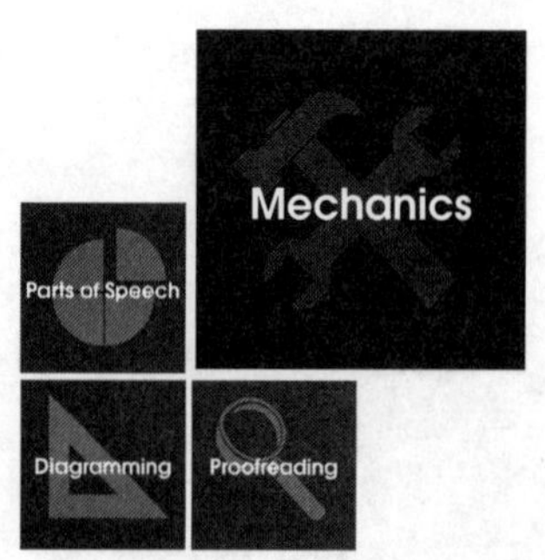

Good Mechanics Are Hard to Find

Fill in the blanks.

1. The object form of the pronoun **we** is ____________.
2. A pronoun following a linking verb should be in the ____________ form.
3. The subject form of the pronoun **me** is ____________.
4. A subject complement follows a ________________ verb.
5. An adjective modifies a ________________ or a ________________.
6. An adverb modifies a ______________, an ____________________, or an ____________________.
7. A compound sentence must be punctuated with a ____________ or a ________________.
8. If a compound subject is connected with **either, or,** then the verb agrees with the subject ________________ to the verb.
9. The adverbial form of **good** is ________________.

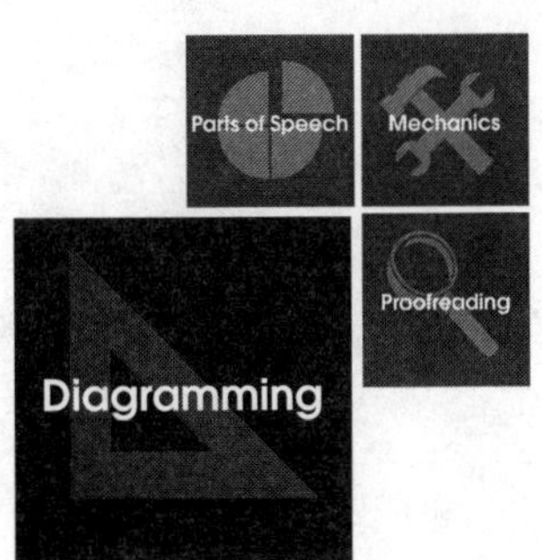

Understand the Structure

Reconstruct the sentence from the diagram.

1.

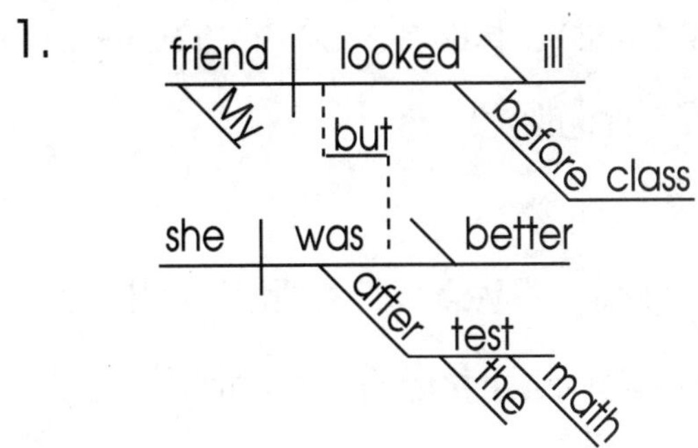

2.

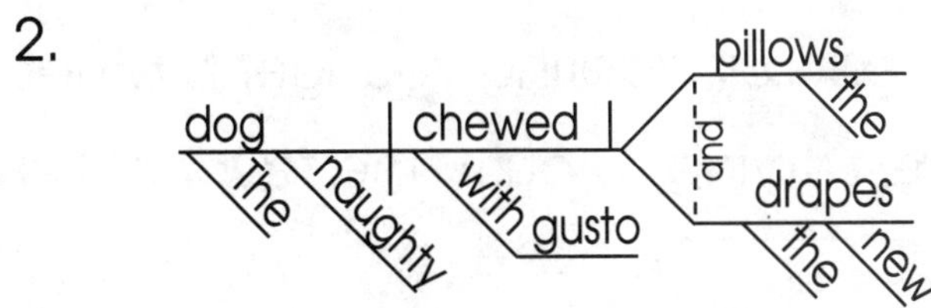

3.

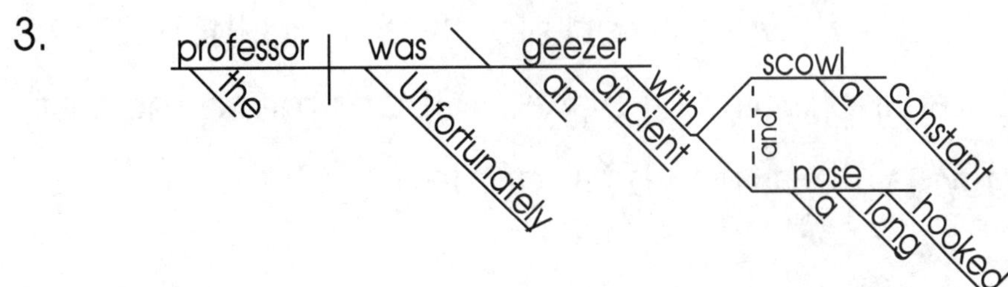

Careless Mistakes Can Cause Big Problems!

Correct the mistakes in the sentences below. ***There are nine mistakes.***

. Four brothers, ***I***, ***Me***, ***We***, and ***Us***, were camped in front of the refrigerator examining the last remaining peice of a apple pie.

"Which of us deserves that piece?" mulled ***Us***.

"It's me!" whined ***Me***.

"In your dreams!" answered ***I*** real quick. "***We*** will split it with me."

"By far the most deserving member of this family is me," snarled ***We***. "However, I have no plans to share it with ***I*** or anyone else for that matter."

"I was sure you would give me, your adoring younger brother, some of the piece," ***I*** simpered, trying to curry the favor of his older sibling.

"That pie smells badly and looks worse," suggested ***Us,*** hoping that the others would lose interest and go away.

While the others argued, ***Me*** slipped silently behind them, snatched the prize and wolfed it down. "That's me, a man of action, gloated ***Me*** with a mouth full of pie.

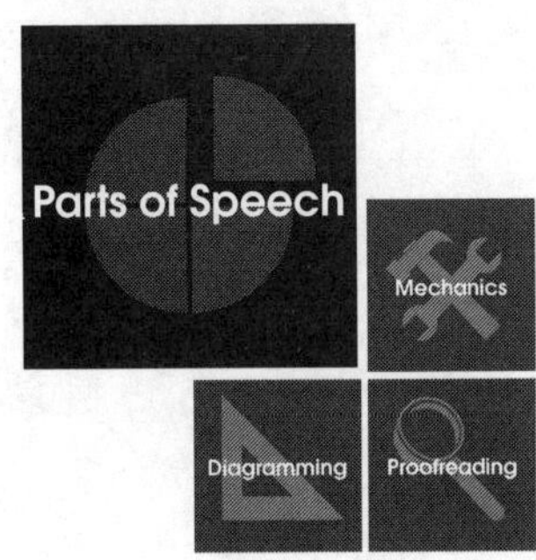

Know Your Building Materials!

Phrases and Clauses

A **phrase** is a group of words without a subject and a predicate. A prepositional phrase and a verb phrase are examples of phrases.

A clauses is a group of words with both a subject and a predicate. Clauses can be divided into **independent** and **dependent** clauses. An **independent clause** can make a sentence by itself. A **dependent clause** modifies an independent clause and cannot stand alone. A compound sentence is made up of at least two independent clauses. A comma follows introductory dependent clauses.

Cross out any prepositional phrases. Underline once any independent clauses and underline twice any dependent clauses. Circle the comma following an introductory dependent clause.

1. Ripe plums splattered from the tree because no one had picked them.
2. The field smelled like fermented fruit, and the cows acted drunk.
3. As the breeze blew brightly, the bees buzzed crazily in circles.
4. Under the spreading oak tree, the young man napped.
5. Because he was dreaming happy dreams, he smiled and snored.
6. Unfortunately, he was resting on an anthill that was full of army ants.
7. Although the dreamer didn't know it, the ants were upset.
8. They plotted their revenge while they imagined fresh meat for dinner.

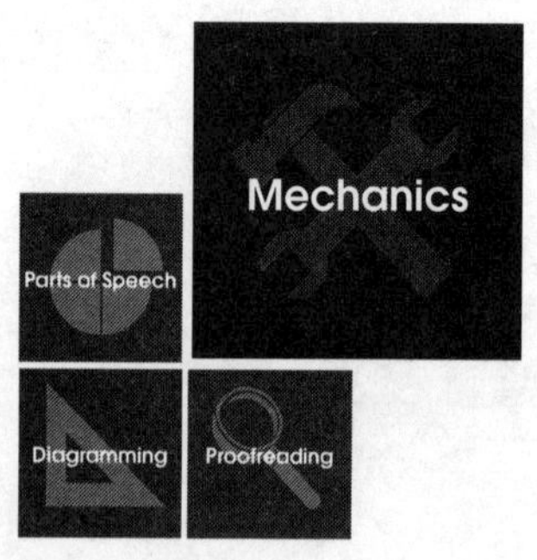

Good Mechanics Are Hard to Find

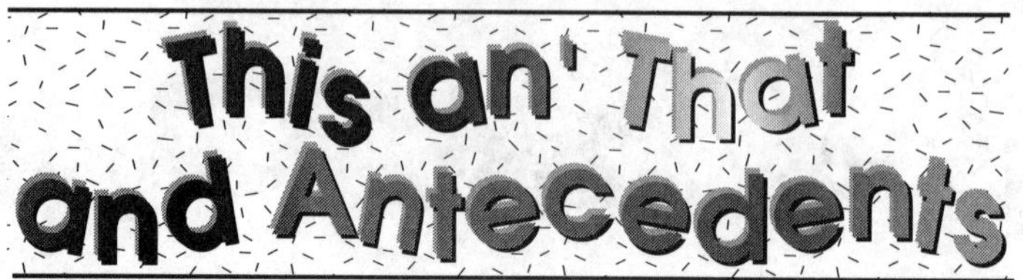

The pronouns **this**, **that**, **which** and **it** must refer to a specific noun in the preceding clause or sentence. They should not refer to a general idea.

Wrong: Plato believed that rulers should be educated in statesmanship. **This** is expressed in The Republic.

Right: Plato believed that rulers should be educated in statesmanship. **This idea** is expressed in The Republic.

Wrong: My brother bites his nails. **That** really bothers me.

Right: My brother bites his nails. **That habit** really bothers me.

Wrong: My mother is a birdwatcher. **It** is a hobby that doesn't interest me.

Right: My mother is a birdwatcher, but that doesn't interest me.

Rewrite the following sentences clarifying the antecedents to the pronouns.

1. My grades are good lately. This shows I have become very responsible.
2. Bud did not stick up for his friend which was very disloyal.
3. Koko is a talking gorilla. That means she seems very human.
4. If criminals are set free, it will force honest people to live in fear.
5. I worry a lot about finishing tasks on time, but this is not true for homework.
6. Your dog is obese which suggests you are overfeeding him.

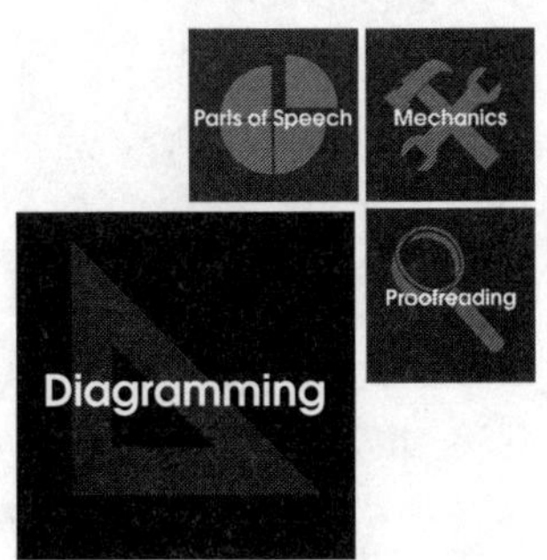

Understand the Structure

More Sentence Patterns

Sentences that have one independent clause are called **simple sentences.** Sentences with two or more independent clauses are **compound sentences.**

Sentences with one independent clause and one or more dependent clauses are called **complex sentences.** Compound sentences with one or more dependent clauses are called **compound-complex sentences.**

Identify the sentences as simple, compound, complex, or compound-complex. Underline the dependent clauses, and cross out prepositional phrases.

1. ________________ Because the Chargers have no quarterback, they haven't a chance this year.
2. ________________ Quarterbacks are important to the team in many ways.
3. ________________ They direct the plays, and they start off the offense.
4. ________________ The special teams often are responsible for the extra points that mean the difference between winning and losing.
5. ________________ During halftime, the coach gives the team a peptalk and encourages his players.
6. ________________ After the players come into the locker room, they shower, and they get dressed.

Careless Mistakes Can Cause Big Problems!

Correct the mistakes in the sentences below. ***There are eight mistakes.***

Tidal waves, or tsunamis, make great subjects for horror movies. In reality, they don't occur frequently but they can cause a great deal of damage along low-lying coastlines. Landslides, earthquakes or if volcanoes erupt deep beneath the surface of the sea cause tsunamis. The underwater disturbance causes waves to spread out quick in all directions. Although the waves can be up to several hundred miles long, they may be only three feet high. That makes them very difficult to detect. A nearby ship might not notice a tsunami that is only three feet high. When the tsunami reaches shallow water near the caost, the height of the wave is amplified. The shape of the sea floor near the coastline determines it's size. Some tsunamis reach 100 feet tall. Often the front of the wave is vertical, and is rushes toward the shore at 30 feet per second. That would be a terrifying sight to see!

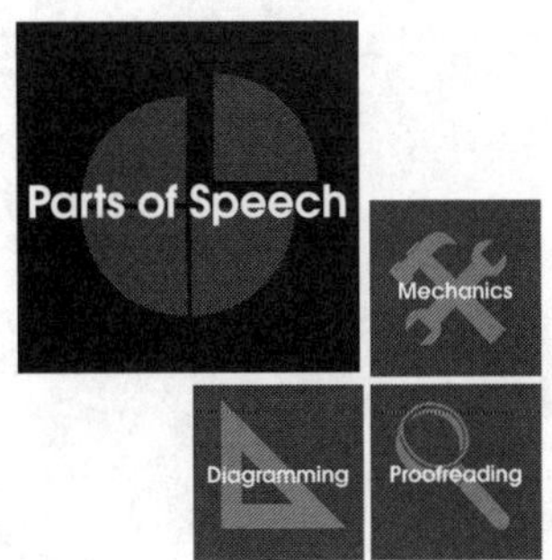

Know Your Building Materials!

Subordinate conjunctions connect dependent clauses to independent clauses.

Some common subordinate conjunctions are **because, although, as, if, when, whenever, until,** and **since**. Notice that sometimes a word functions as a preposition and sometimes the same word is a subordinate conjunction.

Circle the subordinate conjunction and underline the dependent clause. Cross out the prepositional phrases. Insert commas after introductory dependent clauses.

1. Until school starts you can sleep until ten.
2. You had better get your work done before it is due.
3. You had better get your work done before the day of reckoning.
4. Since your teacher is heartless you have no chance unless you work hard.
5. Because you are a hard worker your friends admire you.
6. If you want free time after school you should finish quickly.
7. Whenever my teacher is in a foul mood he gives tons of homework.

Fill in the blanks.

A clause is a group of words with a ____________________ and a ____________________.

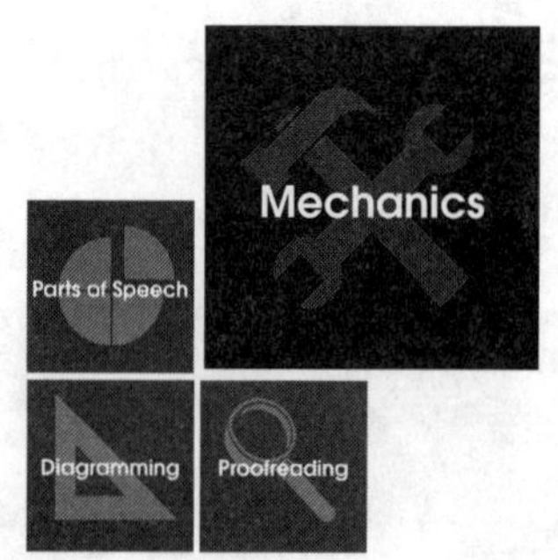

Good Mechanics Are Hard to Find

Like is commonly used as a preposition while **as** and **as if** are subordinate conjunctions.

Choose the correct word or words.

1. His father looked (like, as) a clown.
2. His father looked (like, as if) he were a clown.
3. Do (like, as) I say, not (like, as) I do.
4. The thunder crashed (like, as, as if) the sky were exploding.
5. The son acts (like, as) his father does.
6. Nobody cooks as well as (him, he does).
7. Nobody adores hot fudge sundaes like (me, I do).
8. Jeff likes you as much as (me, I do).

Fill in the blanks.

A clause must have a ______________________________, and a ____________________________.

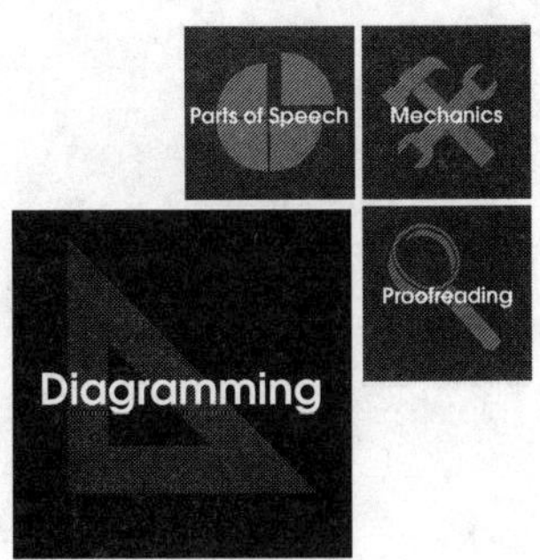

Understand the Structure

An adverb clause is placed on a line below the main clause. A dotted line connects the verb in the adverb clause to the word it modifies in the main clause. The subordinate conjunction is placed on the dotted line.

After he finishes his homework, John goes to work.

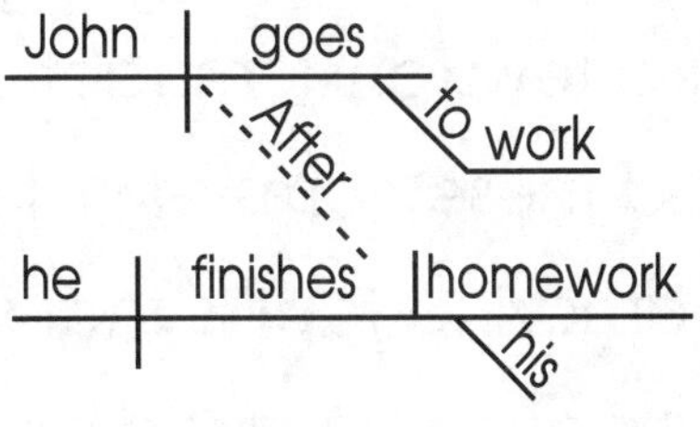

Diagram the following, paying special attention to adverb clauses.

1. I love my slippers because they tickle my toes.
2. When you get a sunburn, you increase your risk of skin cancer.

Careless Mistakes Can Cause Big Problems!

Correct the mistakes in the sentences below. ***There are nine mistakes.***

The urban myth tells us that 90% of our brain is unused. Of course, that is not true, but most of us do have some extra spots available for a few random facts. I thought you might appreciate like I did these items of animal lore gleaned off the Internet. The first amazing fact is that snails can sleep for three years without eating. Around my house, they don't live that long because the garden snails chief archenemy is me. The next fascinating fact is that koala bears fingerprints are virtually indistinguishable from human prints, so they could be confused at a crime scene. This seems quite likely, considering all the rabid koalas that are running around our inner cities in gangs like Al Capone's buddies. Finally, did you know that a ostrich's eyeball is bigger than it's brain? It is also bigger then many people's brains if their actions are any indication of brain size. Lest you complain about the brain size of the author of this piece, I'd better draw it to a hasty conclusion.

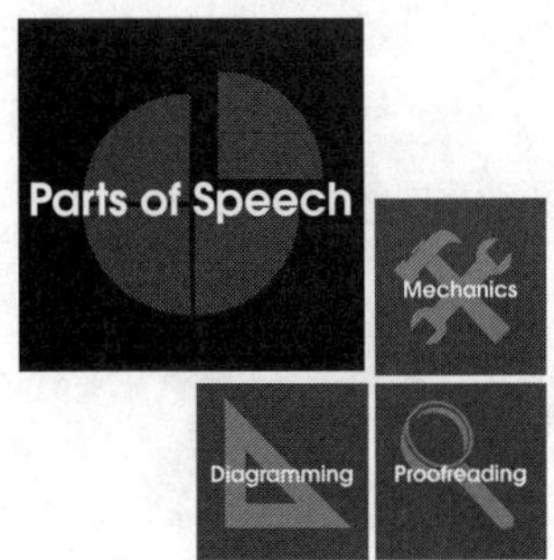

Know Your Building Materials!

Relative Pronouns

Relative pronouns connect adjective clauses to an antecedent in another clause. The most common relative pronouns are **who, whom, whose, which,** and **that**.

The car **that caused the accident** was speeding.

That is a relative pronoun in an adjective clause. The antecedent of **that** is **car**.

Underline the adjective clause once. Circle the relative pronoun, and underline its antecedent twice.

1. A Mustang is the most exciting car that is on the road today.
2. Joel is the only student to whom the teacher gave an "A."
3. Ginger was embarrassed by a remark that was unkind.
4. The boy, whose jacket was lost, was very cold that night.
5. The citizens, over whom the helicopters fly, are irate.
6. After the kids who were at the football game came home, the family ate.
7. The dust puppies, which were under the bed, were as big as Great Danes.
8. The lake in which the Loch Ness monster supposedly lives is very deep.

Fill in the blanks.

A clause has both a _________________ and a _________________.

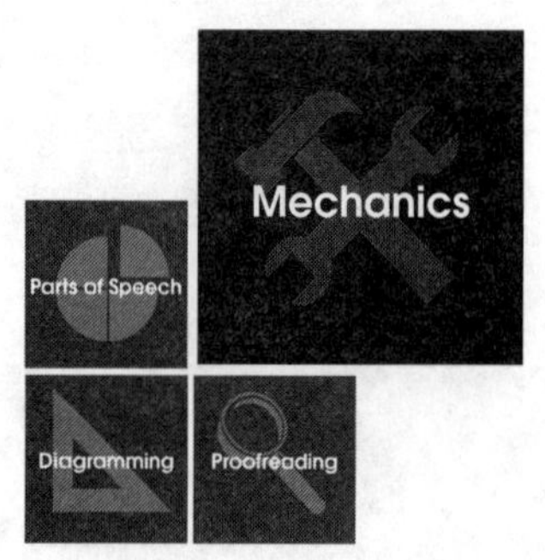

Good Mechanics are Hard to Find

When a relative pronoun is used as the subject of an adjective clause, the subject form, **who,** is used. When a relative pronoun is used as a direct object, an indirect object or an object of a preposition in an adjective clause, the object form, **whom**, is used.

The child **who is first** will have to wait.
(**Who** is the subject of the adjective clause, **who is first**.)

The child **whom you scolded** is crying.
(**Whom** is the direct object in the adjective clause **whom you scolded**.)

Underline the adjective clause and choose the correct form of the relative pronoun.

1. The detective (who, whom) found the prints was careless with the evidence.
2. The criminal, (who, whom) the detective shot, was wanted in three states.
3. The partner, with (who, whom) he investigated the crime scene, was crooked.
4. The policeman, to (who, whom) he gave the evidence, was incompetent.
5. I believe that the witness (who, whom) testified about the gun was lying.
6. He arrested a thief (who, whom) he caught red-handed.

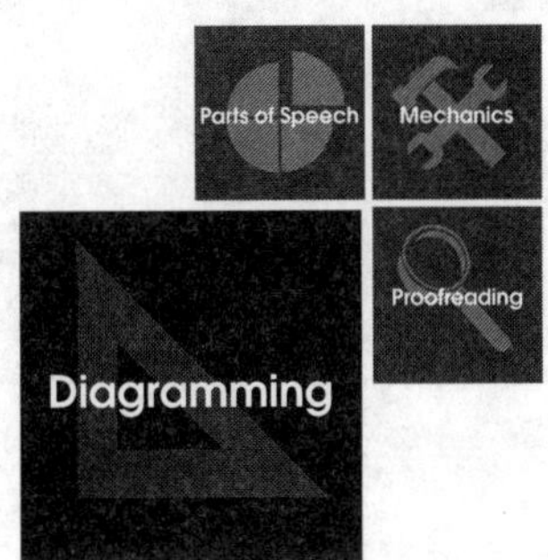

Understand the Structure

An adjective clause is placed on a line below the main clause. A dotted line connects the relative pronoun with its antecedent in the main clause.

I like the restaurant that serves potstickers.

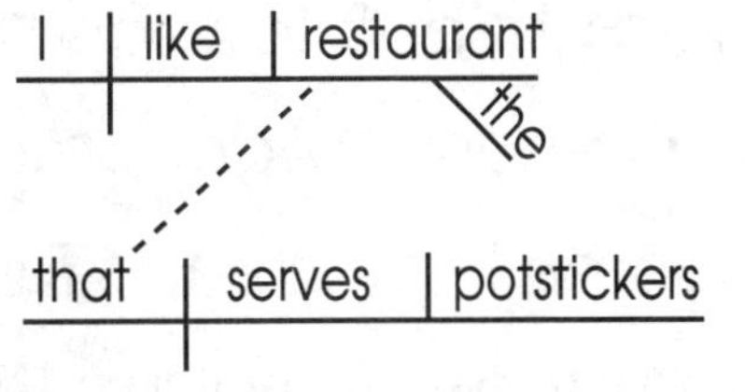

Diagram the following, paying special attention to adjective clauses.

1. The pitcher who got the two-year contract broke his arm.
2. My friend, to whom you sent the card, feels better.
3. I sent a letter that described my situation to the man who overcharged me.

Careless Mistakes Can Cause Big Problems!

Correct the mistakes in the sentences below. ***There are seven mistakes.***

Teachers are sometimes more astute then students expect. An incident that occurred several years ago at Duke University illustrates this. The night before finals, two students decided to go to a party at another college some distance away. Like college students sometimes do, this fun-loving pair spent the night at the party instead of making the long drive back to their dorm. Unfortunately, the next morning they realized that they had missed there exam. To avoid failing, they decided to concoct a excuse about how they were returning to campus when they got a flat tire. The professor who they told their sad tale to seemed real sympathetic and gave them permission to take the exam the next day. Well rested and right on time, the two students showed up the next day. The professor gave each of them a copy of the exam and sent them into separate rooms to take it. The exam was short—just two questions. The second question was the hard one: "Which tire?"

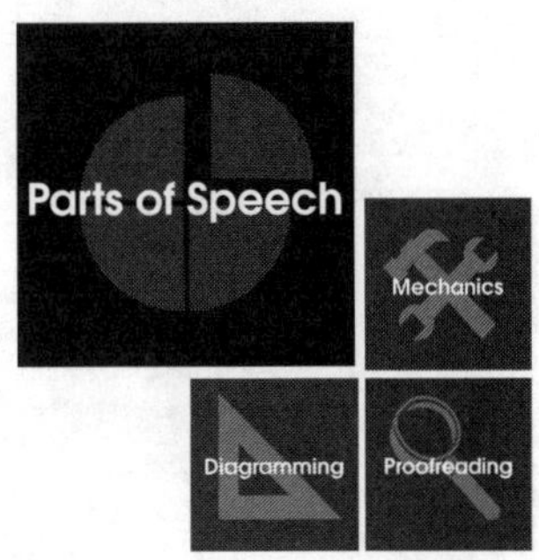

Know Your Building Materials!

Sometimes an entire clause functions as the subject, a predicate nominative, a direct or indirect object, or an object of a preposition. These clauses that take the place of a noun are called **noun clauses**.

Whoever is going needs to buy tickets.
(**Whoever is going** is the subject of the main verb **needs**.)

Underline the noun clause and label the job it does in the sentence: subject, direct object, object of a preposition, and so forth.

1. What I saw today on Mulberry Street was astonishing.
2. I will give my leftovers to whoever wants them.
3. Who you are makes no difference to me.
4. My classmates agree that Mrs. Fink is obnoxious.
5. Young readers think that the Harry Potter books are the best new series.

In a noun clause, the pronoun **who** or **whoever** is in subjective or objective form depending on **the job it does in the noun clause**.
Some colleges give scholarships to **whoever** needs them.
The noun clause **whoever needs them** functions as an object of the preposition **to,** but **whoever** is in the subjective form because it is the subject of the clause.

Underline the noun clause and choose the correct pronoun.

1. I will destroy (whoever, whomever) gets in my way.
2. (Whoever, Whomever) the teacher likes will get an "A."
3. The prize will go to (who, whom) you choose.

Good Mechanics Are Hard to Find

Sentence Fragments

Every sentence must have an independent clause. A group of words without a subject or a predicate in an independent clause is called a **sentence fragment**.

*If the following is a sentence, underline the independent clause and label it sentence (**S**). If the following is missing a subject or predicate or is a dependent clause, label it fragment (**F**).*

1. _____ The individual who owns this backpack.
2. _____ The owner of the backpack who has a runny nose needs a tissue.
3. _____ Students carry backpacks with too much junk in them.
4. _____ Whoever carries a loaded backpack will have back spasms.
5. _____ Whenever he overloads his backpack with homework.
6. _____ This load of books will destroy whoever has to carry it.
7. _____ Old candy bar wrappers and half-eaten lunches in the bottom.
8. _____ Without any thought of student health, teachers who assign loads of homework.
9. _____ Because the students need to develop better posture, they should not carry backpacks over one shoulder.
10. _____ Homework is the root of all evil, and teachers should not assign it.

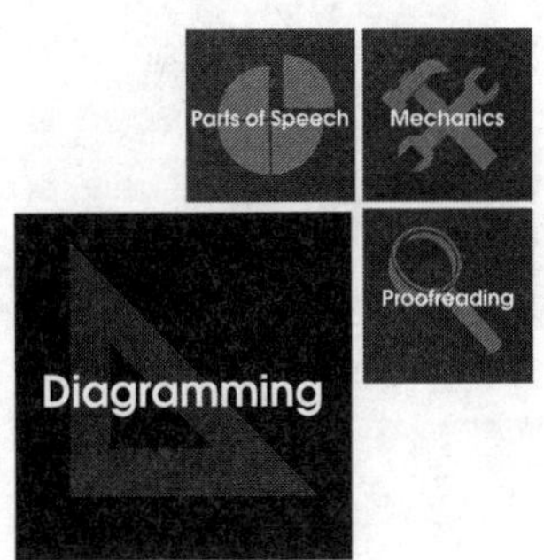

Understand the Structure

A noun clause takes the place of a noun. It is diagrammed on a separate line that stands on a stilt. If the clause does the job of the subject, the stilt sits on the subject line. If the clause does the job of an object of a preposition, the stilt sits on the object of the preposition line and so on. Sometimes a noun clause has an introductory word that only serves to introduce the clause. That word lies along the stilt.

He gave the candy to whoever wanted it.

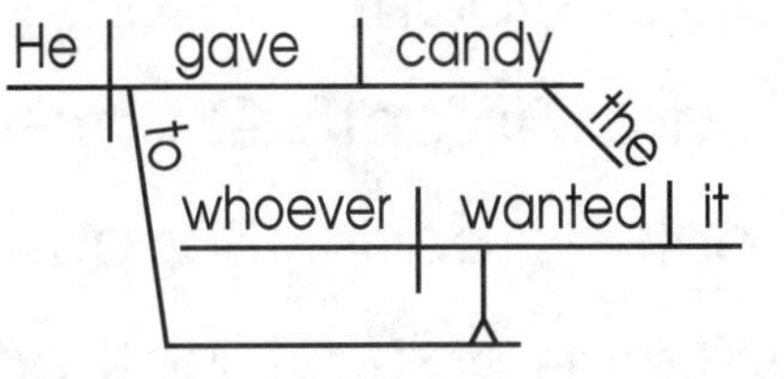

Diagram the following, paying special attention to noun clauses.

1. We thought that the test was difficult.
2. What computers can do is unbelievable.
3. We will give passes to whomever the coach chooses.

Careless Mistakes Can Cause Big Problems!

Correct the mistakes in the sentences below. ***There are eight mistakes.***

"Children should be seen but not heard" is an old saying propounded by an earlier generation. In victorian england, mothers used opium to make their offspring behave like mannerly children should. Opium solutions like "Mother's Helper," "Soothing Syrup," and "Infant's Quietness" were sold in large jugs. Children drank it greedy. Because it was often mixed with sweet syrup. Since opium is not readily water soluble, it tended to become concentrated in the bottom of the jug. Thus the child who got the last dose became totally intoxicated. Women of the upper classes as well as the poor sought the relief from their fractious offspring by sedating them. If a child was inconvenient to her social life. If she couldn't afford to come home from her sweatshop job to nurse her baby. Mom could quiet him with a dollop of syrup. Imagine the long-term effects of drug dependency on a whole generation of children who were "seen but not heard.

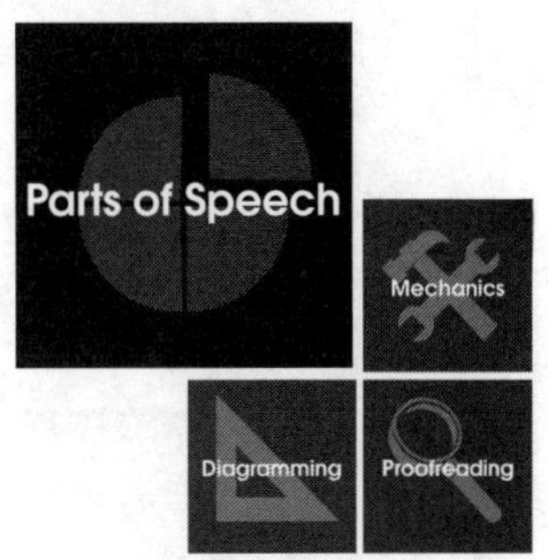

Know Your Building Materials!

Conjunctive adverbs show a relationship between independent clauses. They often act as transitions.

Some common conjunctive adverbs are **therefore, thus, nevertheless, moreover, still, accordingly, for example, however** and **hence**. Since conjunctive adverbs connect **independent clauses**, a period or a semicolon must separate the clauses.

Label the appropriate clause as independent (Ind.) or dependent (Dep.) and punctuate properly. Underline any conjunctive adverbs once and any subordinate conjunctions twice.

1. It is raining, however I am going to the beach anyway.
2. The tide is low, therefore the waves will be puny.
3. When I surf, I get good exercise.
4. Paddling out through the breakers is tough work, still lying on the board waiting for a wave is restful.
5. Although surfing can be dangerous, it is worth the risk.
6. I go to the beach every day unless it is stormy.
7. After a long day at work, a dip in the ocean is refreshing because it clears my mind.
8. I get a rush when I see a huge wave bearing down on me and my adrenaline starts to pump.

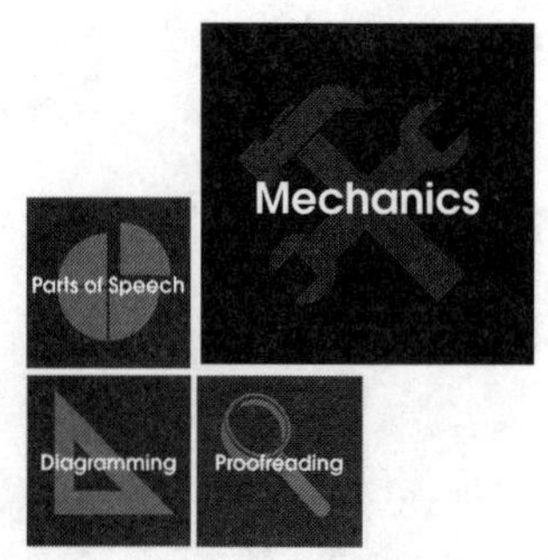

Good Mechanics Are Hard to Find

Run-On Sentences

A **run-on sentence** is two or more independent clauses improperly strung together. Connect independent clauses correctly by using a semicolon or a coordinate conjunction. A run-on sentence omits these connectors and often uses a comma (comma splice) or a conjunctive adverb by mistake.

*Label the run-on sentences (**r-o**) and the correct sentences (**ok**).*

1. ______ I washed my car yesterday hence it will rain today.
2. ______ I think, therefore I am.
3. ______ Although I don't believe in destiny, I am convinced that we were meant to be together.
4. ______ Karma means that what you do comes back to you, for example, if you are cruel to others, others will be cruel to you.
5. ______ I am a fatalist, thus I believe that what I do makes no difference.
6. ______ Unless I was an evil person in my last life, I don't deserve the predicament I am in now.
7. ______ The pirate's parrot is pecking painfully at my proboscis.
8. ______ My nose hurts , moreover I have feathers in my eyes.

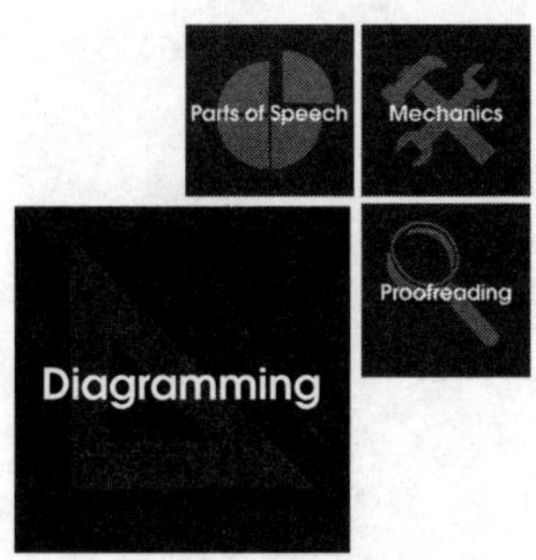

Understand the Structure

Diagram the following sentences. Choose the correct pronoun based on its position in the diagram.

1. Give the raise to (whoever, whomever) deserves it.
2. The parent (who, whom) I detest will chaperone the dance.
3. Although the treasurer was (he, him), George still believed that the money was handled carelessly.

Careless Mistakes Can Cause Big Problems!

Run-on sentences can be corrected using three different techniques. The easiest way is to insert a period or a semicolon between the independent clauses. Another method is to use a coordinating conjunction between the independent clauses. Finally, one of the independent clauses can be changed to a dependent clause.

Correct each of the following run-ons. Use each method at least once.

1. I came, I saw, I conquered.
2. My heart pounded, still I waited patiently.
3. I fear the future, I don't know how I will support myself.
4. After I graduate from high school, I will start a software company, hence I will become an instant millionaire.
5. I am very good at dealing with financial matters except balancing my checkbook, my totals never seem to add up.
6. Unlike many high school students, I am very responsible financially, I spend within my budget.
7. I wouldn't like to have to pay for all my own expenses, however, living on my salary wouldn't be much fun.

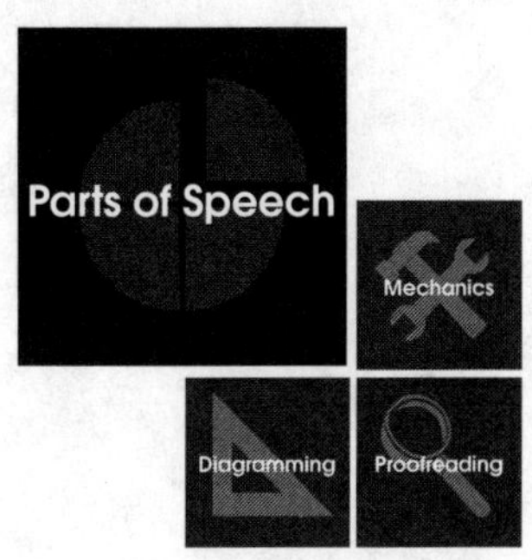

Know Your Building Materials!

Rewrite the following sentences, changing the sentence patterns to the one indicated.

1. The student finished his homework. Then he went to the mall. (Complex with adverb clause)
2. The unfortunate player who made the error sulked. He was sorry afterward. (Compound-complex)
3. My parents are behind the times. They still like the Beatles and the Rolling Stones. (Complex with adjective clause)
4. I am absolutely addicted to my new computer game and I play it day and night. (Complex with adverb clause)

Good Mechanics Are Hard to Find

Place a comma after an adverbial dependent clause at the start of a sentence. **Because he burps loudly, his table manners are questionable.**

Place a comma after an introductory phrase. **In the dining room, burping is not permissible.** Do not use a comma when the clause or phrase is in the middle of the sentence. Do not use a comma after a noun clause used as the subject of a sentence.

Correct the punctuation in the following sentences.

1. After the ball game we'll stop for burgers and fries.
2. We'll pick up some pizza after the ball game.
3. Because we stuff ourselves with junk food at the game we rarely are hungry when we get home.
4. Going to the game and stuffing myself with junk food are my favorite activities.
5. When we get home we often have work to do but we don't have the energy to do it.
6. We lie down we watch television and nap.
7. Whatever is most fattening is always most delicious.
8. If you consider all the pain involved in losing weight it probably is better to eat vegetables fruits and whole grain products instead of cotton candy hot dogs and ice cream but it certainly isn't as much fun.

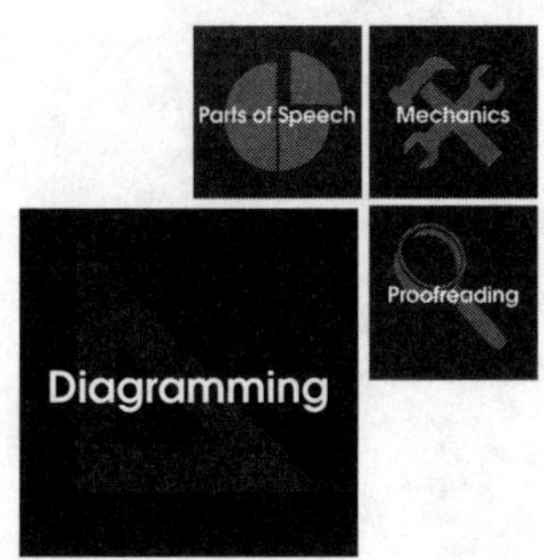

Understand the Structure

Diagram this monster. ***Hint:*** *Find the independent clause first, and add in the dependent clauses afterward.*

1. Before the hero who felt no fear and the villain who seethed with unbridled rage could cross their swords, the townspeople rushed to the scene and destroyed whatever was left of the peace in the castle.

Careless Mistakes Can Cause Big Problems!

Correct the mistakes in the sentences below. ***There are six mistakes.***

Pranks that require great engineering skill but cause no damage are legendary at Massachusetts Institute of Technology (MIT). One of the most famous occurred during a Harvard-Yale football game in 1982. Since MIT is located right down the street from Harvard. The rivalry between the two schools is fierce, thus Harvard's big game was the perfect site for an MIT caper. The night before the big game, students smuggled a weather balloon into the stadium and buried it on the 46-yard line. A device to inflate the balloon was attached and wires were run out to an undergraduate who the students had chosen to trigger the spectacle. In the middle of the game a black weather balloon with "MIT" emblazoned on it emerged in a puff of smoke, inflates to full size, and floated away. The actual weather balloon now resides in a museum dedicated entirely to MIT's technological pranks.

Lessons 21-30

Choose the correct pronoun.

1. All of the contestants failed to answer (his, their) first question correctly.
2. Nobody trying on the new jackets liked the color of (his, their) necktie.
3. The photo of Pia and (I, me) is not very flattering.
4. Anyone who tries out for football must bring (his, their) permission slip.
5. The bottom man on the totem pole seems to be (I, me).
6. Josh is the friend (who, whom) I sent the letter to.
7. (Whoever, Whomever) the coach most respects is his first choice.

Identify each of the following as a run-on (r-o), a fragment (frag), or a correct sentence (C).

1. _______ The roller coaster dipped and turned ceaselessly, but most of the white-knuckled riders refused to open their eyes.
2. ________ The parents down below worried, they hoped the ride would end soon.
3. ________ Some happy screeches filled the air, therefore some of the children were enjoying the ride.
4. ________ Because the track with its excellent safety record was known throughout the world.
5. ________ Most carnival rides have the occasional accident for example the brakes on a car might not work.

Lessons 21-30, continued

Rewrite the sentences, changing the pattern to the one indicated.

1. Many viewers watch the Oscars on television, and the stars attending dress in their most spectacular outfits. (Complex)
2. There are always winners and losers. Some actors are bound to be unhappy. Others, of course, will be ecstatic. (Compound-complex)
3. The actress is half naked. She is wearing a dress slit all the way up to her waist. (Complex with adjective clause)

Correct the eight errors.

In the theater, popcorn covers the floor, bubblegum is stuck to the seats, and some viewers spill pop on the floor. While the cleaning crew quickly grabs brooms and sponges the line at the door stretches into the parking lot. Patrons hate to have their feet stick to the floor like they are encased in cement, however the employees rarely have enough time to clean up after the pigs that watched the previous show. People are often slobs in movie theaters which seems a bit unfair to the cleaning crew. Most employees despise whoever they catch spilling and littering in their theater.

Diagram the following sentence.

The long white limousine stopped at the curb while the crowd cheered wildly.

Lessons 21-30

Choose the correct pronoun.

1. My parents complain that the laziest person in the family is (I, me).
2. I want to go with (whoever, whomever) is brave enough to climb it.
3. Every cadet will take (his, their) turn at peeling potatoes.
4. The crook (who, whom) the police caught will get ten years to life.
5. Anyone going to prom should get (her, their) dress early.
6. The dope who dented the car seems to be (I, me).
7. The prize will be awarded to (whoever, whomever) deserves it.

Identify each of the following as a run-on (r-o), a fragment (frag), or a correct sentence (C).

1. ______ Backpacking can be a great adventure however it can be dangerous if the planning isn't done carefully.
2. ______ Remember to bring a water purification system.
3. ______ Ziplock bags are great for keeping clothes dry in your pack during a thunderstorm or heavy dew.
4. ______ Since wet clothes can be really uncomfortable on a cold morning.
5. ______ Moreover, dry socks are required for keeping your feet healthy.
6. ______ Freeze-dried food is convenient, it doesn't taste good though.

Lessons 21-30, continued

Rewrite the sentences, changing the pattern to the one indicated.

1. Hot dogs are not healthy fare. They are usually high in fats. (Complex)
2. Some brands of ice cream are low in fats. They often have a good flavor but a gummy texture. (Compound-complex)
3. Vegetarian food should be available in the lunchroom. It should be provided for whoever wants it. (Complex with noun clause)

Correct the seven errors.

For almost fifty years game shows have been popular on television. In the fifties gullible viewers enjoyed rooting for their favorite contestants each week. Shows awarded big money to whoever answered the most questions on the $64,000 Question and Twenty-one, however, the outcome of the contests were often rigged. The producers chose the most popular contestants and gave them the answers before the show. That allowed them to practice their acting skills on the air while they agonized over each answer. One contestant who was not given answers complained that the shows were rigged, as a result, Congress held hearings to expose the fraud. One contestant, who the producers had chosen to fail, instead won the top prize in the category of prize fighting. She was Dr. Joyce Brothers who later became a famous television psychologist.

Diagram the following sentence.

One contestant who was given answers made a mistake unintentionally.

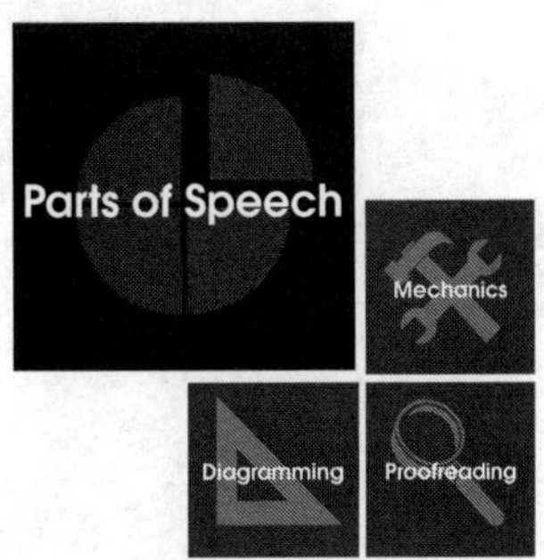

Know Your Building Materials!

An **appositive** is a noun or pronoun that identifies another noun or pronoun near it. Commas usually set off an appositive. An appositive must be in the same subject or object form as the word or group of words it identifies.

My brother, **the annoying fiend**, bothers me daily.

The annoying fiend identifies **My brother**.

The teacher was angry at the noisemakers, **Bess and me**.

Noisemakers is an object of a preposition so the pronoun, **me**, must be in the object form.

Underline the appositive word or phrase.

1. The cook, my loyal friend, slipped me an extra piece of apple pie.
2. The prize went to Jason, the hardest worker in the class.
3. Charles Dickens, the author of A Tale of Two Cities, was a prolific writer.

Choose the correct word.

1. The Johnson brothers, Jack and (he, him) are exceedingly tall.
2. The invitation was addressed to us, Joan and (I, me).
3. Two of us, Derek and (I, me) are known for our loud voices.

Good Mechanics Are Hard to Find

Use interesting new expressions instead of worn-out phrases in common usage. Hackneyed expressions are not as effective as fresh new images.

Underline the clichés and replace them with better word choices.

1. My aunt went ballistic when she discovered her car was dented.
2. You had better shake a leg if you expect to get to the game on time.
3. There are many creative ideas out there.
4. He is not the brightest star in the sky, but he works like a dog.
5. I died laughing when Hilary went ape over the student teacher.
6. We have a sneaking suspicion that Charles has a thing for Dana.
7. We can't agree to disagree; we'll fight to the bitter end.

Fill in the blanks.

A clause contains both a ________________ and a ________________.

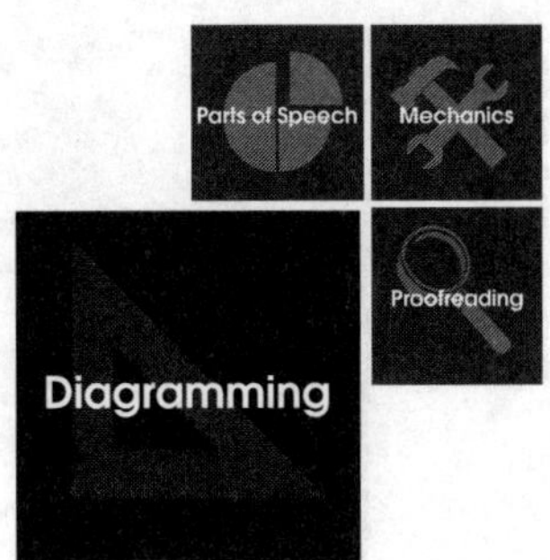

Understand the Structure

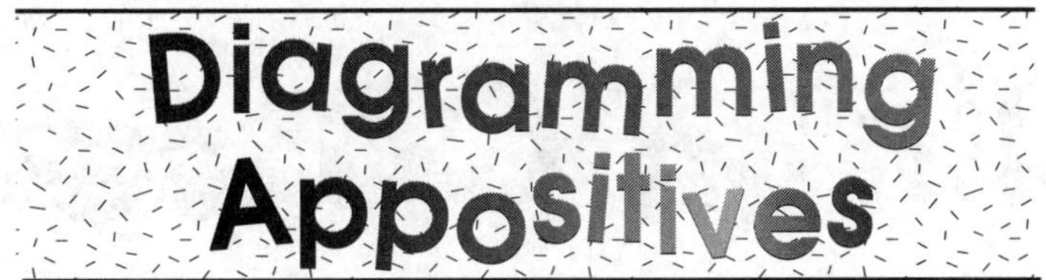

An appositive is placed in parentheses on the line next to the word it describes. Modifiers are placed on slanted lines below the appositive.

I brushed Blackie, my filthy setter.

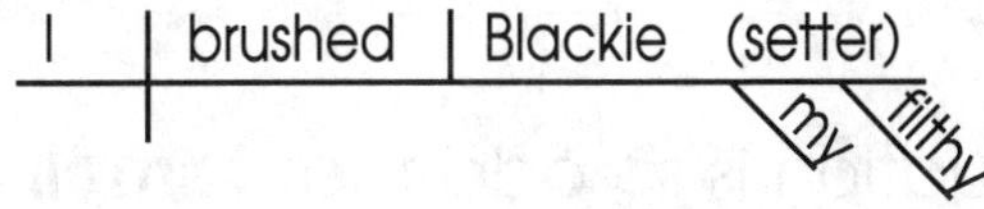

1. I felt sorry for my only sibling, Ben.
2. Because we won the championship, the local newspaper interviewed Josh, the captain of the team.
3. The student council president, Laurie, chose who would represent us.

Careless Mistakes Can Cause Big Problems!

Identify the clichés from their literal translation.

Example: This situation is so odd that I sense with my nose a small rodent.

This situation is so odd that **I smell a rat**.

1. While you are visiting your grandparents, pay attention to the 16th and 17th letters of the alphabet.
2. Jen is such a hard worker that you can always count on her to travel 5,280 feet farther.
3. Three-year-old Tim is so active that in a restaurant he behaves as if his trousers are being invaded by insects of the order *Hymenoptera.*
4. Surprisingly, during my first speech, I was the temperature of a common, cylindrical garden vegetable.
5. My father says he will buy me a new sports car when Hades reaches a sustained temperature below 32 degrees.
6. When you really want something, you need to use adhesive on yourself and your firearms.

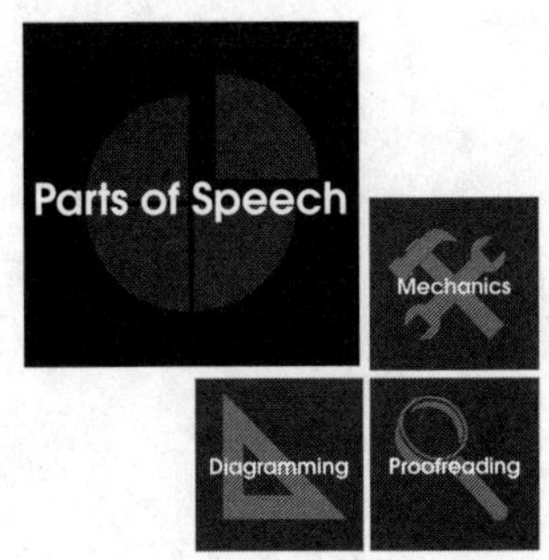

Know Your Building Materials!

A **participle** is an *-ing, -ed,* or *-en* verb form that can be used as an adjective.

The **running** boy was tired.

Running is a form of the verb **to run**, but in this sentence it functions as an adjective modifying **boy.**

Sometimes a participle has an object.

The girl **hitting the ball** was confident.

Hitting the ball is a participial phrase that modifies **girl. Ball** is the object of the participle **hitting.**

Underline the participles and participial phrases used as adjectives. Cross out participles used as verbs.

1. The dancer, gyrating wildly, was discovered to be insane.
2. My brother, taking a calculus class, has forgotten all his algebra.
3. The crazy dancer was taking a basic basket-weaving class instead of calculus.
4. Pushing aside all his inhibitions, my brother will dance while he is memorizing his geometric formulae.
5. Unfortunately, the Spanish class fulfilling my language requirement includes my brother and the dancer.
6. Usually, a class harboring insane dancers and incompetent brothers is a difficult learning environment.

Name the present participle form of the following verbs:

To be ____________, to go______________, to find ____________.

Good Mechanics Are Hard to Find

Dangling Participles

Wrapped in cellophane, the model held a box of bonbons.

Who or what is wrapped in cellophane: the model or the bonbons?

The participle **Wrapped in cellophane** dangles because it is too far from the word it modifies.

Underline the participles in the following sentences and draw an arrow to the words modified.

1. Ignoring the danger of the searing flames, the fire was contained by the firemen.
2. Hiding in the back room, the babysitter searched for the toddler.
3. The motorist gunned his engine frazzled by the frustrating traffic jam.

Sometimes the word modified by the participle is left out completely. To correct the sentence, add the word modified and place the participle next to it. Rewrite the following sentences adding words if necessary.

1. Fighting off an attack of hay fever, the grass was mowed.
2. Hidden among the fresh daffodils, I found a plastic flower.
3. Outsmarted by the gophers once again, more traps were set.
4. Running to catch the school bus, my books fell in a puddle.
5. Lying in the gutter, scummy and dirty, I picked up my books and stuffed them into my backpack.

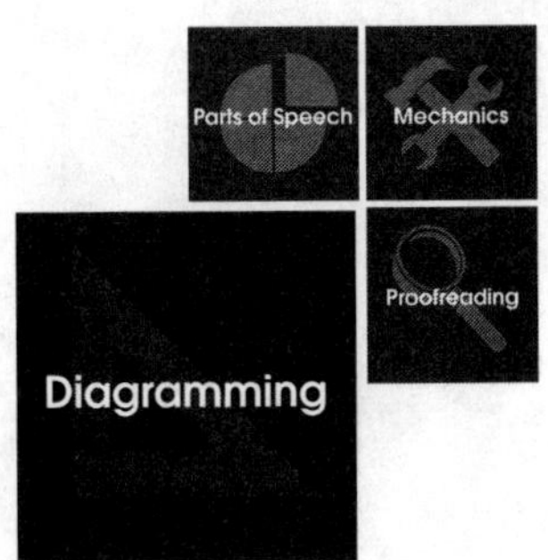

Understand the Structure

A participle is placed on a line like this _____ below the word it modifies. Any object is placed on the same line separated by a vertical line.

The child sucking his thumb is hungry.

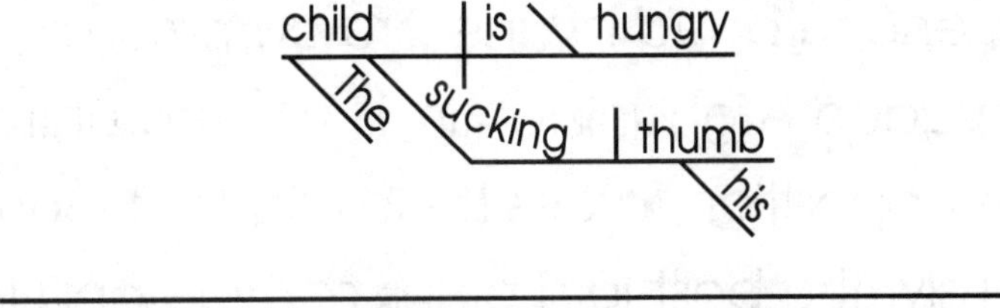

Diagram the following, paying special attention to participles.

1. Running through the fields, my sweetheart stumbled.
2. Her filmy dress covered with mud clung to her body.
3. She smiled, embracing me fondly while she covered me with muck.

Careless Mistakes Can Cause Big Problems!

Eliminate clichés and correct the mistakes in the sentences below. ***Find at least one cliché and more than six mistakes.***

The Soviets, encouraged by the pro-communist Afghan government, invaded Afghanistan in 1979. The United States backed the opposition forces believing that Communism was evil. Obviously, the best-laid plans of mice and men often go awry. In 1996, the US-backed Islamic Taliban ousted the pro-communist government. Since then, human rights and the rights of women, in particular, has deteriorated by leaps and bounds. Before the Taliban came to power, women worked as schoolteachers and nurses. However, under the Taliban regime, women are not allowed in the workplace. In fact, a woman is not allowed to leave the home accept when accompanied by their husband. Even then, a woman must be fully covered from head to toe so that no male other then their husband sees them. Thus, a woman is not allowed to go to school or visit a doctor. If a woman is sick, her husband goes to the doctor for her. Clearly, the US had no clue as to the affect of its policy toward Afghanistan.

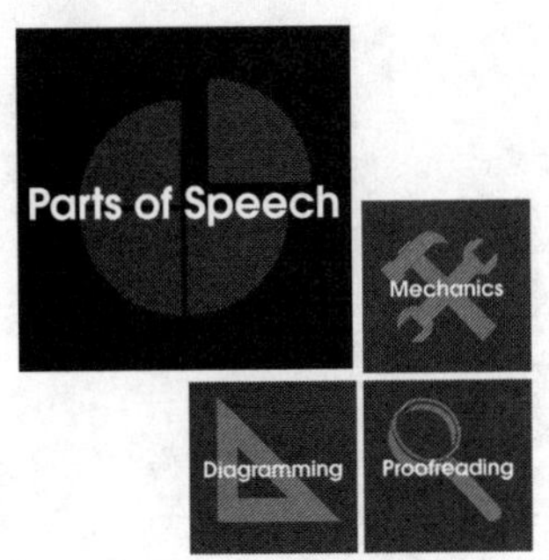

Know Your Building Materials!

A **gerund** is an "ing" verb form used as a noun. A **gerund phrase** contains an object, a complement or some modifiers.

Running is exhausting.

Running is a form of the verb **to run**, and in this sentence, it is used as the subject.

Being pretty is sometimes difficult.

Being is a form of the verb **to be,** and **pretty** is a predicate adjective.

Underline the gerunds and gerund phrases in the following sentences. Write in the blank the job the gerund does in the sentence (subject, direct object, etc).

1. __________ Taking photos of insects is Alan's passion.
2. __________ Alan hates running out of film just as a spider catches its prey.
3. __________ Termites are associated with building huge mounds and making mud tunnels.
4. __________ Chasing after the perfect shot is taking too much of his time.
5. __________ After seeing a black widow eat her husband, Alan was ecstatic.
6. __________ Watching cockroaches scurry into dark corners is fascinating to him.
7. __________ He gets the perfect shot by waiting patiently and by sitting absolutely still.

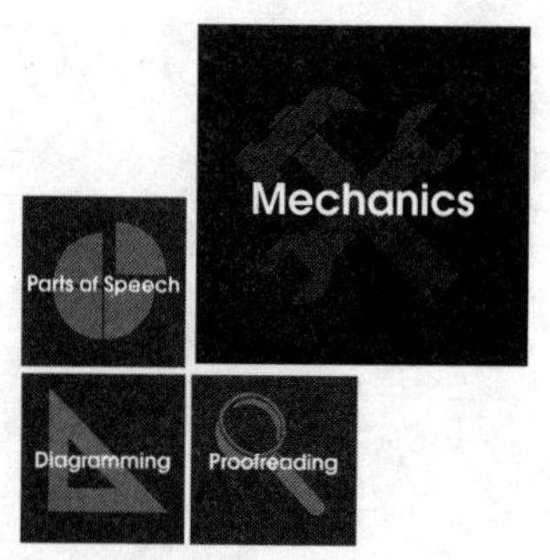

Good Mechanics Are Hard to Find

Watch out for sentence fragments that are gerunds or participles without predicates. Gerunds are preceded by possessive adjectives, not pronouns.

My studying was not sufficient.

Correct the following gerund and participle errors. If the sentence is correct, mark it OK. If it is a fragment, mark *Frag.*

1. Being that I am really tired.
2. Him staying up late is what made him oversleep.
3. For my roommate, waking up is not difficult.
4. Seeing as I like to get my work done and to go to bed early.
5. My sister usually feeds the dog getting up at daybreak.
6. Jim checking my papers has helped me get good grades.
7. Hearing the alarm, the blankets were pulled over my head.
8. Me using a word processor has certainly helped me spelling.
9. Seeing the sunrise while picking up the newspaper at daybreak.

Fill in the blanks

A verb form used as an adjective is called a ____________________.
A verb form used as a noun is called a ____________________.

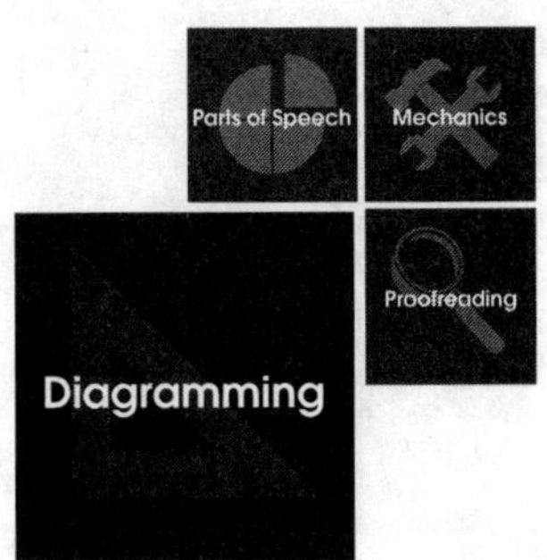

Understand the Structure

A gerund takes the place of a noun. It is diagrammed with its objects or modifiers on a line like this ⌐——. It is placed on a stilt above the main line.

Eating fish is good for you.

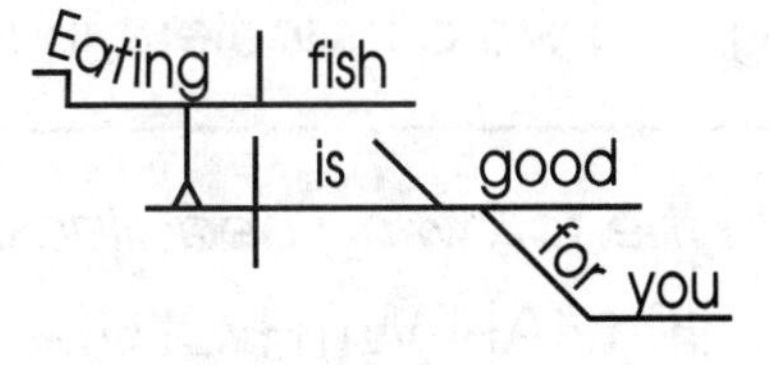

Diagram the following, paying special attention to gerunds.

1. I enjoy munching popcorn at the movies.
2. I am gaining weight from eating too much candy.
3. After drinking diet pop, my belching is heard statewide.

Careless Mistakes Can Cause Big Problems!

Murphy's Law: Section I, Article 369

"That which can be misunderstood will be misunderstood."

A sentence is ambiguous when it can have more than one meaning. Sometimes ambiguity is caused by misplaced modifiers and other grammatical confusions.

Sometimes the meaning of a word is unclear in the context.

Correct the ambiguity in the following headlines.

1. WOMAN BEATS UP MAN WITH CLUB
2. PLAYERS FIGHT BEFORE FANS
3. GERBILS IN TESTING FACILITY SMELL
4. REVOLTING STUDENTS DEMONSTRATE AGAINST DRESS CODE

Describe the role of the ambiguity in the following story.

One day a panda bear came into a restaurant and sat down at a table. The waiter approached politely and took his order for a large bamboo salad with sesame dressing. The panda ate his salad with gusto and then called for the check. This time as the waiter approached, the panda whipped out a pistol and shot the waiter. Calmly, he got up from the table and walked toward the door. The restaurant manager watched the scene in horror and amazement. At last he couldn't control himself. Running to the door he called to the panda, "What was that all about?"

The panda answered, "I'm a panda. Look it up!" Confused, the manager went to the dictionary and looked up "panda." He found "panda: Asian mammal; eats bamboo, shoots and leaves."

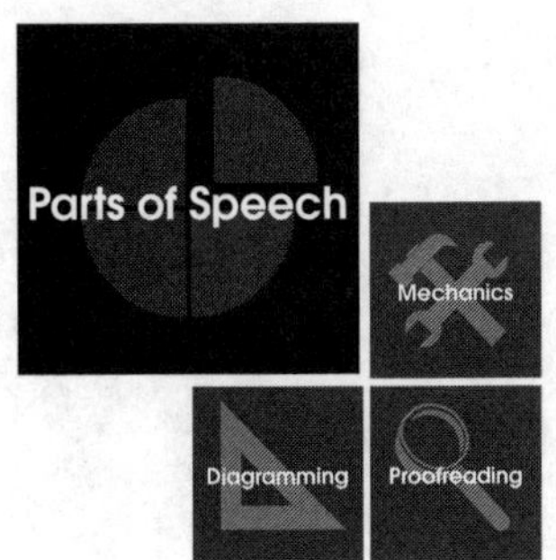

Know Your Building Materials!

An **infinitive** is a verb form that is preceded by **to: to read, to jump, to be, to hop.** Infinitives can take objects and other modifiers like participles and gerunds. They can function as nouns, adjectives or adverbs.

I like to go home early.

To go home early is an infinitive phrase that functions as a noun.

The player to watch carefully is the tight end.

To watch carefully is an infinitive phrase that functions as an adjective modifying **player**.

Underline the infinitive or infinitive phrase and write the part of speech it represents.

1. _________I love to eat potato chips.
2. _________To learn self-control when faced with a bowl of chips is difficult.
3. _________I find it difficult to control myself when I see guacamole.
4. _________The best chips to buy are triangular tortilla chips.
5. _________Onion dip tends to make people gorge themselves.
6. _________I made the bean dip to go with the mini tacos.

Fill in the blanks.

An adjective modifies a _______________. An adverb modifies an _______________, an _______________, or a _______________.

Good Mechanics Are Hard to Find

Too Many Words!

Eliminate wordiness by using participles, gerunds and infinitives.

Wordy: George was worried about tornadoes. He begged to sleep in the cellar.

Better: Worried about tornadoes, George begged to sleep in the cellar.

Rewrite the underlined portions of the following sentences using the construction indicated.

1. I was terrified while I was seeing the black funnel cloud on the horizon. (Infinitive)
2. The winds twisted and swirled. They picked up a truck as though it were a toy. (Participle)
3. It doesn't accomplish much when you run in the other direction. (Gerund)
4. Soon, the winds that roared like wild beasts were upon us. (Participle)
5. It is a wise idea to build a storm cellar in tornado alley. (Gerund)

Eliminate wordiness in the following sentences.

It is not cowardly when you run away from something that can really hurt you. It is foolhardy to put yourself in danger if you don't need to.

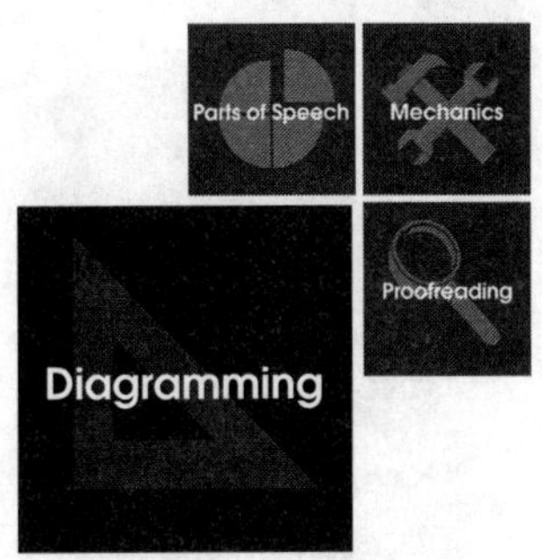

Understand the Structure

Infinitives and infinitive phrases used as nouns are placed on a stilt above the main line.

I love to eat chocolate.

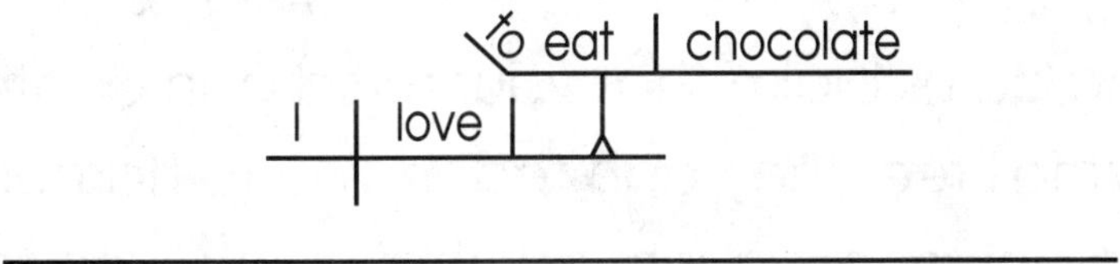

Diagram the following, paying special attention to infinitives.

1. To eat fried chicken with your fingers is acceptable nowadays.
2. Since you want to be polite, you need to put your napkin under your chin.

Careless Mistakes Can Cause Big Problems!

Correct the mistakes in the sentences below. Eliminate any clichés and ambiguities, and change two adjective clauses into participles. Find at least one cliché, one ambiguity, and more than four other mistakes.

Firewalking gurus claim that your mind can control mater. For a not-so-small fee, they can teach you to harness the untapped power of your mind, that allows you to walk across a bed of hot coals without being burned. Actually, anyone can walk across a bed of hot coals without harnessing any mental powers. But don't try this at home, kids. If the coals are properley prepared and the participants and walk at a rapid rate having dry feet, they will emerge unburned, this has nothing to do with occult forces and everything to do with physics. The ash layer that covers the hot coals does not conduct heat well, instead it insulates the feet. If you put your hand briefly into a 400-degree oven it won't burn. If, however, you touch the metal rack that is also 400-degrees, it will burn. Like the ash layer, the air in the oven doesn't conduct heat, whereas the metal rack does. Science is full of amazing facts and if you don't know those facts, charlatans will happily take your money.

Know Your Building Materials!

Phrase and Clause Review

Match the number of the phrase or clause with the underlined sentence part.

1. Prepositional phrase
2. Appositive phrase
3. Participial phrase
4. Gerund phrase
5. Infinitive phrase
6. Adjective clause
7. Noun clause
8. Adverb clause

1. ____ When I turned two, my father gave me a teddy bear.
2. ____ He has one cracked glass eye and an ear that I ripped ages ago.
3. ____ His fur is brown and matted with years of love.
4. ____ His name is Grizzler, the brave and ferocious guardian.
5. ____ Sitting on my bed, he listens patiently to all my problems.
6. ____ My mother always said that Grizzler would go to college with me.
7. ____ I wanted to take him to college, but I was concerned about what my new roommate would think.
8. ____ I shouldn't have worried because sitting on my roommate's pillow was the mangiest specimen of a teddy bear I had ever seen.

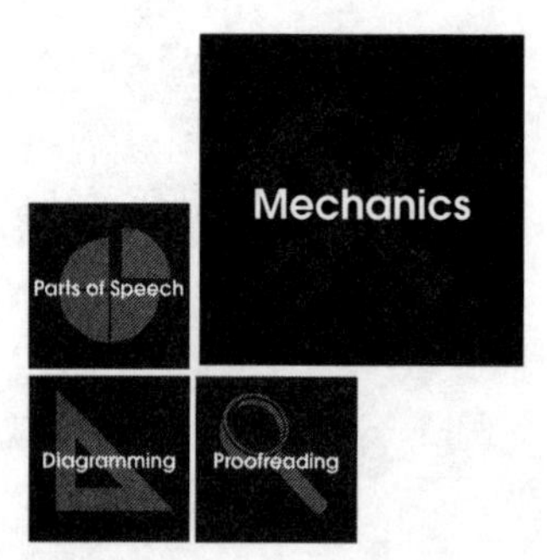

Good Mechanics Are Hard to Find

Sentences that are all the same length are boring. Vary your sentences using different grammatical patterns to make your writing more interesting.

Rewrite the following. Use at least one compound sentence, one adverb clause, one adjective clause, one appositive, one participial phrase, one gerund, and one infinitive.

It is six o'clock. I am starving. My stomach is gurgling. I had only a small lunch. It was a Cobb salad. I ate it at my desk. I will make some pasta with marinara sauce. It always fills me up. I'll throw together a green salad and some garlic bread too. That menu should subdue my hunger pangs. If that isn't enough, I can go out for pizza later.

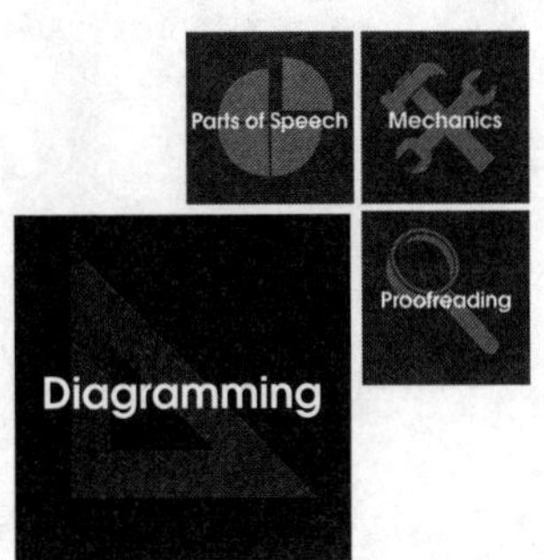

Understand the Structure

Infinitives used as adjectives or adverbs are diagrammed on a stilt below the word modified.

I am too busy to waste time.

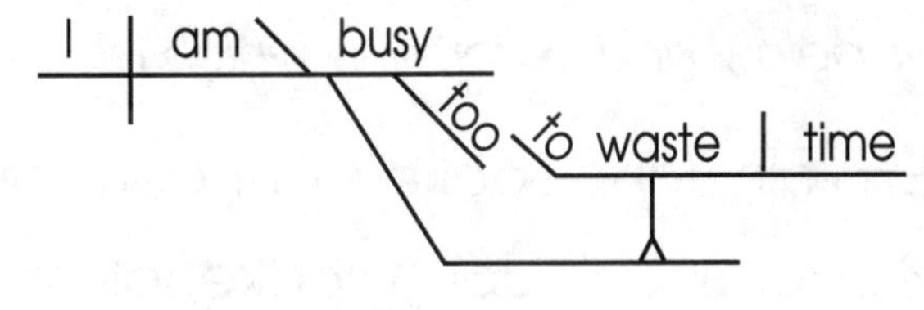

Diagram the following, paying special attention to infinitives used as adjectives or adverbs.

1. The chapters to read are lengthy.
2. After you have learned to hum the melody, the lyrics are easy to memorize.

Careless Mistakes Can Cause Big Problems!

Sometimes your grade on an essay test depends more on how you write your essay than on how much information you know.

Read the two essays below and determine which received the higher grade.

Question: Explain John Locke's concept of "natural rights."

Essay # 1. According to John Locke, all men have God-given natural rights including the right to life, health, liberty, and property. If a man works to create property (if he chops down a tree to build a house), he has the right to keep that property. In fact, a man has the right to collect as much property as he can use as long as enough is left for the needs of others and as long as he doesn't harm others in the process. According to Locke, a government that does not protect these natural rights is illegitimate.

Essay # 2. John Lock believed that if a man builds a house or plows a field he should be allowed to keep them. This is a right given by God. A man should be able to get as rich as he wants so long as he doesn't hurt other people in the process or corner the market. Liberty and life and health are other natural rights. A good government would protect men and their rights. Citizens can overthrow a government that doesn't protect rights.

What makes one essay better than the other? Evaluate the essays for content, organization, grammar, spelling, and expression.

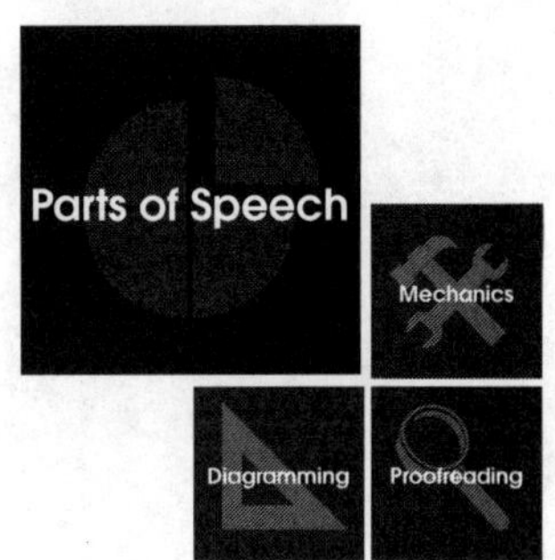

Know Your Building Materials!

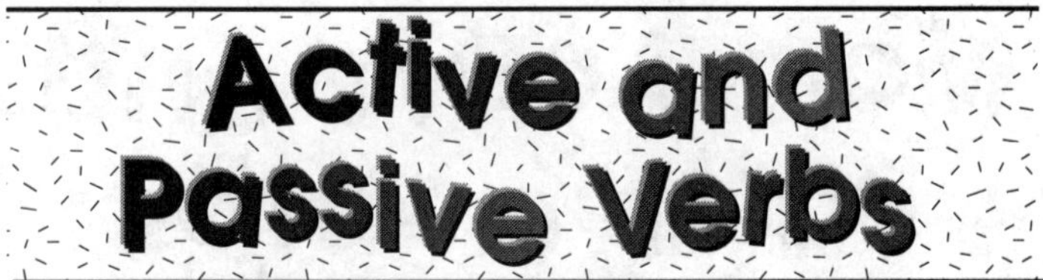

Verbs that can take direct objects are either active or passive.

When a verb is **active**, the subject does the acting.

The boy hit the ball.

When a verb is **passive**, the thing that is acted upon, the direct object, becomes the subject of the sentence.

The ball was hit by the boy.

Sometimes the person or thing that does the acting is unknown. Then the verb is passive.

Underline the verb and identify if it is active ***(A)*** *or passive* ***(P)***.

1. _____ The carpenter struck the nail on the head.
2. _____ Then, a thumb holding the nail was struck by the unfortunate carpenter.
3. _____ Several disgusting but colorful words were uttered by the workman.
4. _____ "I will never hammer another nail," screamed the enraged carpenter.
5. _____ However, nails would be pounded tomorrow by this man.
6. _____ The next day, his thumb was bandaged by yards of gauze.
7. _____ His pride was also wounded.
8. _____ Carpenters should not mash their digits.
9. _____ This carpenter decided to switch to plumbing.

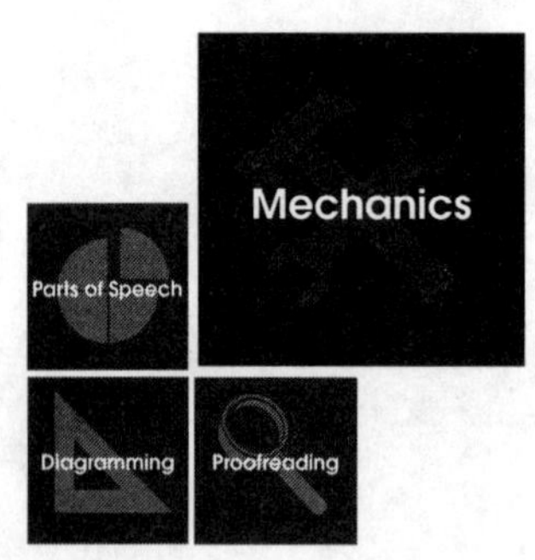

Good Mechanics Are Hard to Find

Active verbs are direct and lively. Passive verbs tend to be wordy and weak. Passive verbs are not incorrect, but active verbs are preferable.

Rewrite the sentences below changing passive verbs to active verbs wherever possible.

1. The aria was sung by the entire choir.
2. An off-key note was struck by the tenor with the cold in the back row.
3. The discordant sound was noticed.
4. The tenor was embarrassed by his mistake.
5. Suddenly, sneezing was heard throughout the concert hall.
6. The tenor was hidden by the singers next to him.
7. He was dragged off the stage into the wings by an irate stage manager.

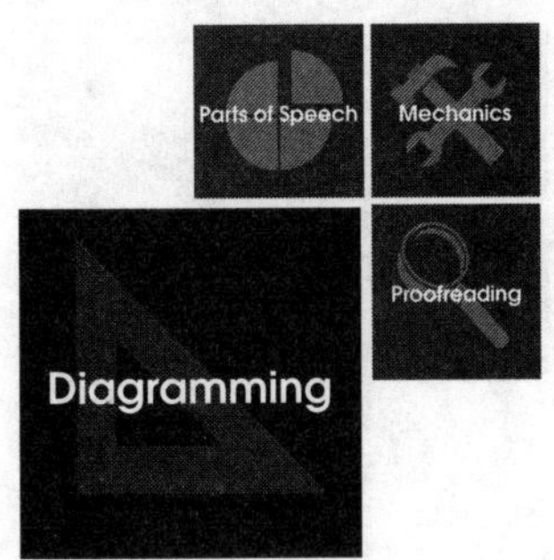

Understand the Structure

Correct the fragments and diagram the corrected sentence.

1. The first baseman hitting the ball into left field.
2. Making loud noises in a movie theater.
3. My friend, the kid with the freckles on his nose.

Careless Mistakes Can Cause Big Problems!

Eliminate wordy expressions and correct the mistakes in the sentences below. Change passive verbs to active verbs if possible.

The Black Death (the bubonic plague) swept through medieval Europe in deadly waves. Though usually associated with Europe, China seems to have been its birthplace in the first century A.D. After it traveled slowly through Asia, it arrived in Eastern Europe in an extremely virulent form. During the worst of its reign, it is estimated that between two-thirds to three-quarters of the population in parts of Europe were killed. The death toll was the worst in cities since the flea which spread the plague lived on rats in densely populated city centers. Death was quick, most people died within two or three days of noticing the first symptoms. The nursery rhyme "Ring around the Rosy" dates from the plague years. The "rosy" is the fleabite, and the "ring" is the inflamed circle around it. The posies are either the black swellings near the lymph nodes, or the flowers to ward off the smell of the dead bodies brought by mourners.

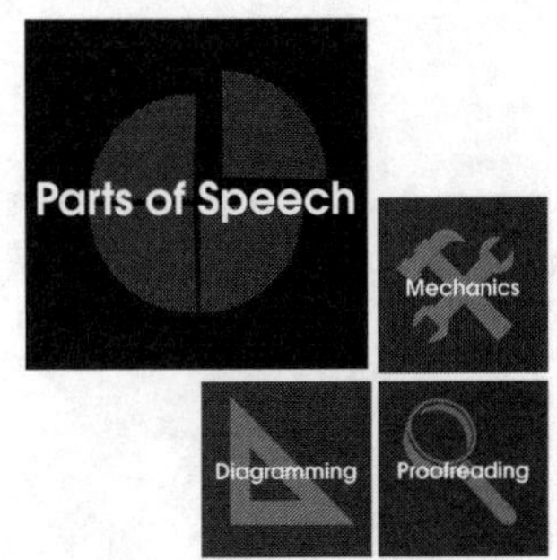

Know Your Building Materials!

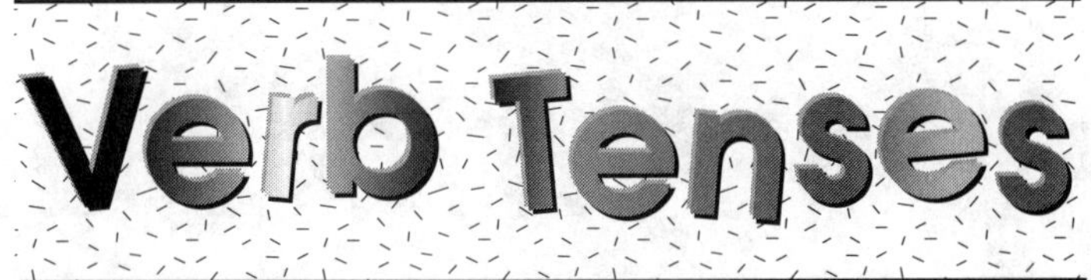

A **verb tense** indicates the time of an action. Different tenses in the same sentence may indicate the sequence of the actions.

Present: I **run.**	Present perfect: I **have run**.
Past: I **ran.**	Past perfect: I **had run.**
Future: I **will (shall) run.**	Future perfect: I **will (shall) have run.**

Each tense also has a **progressive** form.

Present: I **am running**.	Present Perfect: **I have been running.**
Past: I **was running**.	Past Perfect: I **had been running.**
Future: I **will (shall) be running.**	Future perfect: I **will (shall) have been running**.

Fill in the blank with the tense of the verb indicated.

1. You jump. (Future) ______________________________
2. We choose. (Present perfect) ______________________________
3. I am. (Past perfect) ______________________________
4. I drive. (Future perfect) ______________________________
5. He finds. (Present progressive) ______________________________
6. They fly. (Future perfect progressive) ______________________________
7. You buy. (Past perfect progressive) ______________________________
8. We take. (Present perfect progressive) ______________________________
9. They rise. (Present perfect) ______________________________

Good Mechanics Are Hard to Find

Tense Ambiguity

Usually, all the verbs in the sentence are in the same tense. Sometimes, however, different tenses indicate the specific sequence of events.

Since I **have been running** for an hour, I **am** tired.
(I am still running, and now I am tired.)

Since I **ran** for an hour, I **am** tired.
(I finished running, but I am still tired.)

The perfect tenses indicate an action begun in the past and continued into the present (present perfect), continued into the future (future perfect), or begun in the past and finished in the past before some other action is completed (past perfect).

Choose the correct verb form to express the meaning indicated.

1. I (arrive)__________________at school when the bell (ring) _______________. (I got there after the bell.)
2. I (arrive)__________________ at school when the bell (ring) _________________. (I got there while the bell was going off.)
3. When I (arrive)_____________________, I (miss) _______________ half an hour of class. (I was half an hour late.)
4. At the end of the term, I (finish) ___________________ three years of Spanish. (The term ends soon, and my Spanish class ends at the same time.)
5. By the end of the term, I (finish) ___________________ seven essays. (The term ends soon, and my essays are due a week earlier.)

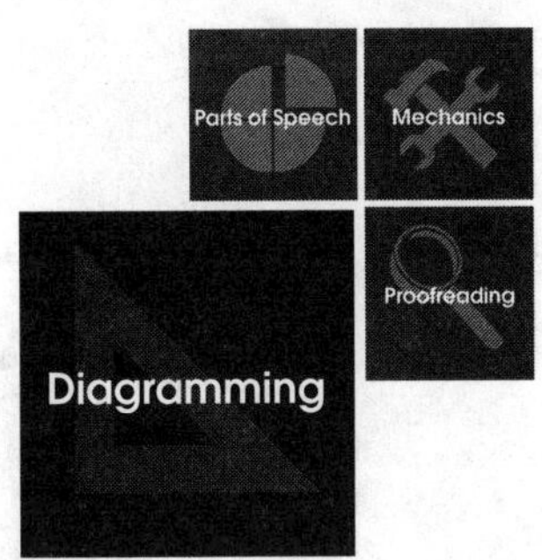

Understand the Structure

From the words listed, create a sentence that fits the diagram.

1. he, fortunately, hurting, he, slipped, himself, avoided, fell, and, seriously, but

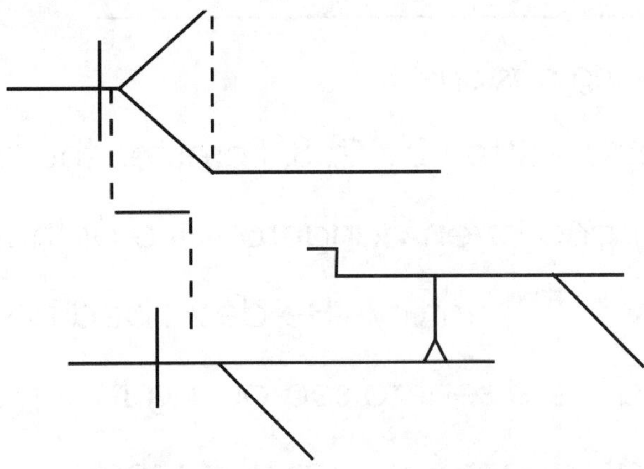

2. by, other, made, light, funky, danced, of, the, chicken, silvery, the, faces, while, other, each, moon, we, we, at

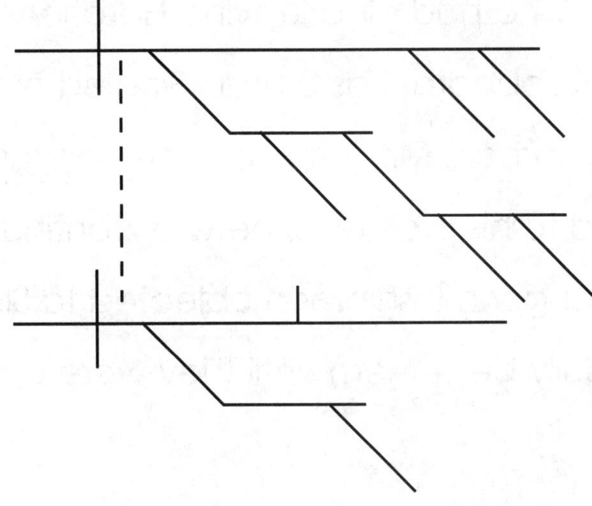

Careless Mistakes Can Cause Big Problems!

Correct the Tenses

When discussing the actions of characters in novels, use the present tense:

With the help of his friends, Tom Sawyer **paints** a fence.

The author, Mark Twain, **describes** life in the South following the Civil War.

Correct the tenses in the following passage.

In the Hornblower saga written by C. S. Forester, the author depicted the difficult and often dangerous life of the young sailor during the early 19th century. He described how boys as young as 10 years old were sent to sea during that period. Horatio Hornblower, at seventeen, was older than most midshipmen when he signed on to his first berth. He was the son of a poor clergyman who had died leaving Horatio with no inheritance. Life on shipboard was brutal. Singled out for hazing by an older midshipman, Mr. Simpson, Horatio was teased and tortured. To add to his problems, he was continually seasick. When other younger midshipmen objected to Simpson's tyrannical rule, the bully beat them until they were unconscious.

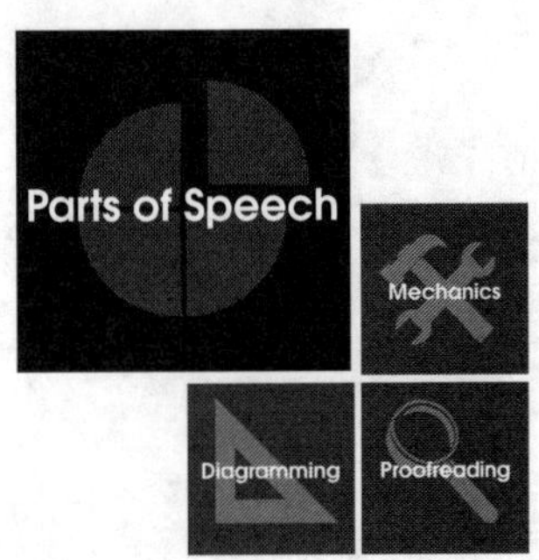

Know Your Building Materials!

Subjunctive Verbs

Subjunctive verbs are used to describe a situation that is contrary to fact. The helping verbs **were** and **would** are signs of the subjunctive.

If I **were** 7 feet tall, I **would be** a basketball star.
(But I'm only 5′4″ so I'm not a star.)

Change the boldfaced verbs to the subjunctive.

1. If I **was** an expert, I would show you how to do it.
2. I wish I **was** climbing Mt. Everest.
3. If my father **was** king, then my mother **is** queen.

*Correct the following sentences. Write **OK** after the ones that need no corrections.*

1. If the sun was out, we could have a picnic.
2. Since it is raining, we can stay warm and cozy inside.
3. I wish it was practical to build a hot tub, but we haven't the room.
4. If it was a warm rain, we could enjoy sitting in the hot tub outside.
5. After we build the hot tub, we will luxuriate in it while we are being tickled with peacock feathers.

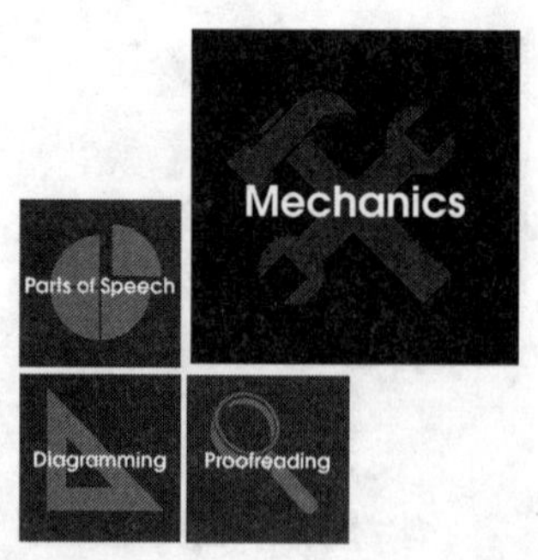

Good Mechanics Are Hard to Find

A **redundant expression** repeats itself. A **complete stop** is redundant. Redundancies are usually wordy and boring.

An **oxymoron** is an expression that contradicts itself. **Diet ice cream** is an oxymoron. Oxymorons unlike redundancies are often humorous.

Underline the redundancy or oxymoron in each sentence and label it either ***R*** *or* ***O.***

1. _____ We need an exact estimate of the cost.
2. _____ This budget cut is absolutely essential.
3. _____ They are alone together in the back room.
4. _____ Anarchy rules!
5. _____ The reason why we are late is because of the traffic.
6. _____ Be ready at 8:00 a.m. in the morning!
7. _____ The ghost appeared to be invisible.
8. _____ The worker was fired at a time when discrimination was legal.
9. _____ Save up to 50% and more.
10. _____ This recipe makes a 12-ounce pound cake.

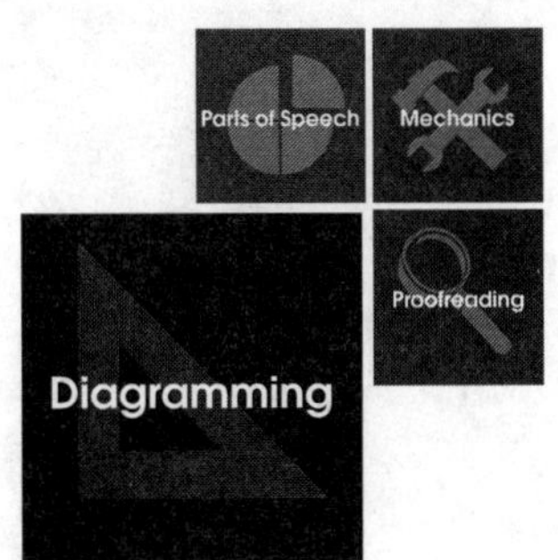

Understand the Structure

Diagram the sentence and then choose the correct word form.

1. If I (was, were) a hero, I would rush into that burning building.
2. The firefighter hands the ax to (whoever, whomever) looks strong.
3. Because of our insistence, the firefighter gave us, Meg and (I, me),the kitten.

Careless Mistakes Can Cause Big Problems!

Correct errors and rewrite wordy or ambiguous passages.

Consider the plight of the poor mermaid, how does she care for her skin? Her chest and upper torso are bathed in salt water a good portion of the day. What kind of moisturizer can handle that abuse? While her bottom half is scalded by the sun when she sits on the rocks. Does sun screen work on fish scales? What SPF do you use to provide protection from sunburn. It must be excruciating when a mermaid has to comb out that long hair filled with salt water. Because of the fact that shampooing several times a day is out of the question, if I was a mermaid I'd chop off my long locks right away. I think it sounds rather boring to be sitting out on the rocks in the sun day after day. For entertainment, a mermaid can sing to attract sailors with a beckoning voice, but suppose they catch a handsome one. What would they do with them? Perhaps mermaids like to toast sailors in the sun and eat them with tartar sauce.

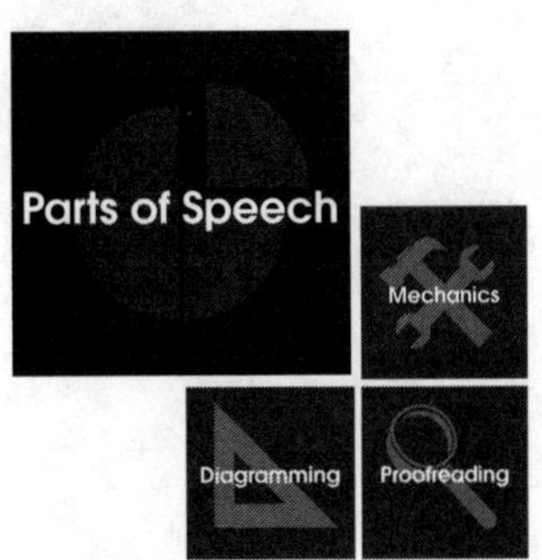

Know Your Building Materials!

Underline the verbals (infinitives, gerunds, participles), cross out the passive verbs and circle the subjunctive verbs (contrary to fact).

1. I am disturbed to see a lot of preteens screaming at some adolescent rock star.
2. Suppose you were a preteen, and you met one of these pimply millionaires.
3. What would you say to someone that rich?
4. Rock stars are not known for their intellectual prowess.
5. They may well be very dull people who have little to say.
6. On the other hand, perhaps they travel widely seeing more of the world than most ordinary people.
7. Most likely, they are just ordinary people fascinated by music.
8. The music produced by such people can be very creative.
9. Still, swooning over performers seems silly to me.

Good Mechanics Are Hard to Find

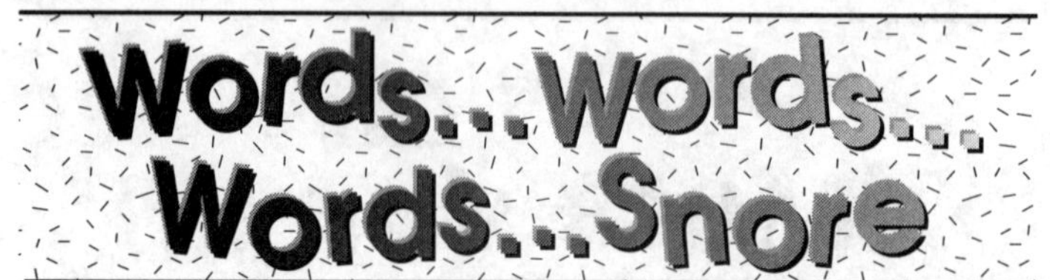

Dynamic writing is concise. Wordy writing puts the reader to sleep. Avoid wordiness by using the following strategies:

Use active verbs instead of passive verbs.

Avoid redundant expressions.

Avoid **it is** or **there is** at the beginning of a sentence.

Instead of **the teacher who was boring,** say **the boring teacher.**

Instead of **the car was swerving** say **the car swerved.**

Rewrite the following sentences eliminating the wordy expressions.

1. There were fireworks dancing across the sky.
2. The dogs that were barking made a racket.
3. On Independence Day, July 4th, there is barbeque smoke in the air.
4. Nothing beats a hot dog that is slathered with mustard and sauerkraut.
5. The grill is manned by my brother while the lemonade is stirred by my sister.
6. There is always a pool party that is fun at my neighbor's house.
7. The teens at the party were ogling the opposite sex, but little conversation was taking place.

Understand the Structure

Misplaced Modifiers

Rewrite the following sentences removing the ambiguity and then diagram.

1. The pre-school needs a 3-year old teacher.
2. After driving for 50 years, Mr. Smith ran into a telephone pole.
3. We need someone to care for Bessie, our cow, who does not smoke or drink.

Careless Mistakes Can Cause Big Problems!

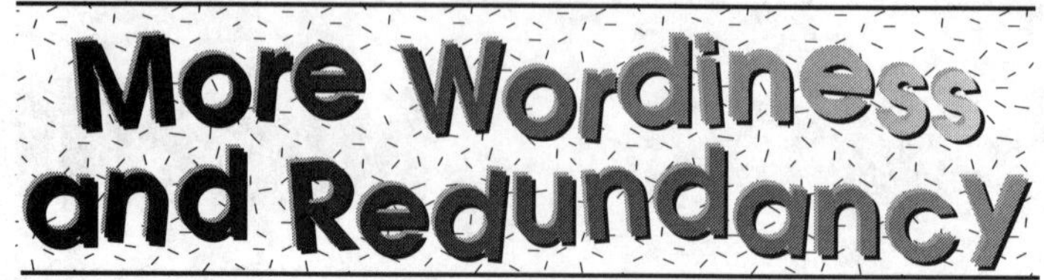

Rewrite the following passage eliminating the wordiness and redundancy.

A number of years ago, eighty-seven to be exact, a new political unit was brought forth on this enormous land mass by the people who moved here first, our forefathers. This new and developing nation was conceived by its founders to be dedicated to the ideal of Liberty and to the proposition that everyone, all men, are the same, or equal. There should be equality for all men.

At this time, we are in the middle of a great big war between factions in the country. We are testing whether or not that nation or any nation for that matter that is conceived and dedicated in this way can endure very long. This is why we are here. We are standing here on a field where a great battle was fought during that war.

Do you recognize this speech?

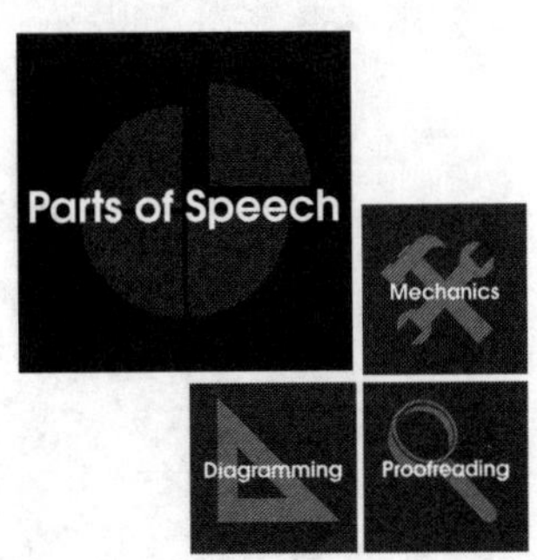

Know Your Building Materials!

Sentence Fragments

A complete sentence requires an independent clause. A dependent clause or a phrase without an independent clause is a sentence fragment.

Rewrite the sentence fragments below to make complete sentences. Write OK after any complete sentences.

1. Television wrestling is nothing like high school wrestling.
2. Seeing as wrestling on television is fixed.
3. High school wrestlers who train as rigorously as any school athlete.
4. In addition, high school wrestlers to watch their weight.
5. Being that it is better to be in a lower weight division.
6. However, television wrestlers are performers and acrobats.
7. Unlike high school wrestlers who do not know what their opponents are going to do.
8. Television wrestlers have all their moves choreographed.
9. I wish high school wrestlers had silly monikers like the television wrestlers.
10. High school wrestlers wearing those great leopard skin outfits.

Good Mechanics are Hard to Find

Commas, Semicolons and Colons

A comma is used before the conjunction in a compound sentence. A semicolon takes the place of a conjunction in a compound sentence. A colon introduces a list that follows a complete sentence. The list should not consist of direct objects or complements.

Correct: The storm was fierce: high winds, pounding rain, and high tides.

Correct: The damage was the following: broken windows, downed trees, flooded streets.

Incorrect: This year, hurricanes are named: Abel, Betty, Charles, and Don.

Correct the punctuation and the sentence structure in the following sentences. If a sentence is correct, mark it ***OK.***

1. Hurricanes frighten me and terrify my dog.
2. I like to go to the beach after a storm, the waves are spectacular.
3. If a storm threatens, you should have: a flashlight, some bottled water, and a first aid kit.
4. The complete list includes the following: matches, rain gear, a whistle, and Granola bars.
5. Hurricanes rarely hit Southern California, in fact they usually miss the entire West Coast.
6. The states that have been extensively damaged by hurricanes in recent years are: North Carolina, Texas, South Carolina, Georgia, and Florida.

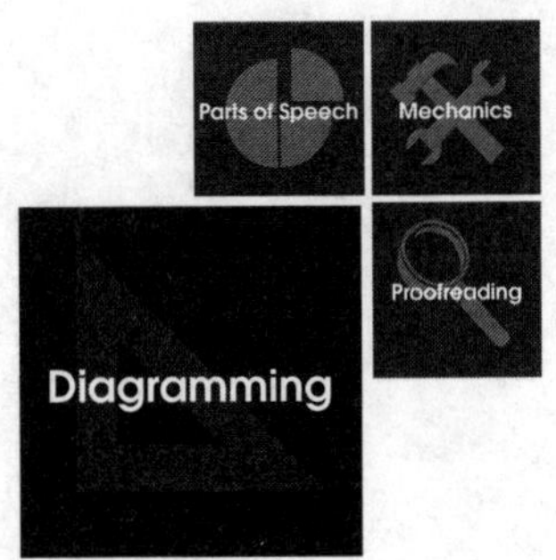

Understand the Structure

Diagram the following. Use your imagination.

1. Although the Braves tried to slip into first place, the Mets were unstoppable.
2. The constant dribbling and shooting of basketball are exciting; in comparison, baseball is boring.

Careless Mistakes Can Cause Big Problems!

Spell-check Goofs

Spell-checks are very useful, but they don't catch all spelling errors. If you have misspelled a word, but your misspelling is another actual word, the spell-check won't notice the error. Always read your papers over before they are printed to find the errors the spell-check missed.

The spell-check says the following poem has no errors. What does it say?

Ida never winnow spilling be,
  Butt anything I right
Is spill-chinked buy Mai knew Pea Sea
  Sew everything is rite.

The tea chairs work king at this cool
  Height spill ink wards Kahn flews,
Sew spill-chick is a use full tulle
  Witch awl weighs should bee ewes.

Ewe Cannes Sea howl well I rite
  With my spill-shaker's aide.
Eye dew my work with conference,
  And know miss steaks are maid.

Lessons 31-40

Rewrite the sentences using the parts of speech indicated.

1. To run on the beach is good exercise. Gerund
2. You should stretch your muscles before you exercise because it is important. Gerund
3. The runner who is panting is out of shape. Participle
4. Personally, I prefer sleeping. Infinitive

Choose the best sentence in each group. Explain what is wrong with each of the others.

A. Displaying them on the blackboard, the teacher encouraged the students to create original paintings.
B. There are paintings displayed on the blackboard that encourage students to be original.
C. The teacher encouraged the students to create original paintings by displaying them on the blackboard.
D. The teacher displayed the students' art on the blackboard, as a result the students created original paintings.
E. Paintings were displayed on the blackboard by the teacher to encourage the students to create original art.

A. Children enjoy a variety of media; painting, sculpting, and collages.
B. Children enjoy a variety of media such as: painting, sculpting, and making collages.
C. Children enjoy a variety of media: painting, sculpting, and making collages.
D. Children enjoy a variety of media: painting, sculpting, and collages.

Lessons 31-40, continued

Choose the correct word.

1. The leads in the play, Jason and (she, her), were unconvincing.
2. If I (was, were) the lead, I'd take a different approach.
3. The villain (who, whom) I detest is quite handsome.
4. (Whoever, Whomever) the director chooses will get the lead.

Correct the errors and eliminate clichés and wordiness in the following passage.

In each and every deck of standard playing cards there is a historical character represented by every king, queen, and jack. Charlemagne, the Emperor of Rome, is represented by the king of hearts, which is odd since he is not well-known for his love life. The king of clubs is Alexander the Great. The king of diamonds, who is sporting a wicked mustache, is supposed to be Julius Caesar however a Roman with a mustache seems unlikely. The king of spades was supposed to be King David of the bible. Do you wonder who chose such a bizarre collection of heros?

Lessons 31-40

Rewrite the sentences using the parts of speech indicated.

1. I like cooking, but mostly I love eating. *Infinitives*
2. It is important to measure ingredients carefully when cooking. *Gerund*
3. The soup that is simmering on the stove smells fragrant. *Participle*

Choose the best sentence in each group. Explain what is wrong with each of the others.

A. Wrapped in an old shawl, the elderly man carried a smelly fish he had caught in the river.
B. The elderly man carried a smelly fish wrapped in an old shawl he caught in the river.
C. The elderly man carried a smelly fish he caught in the river wrapped in an old shawl.
D. The elderly man carried a smelly fish that he caught in the river, it was wrapped in an old shawl.

A. There are old boots, tires, and dead fish floating in the rivers of most major cities which shows how polluted they are.
B. The old boots, tires, and dead fish floating in the rivers of most major cities show how polluted they are.
C. The old boots, tires, and dead fish floating in the rivers of most major cities. This garbage demonstrates how polluted our waterways are.
D. Floating in the rivers of most major cities, the old boots, tires, and dead fish show how polluted our waterways are.

Lessons 31-40, continued

Choose the correct word.

1. (Me, My) dancing is a sight to see.
2. Either the boys or I (am, are) responsible.
3. I washed my hair after I (finished, had finished) my homework.
4. I would feel more relaxed if my science project (was, were) finished.
5. Elect the two candidates best for the job, Jason and (I, me).

Correct the errors and eliminate clichés and wordiness in the following passage.

There was a dead whale that had washed up on the beach that caused a nuisance in a small Oregon town. The highway department that was asked to clean up the odiferous object, decided to dispose of it like they dispose of old highways; blow it up. They stacked dynamite underneath the beached behemoth and sent the onlookers well back into the dunes. When they pushed the plunger, quick as a flash, the whale exploded, raining rancid whale parts all over news crews and onlookers. A parked car more than a quarter mile away was crushed by falling whale guts. The worst thing was that the whale didn't disintegrate sufficiently for the sea gulls and crabs to finish the clean-up job. Instead the highway crew was forced to bury the remains.

Glossary

adjective. A word that modifies a noun or a pronoun.

predicate adjective. An adjective that follows a linking verb and describes the subject. *The sky is blue.*

adverb. A word that modifies a verb, an adverb or an adjective.

conjunctive adverb. A word, such as *therefore, thus, however,* that introduces an independent clause and shows a relationship to a previous independent clause.

appositive. A noun or pronoun that identifies another noun or pronoun near it. *My brother, John, is here.*

article. The adjectives *the, a,* and *an.*

clause. A group of words with both a subject and a predicate.

adverb clause. A dependent clause that modifies a verb, an adverb, or an adjective.

adjective clause. A dependent clause that modifies a noun or a pronoun.

dependent clause. A clause that cannot stand alone.

independent clause. A clause that can make a sentence by itself.

noun clause. A dependent clause that takes the place of a noun.

cliché. A worn-out phrase in common usage.

complement. A noun or an adjective that follows a linking verb and describes the subject.

predicate adjective. An adjective that follows a linking verb and describes the subject. *The sky is blue.*

predicate nominative. A noun that follows a linking verb and describes the subject. *Josh is a voter.*

conjunctive adverb. A word such as *therefore, for example, moreover,* or *however* that introduces an independent clause and shows a relationship to a previous independent clause.

conjunction. A word that joins other words, phrases, or clauses.

coordinate conjunction. A word such as *and, but, so, or, for* that joins equal partners.

subordinate conjunction. A word such as *because, if, although, when,* or *since* that connects a dependent clause to an independent clause.

contraction. A verb and another word combined with a letter or letters left out and replaced with an apostrophe.

Glossary, continued

gerund. An "ing" verb form used as a noun. *Running is hard work.*

gerund phrase. A gerund that is teamed up with an object, a complement, or modifiers.

infinitive. A verb form preceded by *to* such as *to swim.*

infinitive phrase. An infinitive teamed up with an object, a complement, or other modifiers. *I like to eat ice cream.*

noun. A person, place or thing.

common noun. A noun that is not naming a specific person, place, or thing.

proper noun. The name of a specific person, place, or thing.

object. A noun or pronoun (or a phrase or clause used as a noun or pronoun) that follows an action verb or a preposition.

direct object. A noun or pronoun acted upon by the verb. *The club hit the ball.*

indirect object. A noun or pronoun that tells to whom or for whom an action is done. *John gave me a cookie.*

object of a preposition. A noun or pronoun that follows a preposition. *Jump over the hedge.*

oxymoron. An expression that contradicts itself.

parallel structure. A list of two or more words or phrases that have a similar structure. *I like to run, to jump, and to race.*

participle. A verb form that usually ends in ing or ed.

past participle. A past-tense verb form such as *painted.*

present participle. A present-tense verb form such as *painting.*

participle phrase. A verb form with modifiers or objects used as an adjective. *The boy painting the house is tired.*

phrase. A group of words without a subject and a predicate.

prepositional phrase. A group of words including a preposition, its object, and any modifiers.

infinitive phrase. An infinitive teamed up with an object, a complement, or other modifiers.

participle phrase. A verb form with modifiers or objects used as an adjective.

gerund phrase. A gerund teamed up with an object, a complement, or modifiers.

predicate. The part of a clause that includes the verb, its objects, its complements, and its modifiers.

predicate adjective. An adjective that follows a linking verb and describes the subject. *The sky is blue.*

predicate nominative. A noun that follows a linking verb and describes the subject. *Josh is a voter.*

preposition. A word such as *in, over, of, after,* or *like* that shows a relationship between a noun or pronoun and another word in the sentence.

prepositional phrase. A group of words including a preposition and its object, and any modifiers.

pronoun. A word that stands for a noun.

indefinite pronoun. A word that stands for an undefined group such as *anybody, nobody,* or *someone.*

interrogative pronoun. A word that asks a question such as *who, whom,* or *which.*

possessive pronoun. A word that indicates possession such as *mine, theirs,* or *ours.*

reflexive pronoun. A word that reflects back on the subject such as *myself,* or *himself.*

relative pronoun. A word such as *who, which,* or *whom* that connects an adjective clause to an antecedent in another clause.

redundancy. An expression that repeats itself.

sentence. A subject and a predicate in an independent clause.

subject. What or who is being talked about in a sentence.

tense. The time when an action occurs.

future tense. A verb form showing the action is in the future. *I will run.*

past tense. A verb form showing the action is in the past. *I ran.*

present tense. A verb form showing the action is in the present. *I run.*

progressive tense. A verb form showing an action is continuing. *I am running.*

subjunctive tense. A verb form that indicates the situation is contrary to fact. *I would fly if I could.*

verb. A word that shows an action or an appearance of something.

action verb. A word that shows an action. *The bird flies.*

active verb. An action verb with the subject of the sentence doing the action. *The boy hit the ball.*

helping verb. A verb such as *might, can, is, would, may, were* that is paired with another verb.

linking verb. A verb such as *appears, becomes, was, seems, smells, looks* that indicates the appearance of something and is followed by a noun or adjective.

passive verb. An action verb with the subject of the sentence not doing the acting. *The ball was hit by the boy.*

Diagramming Patterns

Subject—Verb

Subject | Verb

Compound Subject

Subject
and
Subject
Verb

Compound Verb

Subject
Verb
and
Verb

Compound Subject—Compound Verb

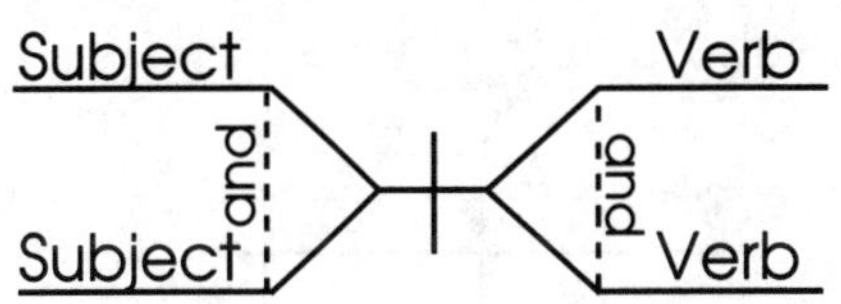

Subject—Verb with Adjectives and Adverbs

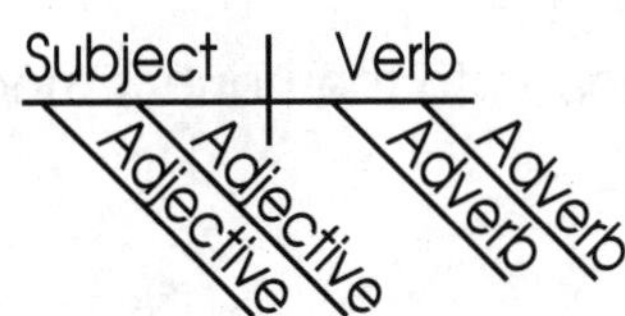

Adverb Modifying Adverb

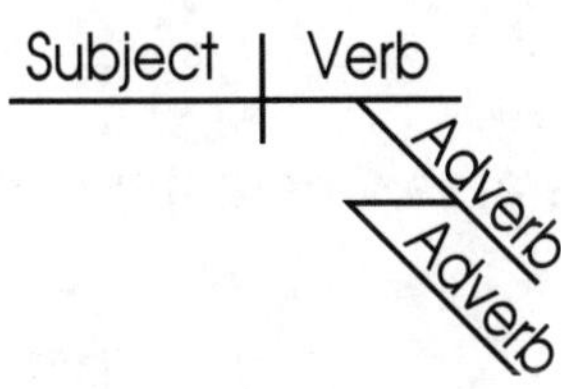

Adverb Modifying Adjective

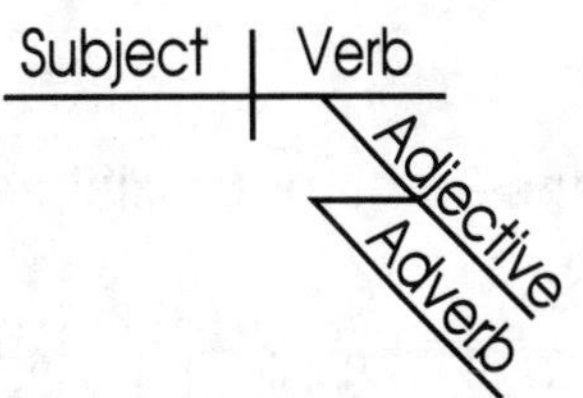

Prepositional Phrase

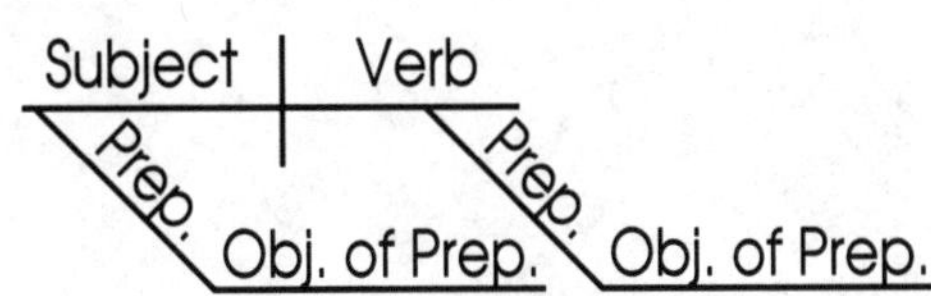

Diagramming Patterns, continued

Direct Object

Subject | Verb | Direct Object

Indirect Object

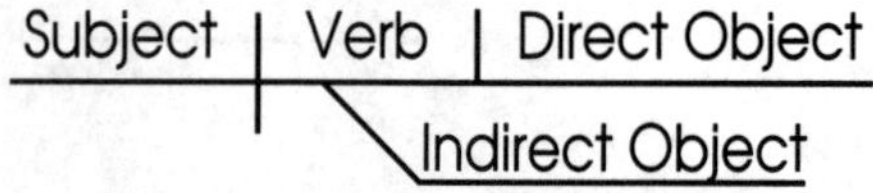

Subject Complements

Subject | Verb \ Predicate Noun or Predicate Adjective

Adverb Clauses—A dashed line connects the verb in the main clause to the verb in the subordinate clause

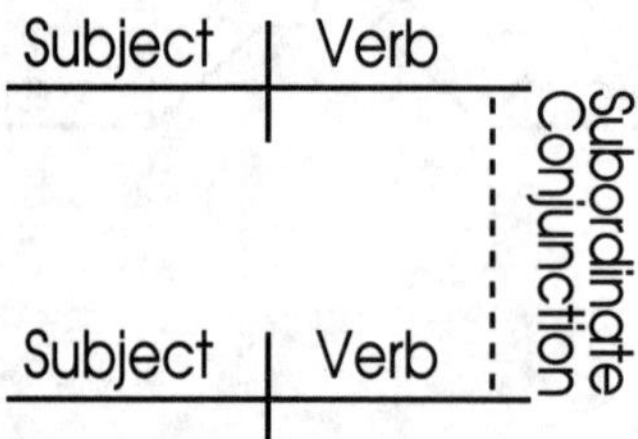

Adjective Clause—A dashed line connects the relative pronoun to the noun it modifies.

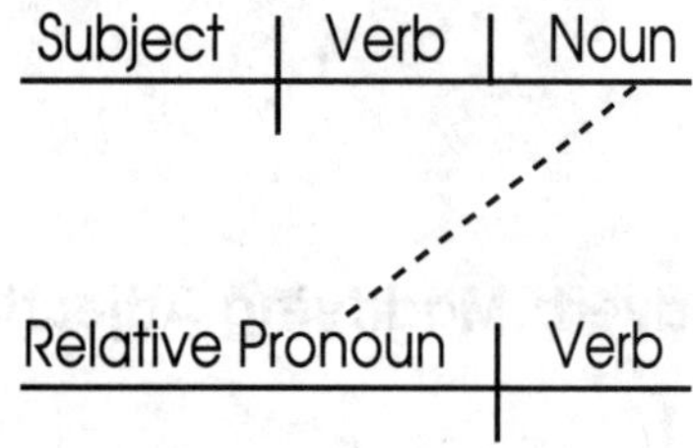

Noun Clauses—The noun clause stands on a stilt above the area where it functions in the sentence.

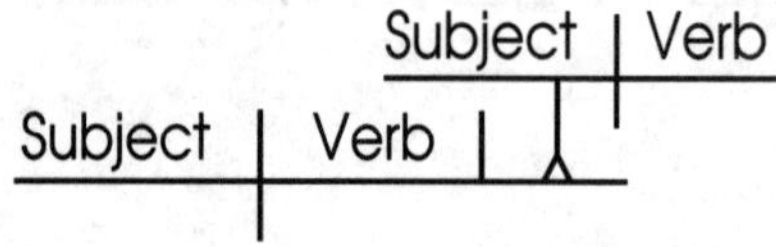

Diagramming Patterns, continued

Appositives—Appositives are placed in parentheses next to the word described.

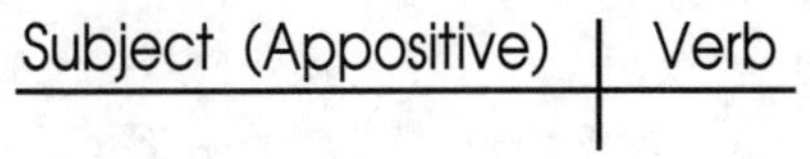

Subject (Appositive) | Verb

Participial Phrases—Participles are placed on a line attached to the word modified.

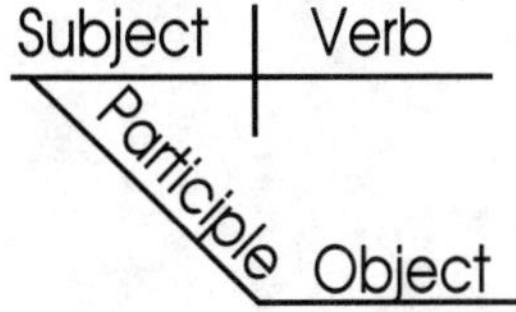

Gerund Phrases—Gerunds are placed on a stilt above the area where they function in the sentence.

Gerund | Object

Subject | Verb |

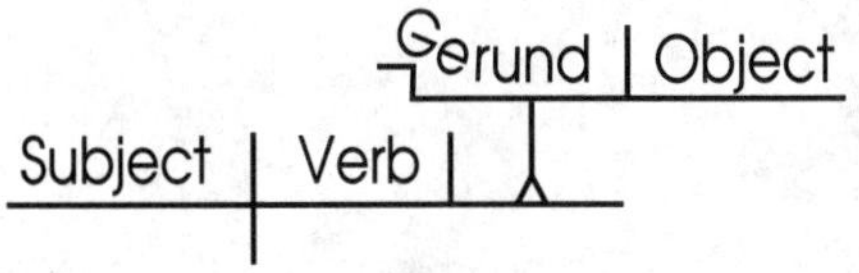

Infinitive Phrase—Infinitives used as nouns are placed on a stilt above the area where they function in the sentence. Infinitives used as adjectives or adverbs are placed on a stilt above a line connected to the word modified.

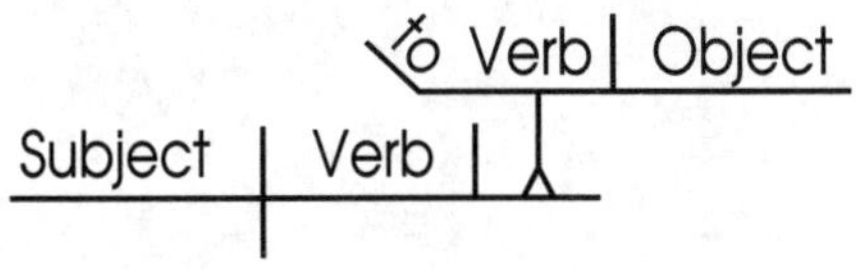

to Verb | Object

Subject | Verb |

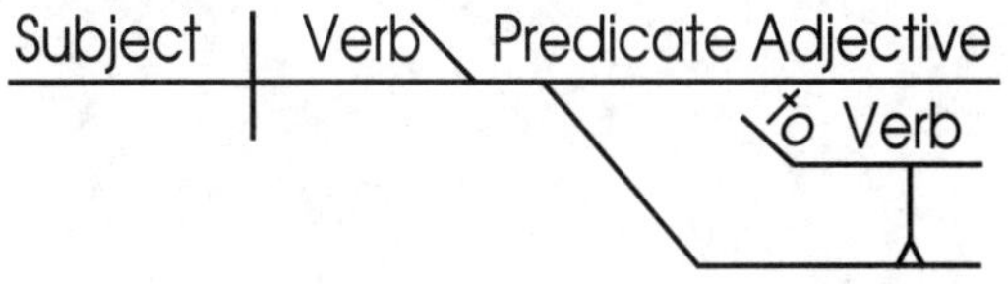

Subject | Verb \ Predicate Adjective

to Verb

Lessons 1-10

1A Nouns—page 1.

Draw a line under each noun.

1. A nasty **dragon** ate the **teacher**. (2)
2. **Desserts** should be eaten before **vegetables**. (2)
3. **Barbie** and **Skipper** are annoying. (2)
4. Ask **Joe** and **Jim** to come. (2)
5. The **Beatles** weere a singing **group**. (2)
6. **Rich** hit the **ball** and then ran around the **bases**. (3)

Fill in the blanks.

A **noun** is a word that names a __**person**__, __**place**__, or __**thing**__.

1B Avoid Slang—page 2.

Cross out slang expressions and replace them with better word choices.

Answers will vary.

1. ~~Well,~~ he ~~hung out~~ with the monkeys.
2. His lifestyle was ~~totally awesome~~.
3. His ~~hood~~ was ~~like~~ a jungle.
4. ~~Like,~~ the world is a jungle ~~out there~~.
5. His ~~buds~~ were ~~animals~~.

Fill in the blank.

A __**noun**__ is a word that names a person, place or thing.

1C Sentence Subjects—page 3.

Underline the subject in each sentence. If it is understood, write it in parentheses.

1. The **cat** ran away with the hat.
2. Where is the **cat** going with the hat?
3. The **man** with the funny hair is going to find that silly cat.
4. Watch out for that cat's claws! **(you)**
5. Those **claws** are sharp.
6. Under the pine tree, **he** lurks.
7. Why am **I** reading about this stupid cat?

Answer Key, Lessons 1-10, continued

1D Proofreading—page 4.

Correct the mistakes in the sentences below. Each line contains one mistake.

My little brother **J**ohn likes to make a snack when he gets home from **school**. He spreads peanut butter on a slice of bread. Then, he puts broccoli in the blender and mashes it **to** a slimy green pulp. Next, he spreads the disgusting green slime **on** another piece of bread and makes ~~**like**~~ a sandwich. Yuck! Does that sound good to you**?**

2A Verbs—page 5.

*Identify the word in **boldface** as an action verb (**AV**) or a helping verb (**HV**).*

1. The girl **jumped** in the lake. **AV**
2. She **was** swimming to cool off. **HV**
3. The lake **may** be freezing cold at this time of year. **HV**
4. Tomorrow, we **might** go to an amusement park. **HV**
5. I **dislike** roller coasters intensely. **AV**
6. My brother and I will **avoid** them if we can. **AV**

Fill in the blanks.

A **noun** is a word that names a **person**, **place**, or **thing**.

2B Singular and Plural—page 6.

Change these singular nouns to plural nouns.

1. fox **foxes**
2. woman **women**
3. fly **flies**
4. tomato **tomatoes**
5. knife **knives**
6. child **children**
7. piano **pianos**
8. rodeo **rodeos**
9. ball **balls**
10. key **keys**

2C More Sentence Subjects—page 7.

Underline the subject in each sentence. If the subject is understood, write it in parentheses.

1. The **tiger** ate the elephant.
2. After his huge meal, the tiger's **stomach** began to ache.
3. What was the **tiger** thinking when he ate that?
4. There is a **limit** to what the stomach can take.
5. Most **tigers** know better than to overeat.
6. From now on, don't eat so much! **(you)**

Fill in the blank

A **noun** is a word that names a person, place, or thing.

2D Proofreading—page 8.

Correct the mistakes in the sentences below. Each line contains one mistake.

My friend Julie and **I** like to visit the candy store at the mall. I like chocolate **candies** best, but Julie prefers the jellybeans. Of course, we both like the fried **potatoes** even more, and sometimes after the candy **store**, we visit the food court. Then we have upset stomachs for the rest of the day**.**

3A Common and Proper Nouns—page 9.

Draw one line under each common noun and two lines under each proper noun.

1. The **kids** on the school **bus** were making loud **noises**. (3)
2. **Jenny** was using bad **language** too. (2)
3. The poor **driver** was unhappy. (1)
4. The **kids** were going to **Skyline School**. (2)
5. The **teachers** were waiting in the parking **lot**. (2)
6. With all the **noise**, **Betty**, the **driver**, was distracted. (3)

Fill in the blanks.

A **verb** is usually an action word.

3B Verb "To Be"—page 10.

Choose the correct verb form.

1. Roger (**is, are**) at least ten feet tall.
2. He (**is, are**) growing very fast.
3. He (**was, were**) huge when he (**was, were**) born.
4. His brothers (**is, are**) all very tall also.
5. His sisters (**is, are**) all going to be very tiny.
6. There (**is, are**) seven kids in the family.
7. Unfortunately, the boys (**is, are**) not very fond of basketball.

Fill in the blanks.

Singular Present, Past Tense	Plural Present, Past Tense
I am , was	we **are, were**
you **are, were**	you are, were
he, she, it **is, was**	they **are, were**

3C Simple Sentence Diagrams—page 11.

Diagram the following sentences.

1. Trees sway.

Trees | sway

2. Bears growl.

Bears | growl

3. A wave will crash.

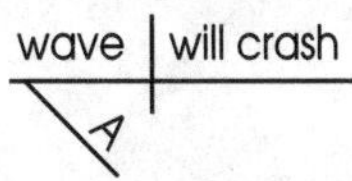

Answer Key, Lessons 1-10, continued

3D Subject-Verb Agreement—page 12.

Write the form of the verb in parentheses that agrees with the noun.

1. A dog (eat) **eats**
2. Parachutes (fall) **fall**
3. Children (swim) **swim**
4. A coyote (sneak) **sneaks**

*Circle the subject and underline the verb in each sentence. If they agree, write **Agree**. If they don't agree, write **Don't Agree.***

1. The enormous wave loom over the surfer. **Don't Agree**
2. The sand on the beach feels hot. **Agree**
3. The hot dog taste great. **Don't Agree**
4. Frisbees flies everywhere. **Don't Agree**

4A More Verbs—page 13

*Identify the word in boldface as an action verb (**AV**), a linking verb (**LV**), or a helping verb (**HV**).*

1. I **am (HV)** going to buy some donuts now.
2. "You **look (LV)** ill," **said (AV)** Mother.
3. I **feel (LV)** fine, but I will **rest (AV)** in case I **am (HV)** getting a cold.
4. Maybe I **should (HV)** eat some donuts to keep up my strength.
5. The cinnamon crumb donuts **are (LV)** the best.

Fill in the blanks.

Run, give, and **go** are **action** verbs.
Seem, look, and **become** are usually **linking** verbs.
Should, will, and **can** are **helping** verbs.

4B Contractions—page 14.

Fill in the blanks.

cannot	can't
I am	**I'm**
we have	we've
had not	**hadn't**
should not	shouldn't
where is	**where's**
it is	**it's**
she will	she'll
you are	**you're**
are not	**aren't**

4C More Simple Sentence Diagrams—page 15.

Diagram the following sentences.

1. The ball is rolling.

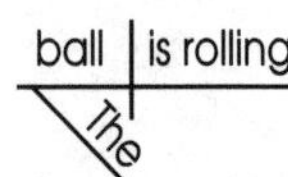

2. You should come.

You | should come

3. A beast snarls.

beast | snarls
A

4. Frogs can jump.

Frogs | can jump

Fill in the blank.
A **verb** is a word that names an **action**.

4D Proofreading—page 16.

Correct the mistakes in the sentences below. Each line contains one mistake.

Jack and Jill **are** good sports. They lugged that bucket of water all the way up the hill without complaining. There **are** many people who whine about doing anything **difficult**. When Jack fell down, he didn't cry even though he broke his crown. **Don't** you think it is a bit silly to wear a crown to climb a hill**?** Still, Jack and Jill are my **heroes**.

5A Nouns and Verbs—page 17.

Underline each ***noun*** *and* ***proper noun****. Label each verb as an action verb (****AV****), a linking verb (****LV****), or a helping verb (****HV****).*

1. Patty and Jill are **(HV)** going **(AV)** to the mall. (3N, 2V)
2. Jill hopes **(AV)** she will **(HV)** find **(AV)** a new dress for school. (3N, 3V)
3. Jill will **(HV)** look **(LV)** great in a bright colored dress. (2N, 2V)
4. Patty hates **(AV)** dresses. (2N, 1V)
5. Both girls adore **(AV)** the pizza at the Fashion Valley Mall. (3N, 1V)
6. The girls will **(HV)** eat **(AV)** too much pizza and become **(LV)** ill. (2N, 3V)

Fill in the blanks.
A **linking verb** shows the appearance of something.
A **noun** is a word that names a person, place, or thing.
A **helping** verb can team up with either an action verb or a linking verb.
An **action verb** shows an action.

5B More Singular and Plural Nouns—page 18.

Fill in the blanks to complete the rules about forming plurals.

1. To nouns ending in **o after a consonant,** like tomato, add **es**.
2. Nouns like **piano** that refer to **music** are exceptions.
3. To nouns ending in **sh, ch, s, x,** like **crutch**, add **es**.
4. To nouns ending in **y after a vowel,** like **key**, add **s**.
5. To nouns ending in **y after a consonant,** like **fairy**, change **y to i** and add **es**.

Answer Key, Lessons 1-10, continued

6. To nouns ending in **o after a vowel,** like **patio**, add **s**.
7. To nouns ending in **f** or **fe,** like **half**, change **f or fe to v** and add **es**.

Change these singular nouns to plural nouns.

1. potato **potatoes**
2. calf **calves**
3. cello **cellos**
4. berry **berries**
5. match **matches**
6. loaf **loaves**
7. hex **hexes**
8. sheep **sheep**
9. house **houses**
10. radio **radios**

5C Compound Subjects—page 19.

Diagram the following sentences.

1. John and Joe were running.

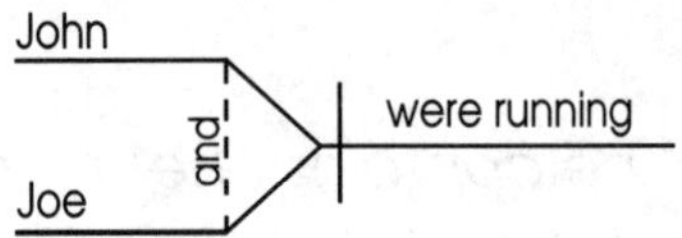

2. Bess and the giraffe raced.

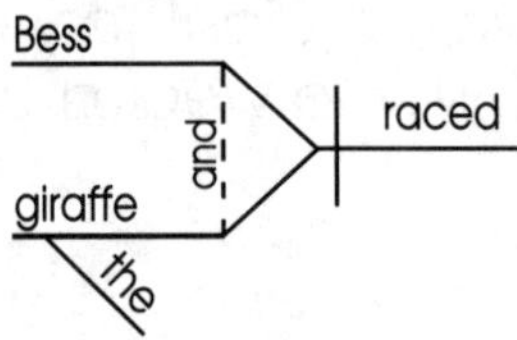

3. Bob or I will go.

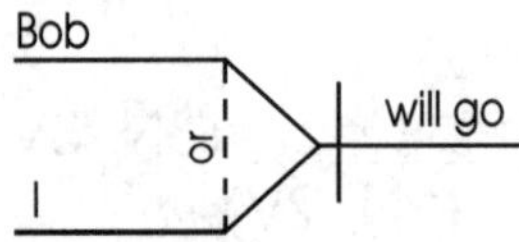

Fill in the blank.

A **verb** is a word that shows an action.

5D Compound Subject-Verb Agreement—page 20.

Underline the subject(s) once and circle the verb that agrees.

1. The beast (howls, howl) throughout the night.
2. The flowers or the dust (is, are) causing my allergies.
3. My brothers and I (is, are) sometimes very noisy.
4. The whole team (was, were) unhappy.
5. Either my sisters or my brother (is, are) in big trouble tonight.
6. On April Fool's Day, my mother (likes, like) to short sheet my bed.
7. My snakes and my iguana (loves, love) to lie in the sun.

6A More Nouns and Verbs—page 21.

Circle the nouns. Draw one line under linking or action verbs and two lines under helping verbs.

1. Fruit can be eaten in a variety of forms. (3N, 3V)
2. My favorite dessert is a pie. (2N, 1V)
3. Because of his sweet tooth, Pat adores snacks. (3N, 1 V)
4. This apple looks rotten. (1N, 1V)
5. Although Travis prefers ice cream, fruit is another favorite.
6. Tyler can spit watermelon seeds farther than Josh.

Fill in the blanks.

A **verb** is a word that shows an action or an appearance of something.

A **noun** is a word that names a person, place, or thing.

6B Possessive Nouns—page 22.

Add apostrophes to show possession.

1. The **dog's** bone was in **Mother's** garden.
2. Both **boys'** minds were on the weekend.
3. Mrs. **Jones's** car was dirty.
4. The **fighters'** noses were broken.
5. The two **ribbons'** colors were a match.
6. The **children's** coats were on the **men's** hooks.

6C Compound Verbs—page 23.

Diagram the following sentences.

1. Toddlers stumble and fall.

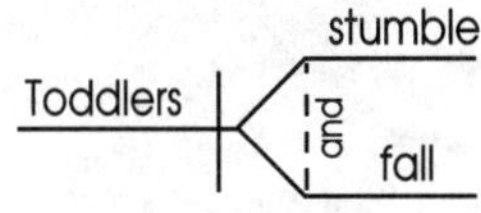

2. The Doberman may growl and bite.

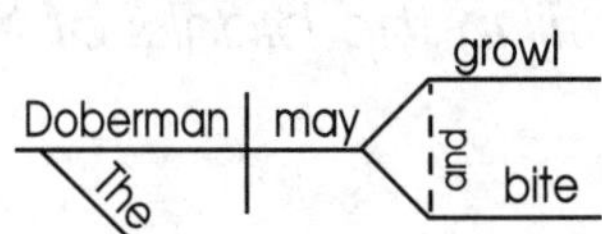

3. Lions and tigers prowl and hide.

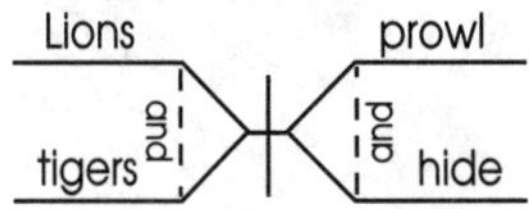

Answer Key, Lessons 1-10, continued

4.The crowd watched and waited.

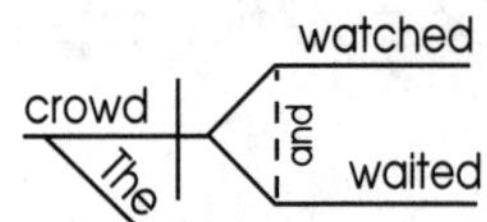

6D Punctuation Pickle—page 24.

Someone forgot to add the punctuation to the sentences. You will need the following:

1. Let**'**s go to the mall right now**!**
2. Unfortunately**,** many of the dogs**'** licenses are unreadable**.**
3. John yelled**,** **"**Can you help me**?"**
4. The boss**'**s father was born in Paris**,** France**.**
5. Why can**'**t you hurry up**?**
6. The two dresses**'** colors were identical**.**

7A Adjectives—page 25.

*Underline each adjective and draw an arrow to the word being described. (Don't forget the articles **the, an,** and **a**.)*

1. The enormous boulder rolled down the hill. (3)
2. The huge rock squashed several tiny bugs. (4)
3. Flattened bugs are invisible. (2)
4. At the bottom of the hill, it stopped. (2)
5. The squashed bugs missed the gorgeous sunset that day. (5)
6. The huge boulder doesn't care if the sunset is ugly or pretty. (5)

Fill in the blanks.

An **adjective** is a word that modifies a **noun** or a **pronoun**.

7B Build Your Own Sentences—page 26.

Choose words from the parts-of-speech list below and fill in the blanks of the story.

Answers will vary.

7C Diagramming Adjectives—page 27.

Diagram the following sentences.

1. The red balloon floated.

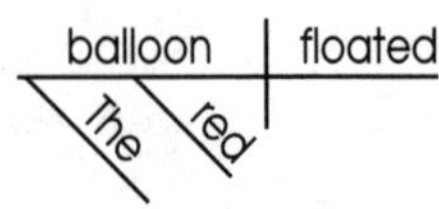

2. An impossible mission failed.

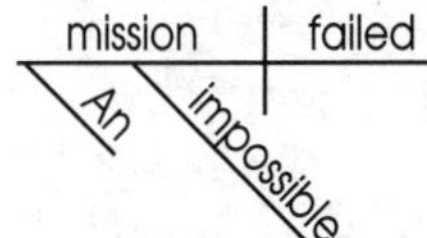

3. A large bear and a small bear charged.

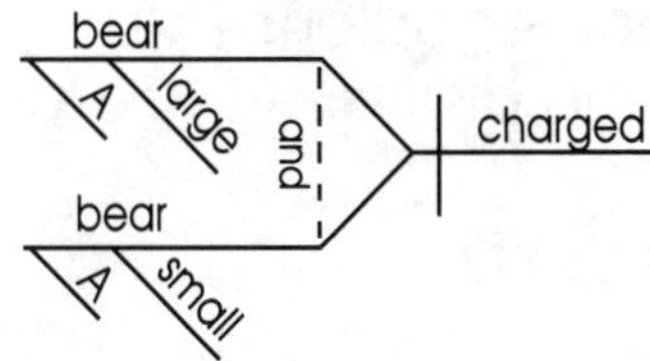

4. An ugly red vase fell and smashed.

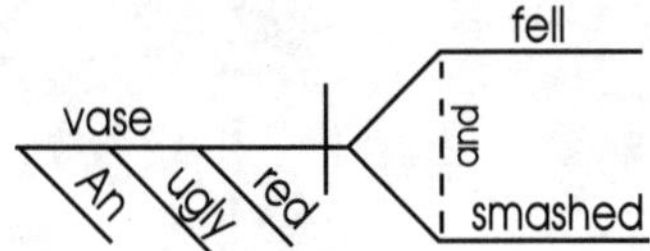

7D More Practice—page 28.

Capitalize each proper noun and add punctuation.

1. At least thirty soldiers**'** mess kits were lost**.**
2. Pick me up on time please**,** **M**other**.**
3. George **R**uth**'**s baseball mitt has holes in it**.**

Write the contraction for each word pair.

1. would not **wouldn't**
2. it is **it's** (Note: The word **its** shows possession.)
3. they are **they're**

Write the plural of each noun.

1. tomato **tomatoes**
2. dish **dishes**
3. monkey **monkeys**

8A Articles—Wimpy Adjectives—page 29.

Choose the correct expression.

1. Find (a, **an**) old, smelly shoe.
2. That was some sort (**of**, of a) large greyhound.
3. Wait for (a, **an**) hour before you go swimming.
4. (**A**, an) hard-boiled egg tastes delicious with lots of salt.

Underline each adjective and draw an arrow to the word being described.

1. A large, smelly dragon lives in the tremendously dank cave.
2. He is very kind and gentle, but he has really putrid breath.

Answer Key, Lessons 1-10, continued

8B Special Forms of Adjectives—page 30.

Write a correct form of the adjective in parentheses.

1. One of the (unusual) **most unusual** animals is the platypus.
2. My (fast) **fastest** teammate is Jean.
3. A tiger is (frightening) **more frightening** than a house cat.
4. A bush is (tall) **taller** than a tree.
5. Cherry pie is (delicious) **more, less delicious** than eggplant.
6. Reading is (fun) **more, less fun** than doing the dishes.
7. Math is my (difficult) **most, least difficult** subject.

8C More Diagramming Adjectives—page 31.

Diagram the following sentences.

1. A red ribbon flew.

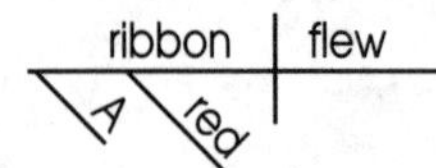

2. A purple shirt and green pants clashed.

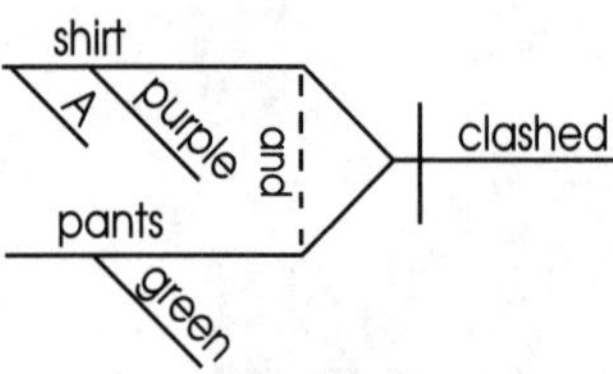

3. A lively dolphin jumped and splashed.

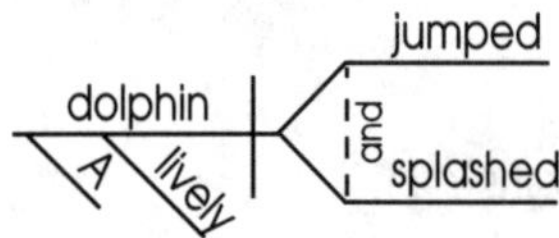

4.The wily fox either ran or hid.

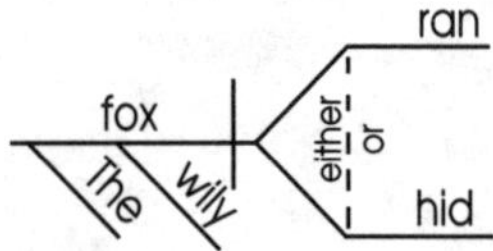

Fill in the blank.

An **adjective** is a word that modifies either a **noun** or a **pronoun**.

8D Proofreading—page 32.

Correct the mistakes in the sentences below. Each line contains one mistake.

Humpty **D**umpty was awfully stupid to sit on that huge wall. What did he expect? **An** egg is exceedingly fragile. Humpty's balance wasn't that great anyway. Everyone knows that **eggs'** shells are very thin. Next time Humpty wants to act **really** hot, he should jump into a frying pan**.**

9A Adverbs—page 33.

Underline each adverb and draw an arrow to the word it modifies.

1. The alarm clock rings early. (1)
2. I get up slowly. (2)
3. Often, I eat breakfast too quickly. (3)
4. Sometimes, the car pool is really late. (2)
5. Tomorrow, I will get to school earlier. (2)

Fill in the blanks.

An **adverb** is a word that modifies a **verb**, or an **adverb**, or an **adjective**.

9B Adjectives and Adverbs—page 34.

Underline each adjective and cross out each adverb.

1. The hungry beast gobbled ~~furiously~~.
2. Without any thought, the hero climbed ~~quickly~~.
3. The photo of the two children was ~~very~~ beautiful.
4. The hasty work seemed ~~quite~~ sloppy.

Draw an arrow from the boldface word to the word modified. Then identify the part of speech of the modified word.

1. **noun** The **enormous** hat looked silly on the man.
2. **adjective** The huge hat looked **very** silly on the man.
3. **verb** The man looked **carefully** at the hat.
4. **noun** The man was exceedingly **careful**.
5. **adverb** Then he walked away **very** quickly.

9C Diagramming Adverbs—page 35.

Diagram the following sentences.

1. Finally, the guests arrived.

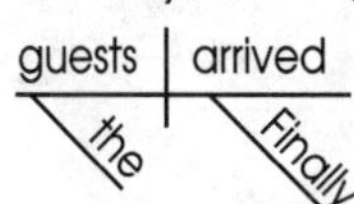

2. The athlete cycled smoothly and ran fast.

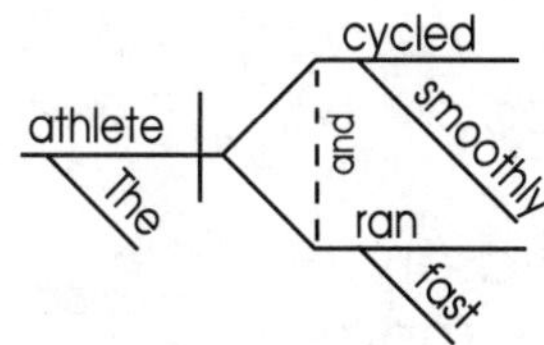

3. Gazelles can leap very well.

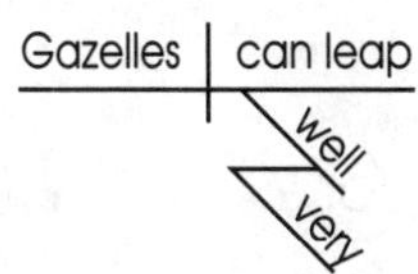

Answer Key, Lessons 1-10, continued

4. The baby cried all night.

baby | cried
The
night
all

9D Good, Well; Bad, Badly—page 36.

Choose the correct word in parentheses and underline the word it modifies.

1. The third baseman hits the ball (good, **well**).
2. He is a (**good**, well) player.
3. Unfortunately, he runs the bases (bad, **badly**).
4. In fact, his base running is very (**bad**, badly).
5. He steals bases (bad, **badly**).

Write the correct adjective or adverb (good, well, bad, badly).

1. A **good** try (positive)
2. **badly** drawn (negative)
3. performs **well** (positive)
4. A **bad** decision (negative)

10A More Adverbs—page 37.

Underline each adverb and draw an arrow to the word it modifies.

1. Charles and Josh dashed quickly away.
2. Unfortunately, they were caught.
3. The big bear ate them greedily.
4. Then the bear barfed* loudly.
5. Charles and Josh emerged very happily.

Fill in the blanks.

An adverb answers the questions **when**, **where**, **how**, or **how often**.

**Editor's note: OK Ok...That word is slang and slang is not acceptable.*

10B Creating Adverbs—page 38

Change the adjective in parentheses to an adverb.

1. I ran (quick) **quickly** to save my buddy.
2. I would (glad) **gladly** help someone in need.
3. He lashed out (angry) **angrily**.
4. The octopus moved (easy) **easily** in the water.
5. The fox stared (wary) **warily** at the raw meat.
6. She was (complete) **completely** happy for once.

Fill in the blanks.

An **adverb** modifies a **verb**, an **adverb**, or an **adjective**.

An **adjective** modifies a **noun**, or a **pronoun**.

10C More Diagramming Adverbs—page 39.

Diagram the following sentences.

1. The odd green stain washed out.

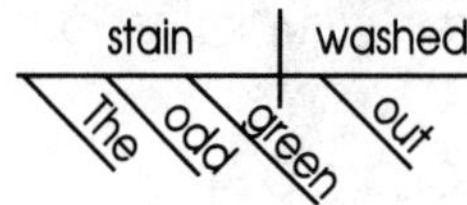

2. James and Rick worked very hard.

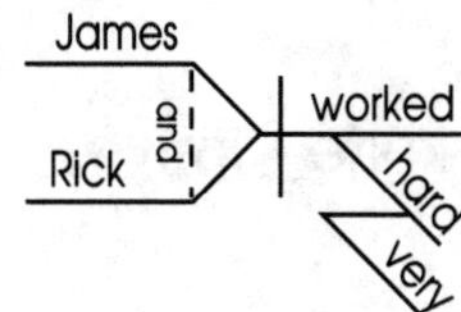

3. The dark green balloon popped loudly.

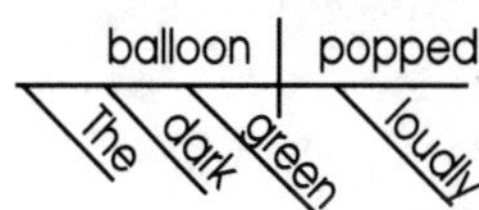

4. The quarterback runs well but throws poorly.

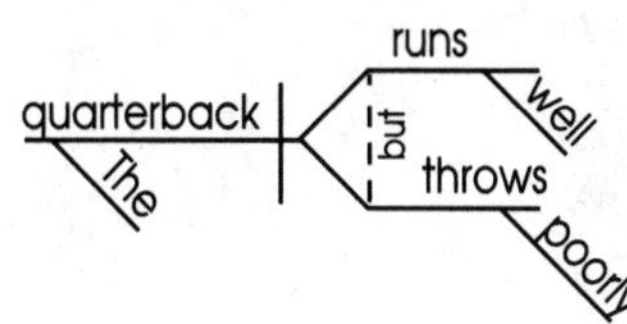

Fill in the blanks.

An **adverb** is a word that modifies a **verb**, or an **adverb**, or an **adjective**.

10D Proofreading—page 40.

Correct the mistakes in the sentences below. Each line contains one mistake.

Little Bo Peep didn't take care of her sheep very **well**. It was silly to assume they would just stand around **and** not run off when she wasn't paying attention. Sheep are about the least **intelligent** of all the farmyard animals. Of course, Bo Peep wasn't so smart either. She must have searched **badly** for her **sheep** since she never found them.

Answer Key, Lessons 1-10, continued

REVIEW Lessons 1-10—page 41.

Connect each part of speech to its partners

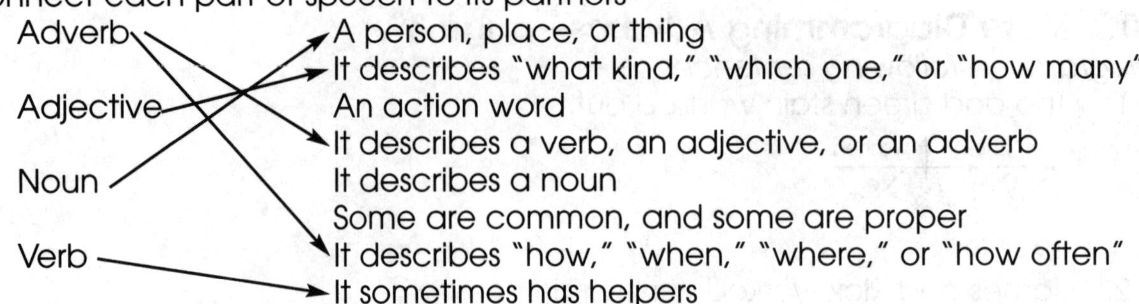

Adverb
Adjective
Noun
Verb
A person, place, or thing
It describes "what kind," "which one," or "how many"
An action word
It describes a verb, an adjective, or an adverb
It describes a noun
Some are common, and some are proper
It describes "how," "when," "where," or "how often"
It sometimes has helpers

Write the plural form

church **churches** army **armies** knife **knives**

Write the possessive form

Mother **Mother's** spiders **spider's**

children **children's**

Fill in the blanks

Adjective	Adverb
glad	**gladly**
complete	completely
good	**well**

Diagram the sentence: John and big Joe ate hungrily.

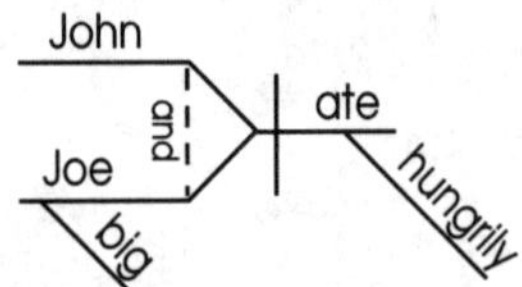

SKILL CHECK Lessons 1-10—page 42.

Identify the part of speech

will be **verb** idea **noun**
swift **adjective** destroy **verb**
bad **adjective** quickly **adverb**
good **adjective** well **adverb**

Write the plural form of the following:

half **halves** duty **duties**
lunch **lunches** key **keys**

Write the possessive form of the following:

boys **boys'** bird **bird's**
children **children's** church **church's**

Fill in the chart:

Adjective	Adverb
good	**well**
light	**lightly**
slow	slowly
noisy	**noisily**

Diagram this sentence: The agile player ran gracefully.

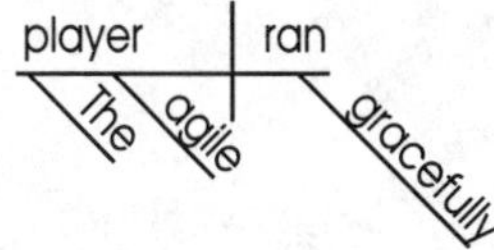

11A Conjunctions—page 43.

Underline the conjunction(s) in each sentence.

1. For dinner, I plan to have a hamburger, some fries, **and** a shake.
2. My mother says I should have some vegetables **and** some milk, **but** I don't believe her.
3. Dinner without grease **or** fats is like living on bread **and** water.
4. **Either** I eat junk food, **or** I eat nothing, **for** junk food is the staff of life.

Fill in the blanks.

An adverb modifies a **verb**, an **adverb**, or an **adjective**.

11B Compound Sentences—page 44.

*Label each compound verb (**CV**), compound subject (**CS**), and compound sentence (**Csen**). Insert punctuation where required. Write **OK** after the sentences that do not need punctuation changes.*

1. John and Jim will go to the movies. **CS OK**
2. Jamie will also go to the movies**,** but I will stay home. **Csen**
3. I will stay home and do my homework. **CV OK**
4. I will write my essay first**;** next I will finish my math. **Csen**
5. I have homework to do because I didn't finish it on time. **OK**
6. Next time, I will avoid procrastinating and finish my work early**,** and then I can go to the movies with my friends. **CV, Csen**

11C Diagramming Compound Sentences—page 45.

Diagram the following sentences.

1. I ran, but he followed.

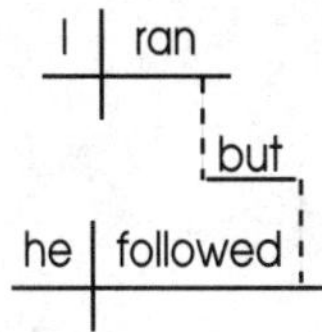

2. The lightning flashed, and the thunder crashed.

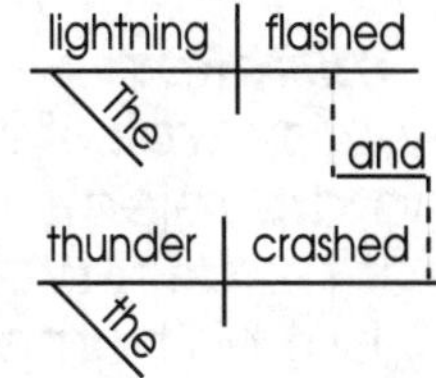

3. The building collapsed suddenly; everything exploded.

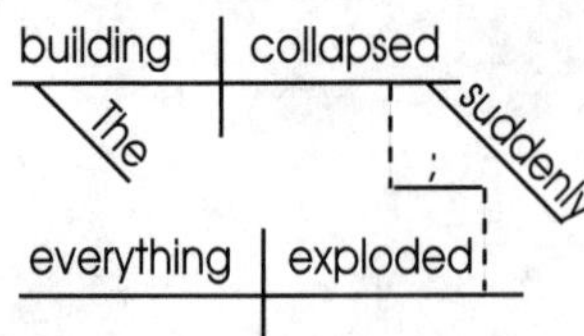

11D Proofreading—page 46.

Correct the mistakes in the sentences below. ***There are seven mistakes.***

Michael Jordan was a great player. The **Bulls really** missed him when he retired. He moved on the court really **well,** and his shooting was completely amazing. I have a bet with my **parents** that he will not come out of **retirement** again. I will be happy **whether** I win or lose the bet.

12A Prepositions—page 47.

Underline the preposition(s) in each sentence.

1. **Under** my hat is a snarl **of** curls.
2. **After** the storm, we are going to assess the damage **near** the barn.
3. Go **into** your room and find the laundry **under** your bed!
4. When we arrive **at** school, run **to** your classroom and apologize **to** your teacher.
5. **Due to** the traffic, we just couldn't get there **on** time.

Fill in the blanks. ***Answers will vary***

Some coordinating conjunctions are **and**, **or**, and **but**.

12B Prepositions Go Fish—page 48.

Card game.

12C Be Creative!—page 49.

Write sentences to fit the diagrams below. Then fill in the words on the diagrams.

1. **Answers will vary.**
2. **Answers will vary.**
3. **Answers will vary.**

12D Proofreading—page 50.

Correct the mistakes in the sentences below. ***There are nine mistakes.***

The Cubs are my favorite underdogs**.** Even when they play **well**, it is a surprise to see them win. The team is full of players who **are** rejects from other teams. Even Sammy Sosa **doesn't** get the respect he **deserves** since his team so rarely wins**.** He hits plenty of homers**,** but his homers aren't game winners. The Cubs may disappoint the fans **more often than** not, but they are loveable even when they **lose**.

13A Prepositional Phrases—page 51.

Draw one line under the prepositional phrase(s) and two lines under the preposition(s) in each sentence.

1. The teenager in the red jacket ran past the door.
2. Under the tree in the back of the lawn is a wrecked car.
3. Among young men, suits and ties are not the fashion.
4. I would love to dance in The Nutcracker like you.
5. Between you and me, I think this exercise is too easy.

List six prepositions not used in the exercise above.
Answers will vary.

13B Of, Off, Have—page 52.

Choose the correct word.

1. Mom should (of, **have**) gotten some milk at the store.
2. I got the answers (off, off of, **from**) my friend.
3. Please get (**off**, off of) my bed.
4. Beth ought to (of, **have**) gone to bed earlier.
5. The box (**of**, off) chocolates disappeared fast.
6. The girl must (of, **have**) been diving (**off**, off of) the cliff.

Fill in the blanks
The parts of a compound sentence can be connected by either a coordinate **conjunction** or a punctuation mark called a **semicolon**.

13C Adjective Prepositional Phrases—page 53.

Diagram the following sentences.

1. The author of the book writes very skillfully.

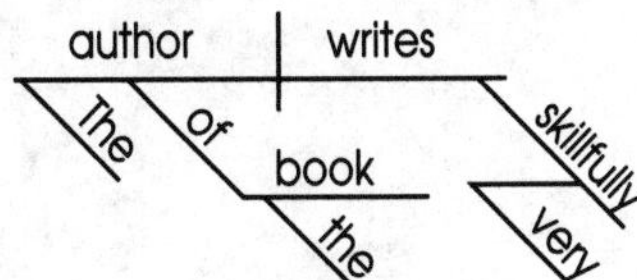

2. The bird with the blue feathers flew overhead.

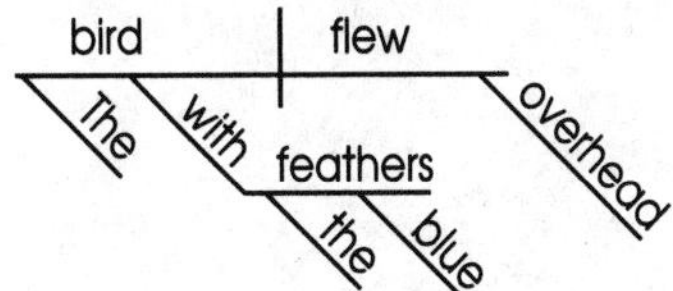

3. The black truck with the dent in the side was speeding.

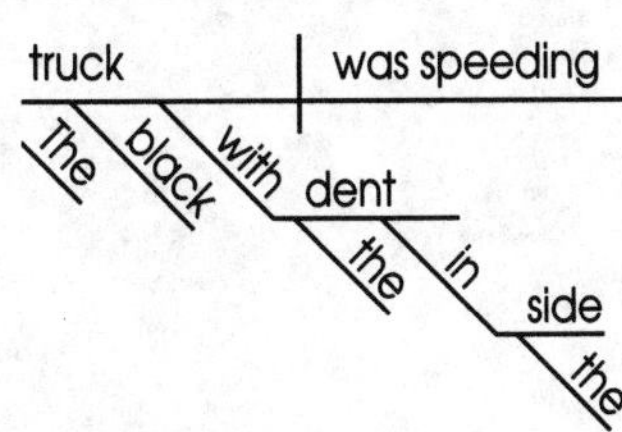

Answer Key, Lessons 11-20, continued

13D Proofreading—page 54.

Correct the mistakes in the sentences below. ***There are eight mistakes.***

Rasputin was one of the **greatest** villains in history. He was **an** advisor to the Czar of Russia in the late 1800s. His enemies tried to assassinate him**,** but he kept refusing to die. First, they **fed** him poisoned wine and cake**,** but he didn't die. Then they shot him in the back and left him to bleed to death. You would **have** thought that was enough, but Rasputin still didn**'**t die. In desperation, they shot him six more times. The **whole** story sounds like a *Three Stooges* movie.

14A More Prepositional Phrases—page 55.

In the following sentences, draw one line under the preposition and two lines under its object. Cross out any modifiers of the object.

1. Without ~~his mother's~~ permission, the teen took the family car to ~~the~~ beach.
2. The repulsive creature waggled his tongue over ~~his enormous~~ teeth.
3. His drool slid over ~~his fuzzy~~ chin and dropped into ~~a~~ puddle on ~~the~~ sand.
4. The teen drove the car directly into ~~the gaping~~ mouth of ~~the horrifying~~ monster.
5. He smashed it like ~~a~~ piece of ~~hard~~ candy.

14B Parallel Structure—page 56.

Rewrite the following sentences to make the structure parallel.

1. I love **the** sun, the sand, and the water.
2. Writing is easy; **writing** well is difficult.
3. The teacher explained the problem, the method, and **the solution**.
4. We want a teammate who is skillful, reliable, and **tireless**.
5. Is it our ideas or **our writing** that matters for our grade?
6. The teacher hopes to improve test scores, and **to develop** a better understanding of the issues.

14C Adverb Prepositional Phrases—page 57.

Diagram the following sentences.

1. The giant oak was struck by lightning.

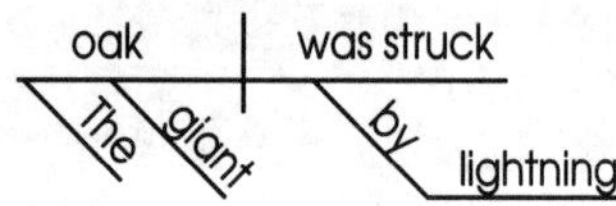

2. My math book fell into the tub.

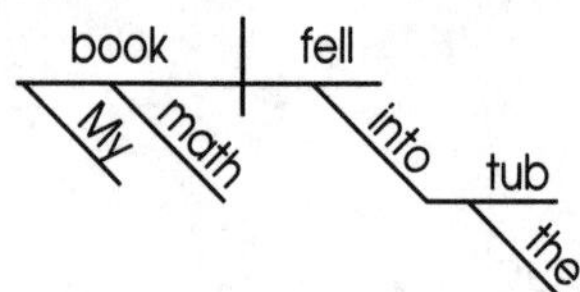

3. I jumped from the tree and fell to the ground.

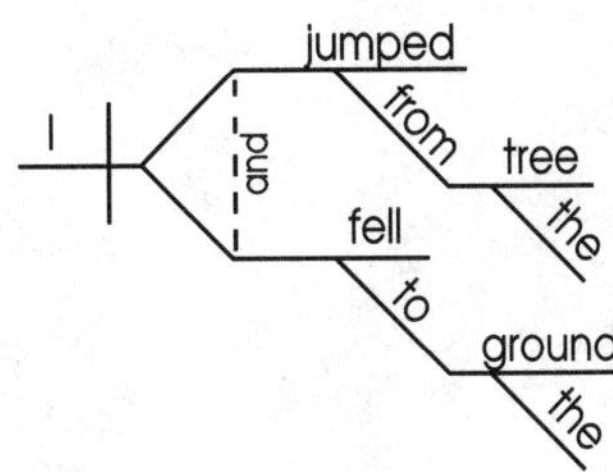

14D Proofreading—page 58.

Correct the mistakes in the sentences below. ***There are eight mistakes.***

The story about how everyone **except** Columbus **thought** the world was flat is **plainly** false. Educated people during Columbus' time **knew** the world was round. They just didn't know how big the world was**.** Many mathematicians thought that the world was much smaller **than** it was. So **when** Columbus and his crew wanted to sail around the world, **to** see new lands, and to find the Indies, they didn't realize what a long voyage they were planning.

15A Direct Objects—page 59.

Draw one line under the verb and two lines under the direct object.

1. My brother hit me.
2. I am arranging a trip to Borneo.
3. The red Mustang hit the little Toyota and the dump truck.
4. Babe Ruth got more hits than anyone on the team.
5. My friend swiped a candy bar from me.
6. Please give a bath to that dog soon!

Fill in the blank.

The most common coordinating **conjunctions** are **and, or,** and **but.**

15B There, Their, They're—page 60.

Fill in the blanks with ***there, their,*** *or* ***they're.***

1. **There** are sixteen students in the class.
2. All the students have **their** own projects.
3. **They're** expected to finish the work independently.
4. As a reward, **they're** going on a field trip to Sea World.
5. **There**, **they're** going to be allowed to feed **their** lunch to Shamu.
6. Unfortunately, Shamu may choose to bite off **their** hands.
7. If **they're** maimed, the students will have to brush **their** teeth with **their** feet.

Answer Key, Lessons 11-20, continued

15C Direct Objects—page 61.

Diagram the following sentences.

1. The baseball player hit the ball into the bleachers.

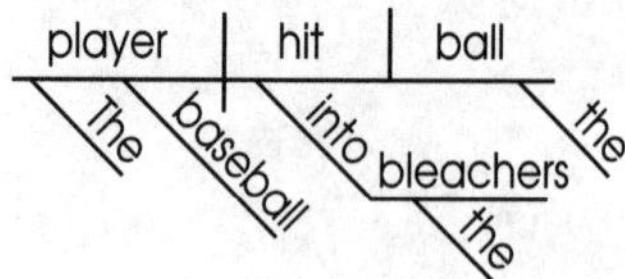

2. Angrily, the teacher threw the papers down.

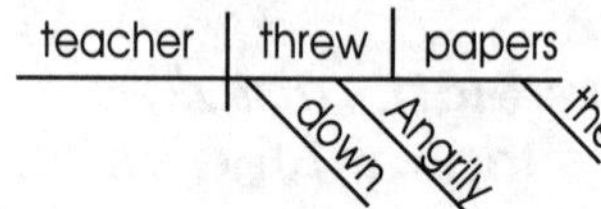

3. My mother baked a cake and frosted it with whipped cream.

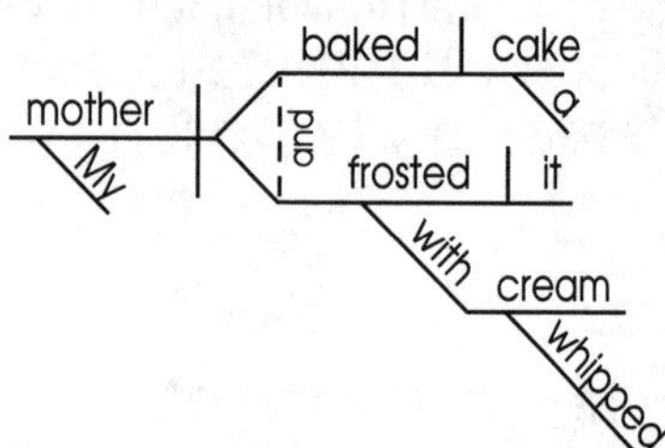

15D Proofreading—page 62.

Correct the mistakes in the sentences below. ***There are eight mistakes.***

Goldilocks would **have** been in big trouble if the police had **caught** her. Think of how many illegal acts she committed! First of all, she **broke** into the three **bears'** house without an invitation. Then, she smashed **their** furniture and stole all **their** dinner. She committed crimes like breaking and entering, destroying property, and **stealing** things. What kind of lesson is this story teaching little kids**?**

16A Indirect Objects—page 63.

Draw one line under the direct object and two lines under the indirect object in the following sentences.

1. I wrote my buddy a long letter.
2. Jean told Jill an embarrassing secret.
3. My dad gave my brother and his friend two tickets to the hockey game.
4. She made Ben chocolate chip cookies and caramel popcorn.
5. I showed William my sister's surprise.
6. On her birthday, I sent my friend a large bouquet of balloons.

16B Verb Tenses and Irregular Verbs—page 64.

Fill in the chart

Pres. tense	Fut. Tense	Past Tense	Past tense & helpers (PP)
paint	will paint	painted	has, have painted

work	**will work**	worked	**has, have worked**
speak	**will speak**	spoke	**has, have, spoken**
ring	will ring	**rang**	**has, have, rung**
ride	**will ride**	**rode**	has, have ridden
eat	**will eat**	ate	**has, have, eaten**
draw	will draw	**drew**	**has, have, drawn**
do	**will do**	**did**	**has, have, done**
know	**will know**	knew	**has, have known**
drive	**will drive**	**drove**	has, have driven
take	**will take**	took	**has, have taken**
begin	**will begin**	**began**	**has, have begun**
see	will see	**saw**	**has, have seen**
move	**will move**	**moved**	**has, have moved**
am, are	will be	**was, were**	**has, have been**
hold	**will hold**	held	**has, have held**

16C Indirect Objects—page 65.

Diagram the following sentences. (Hint: Understood subjects are placed in parentheses on the subject line.)

1. José sent me a letter on the first day of camp.

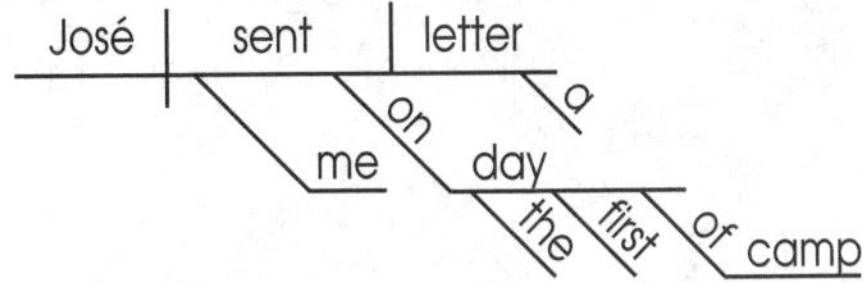

2. Sadly, Lee told Jenny the story about the accident in school.

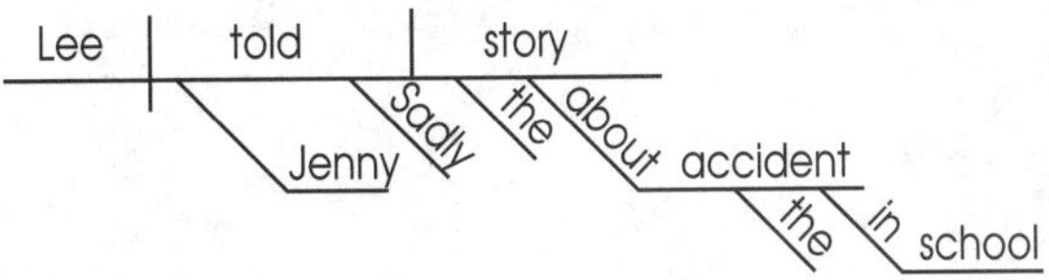

3. Bring him the large purple canister from the kitchen.

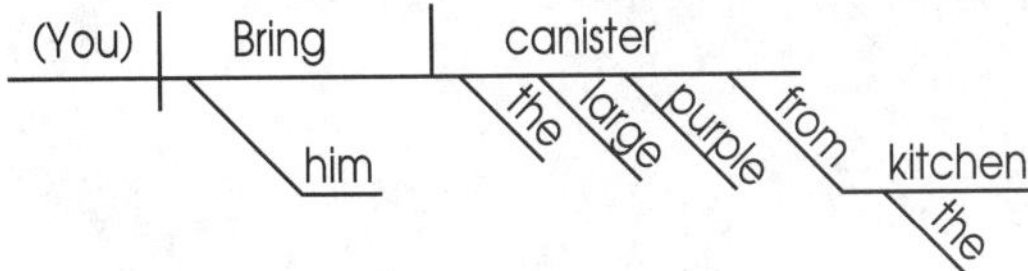

16D Proofreading—page 66.

Correct the mistakes in the sentences below. ***There are eight mistakes.***

Remember all those pictures of the Pilgrims at the first Thanksgiving? **Their** hats and clothes were black and white**,** and they had buckles on **their** shoes. Original letters from the period tell us **that's** not how the Pilgrims dressed. They **wore** colorful clothes, not just black and white. **Putting buckles** on shoes and wearing only black and white didn't come into fashion **until** years later.

Answer Key, Lessons 11-20, continued

17A Pronouns—page 67.

Underline the pronouns in the following sentences.

1. **My** friend and **I** got tickets to the concert **that** is at the Sports Arena. (3)
2. **I** would have earned the money **myself,** but **my** parents gave **it** to **me.** (5)
3. **Everybody** at school is jealous **that** **we** have tickets. (3)
4. **I** don't know **who** is performing before the main act, but **I** bet **it** is a band **that** is going to be good. (5)
5. **Nobody** who sits near the back can see **anything** because **everyone** else stands up through **it** all. (5)

17B Pronouns and Contractions—page 68.

Choose the correct word in the following sentences.

1. (Your, **You're**) a lucky snake!
2. (**Its**, It's) skin is scaly.
3. (Theirs, **There's**) the python in the cage.
4. (Whose, **Who's**) going to feed that creature?
5. Look at the size of the lump in (**its**, it's) stomach.
6. (Its, **It's**) likely to be full now.
7. Don't stick (**your**, you're) hand in the cage.
8. (**Whose**, Who's) food is that?

17C More Objects—page 69.

Diagram the following sentences.

1. Juan bought a record and gave me the change.

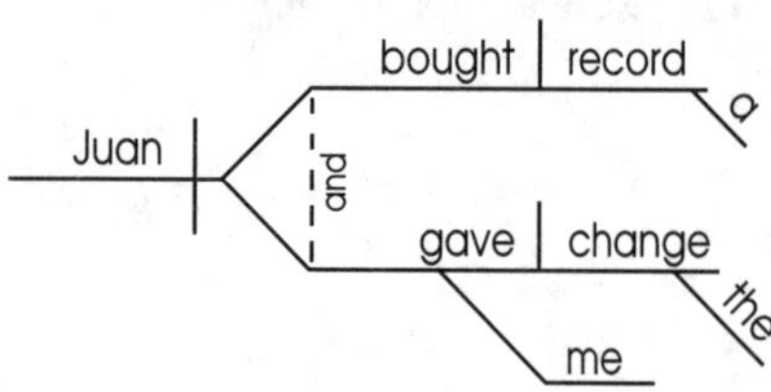

2. Lee sent Bill the tickets, and he tossed me the parking pass.

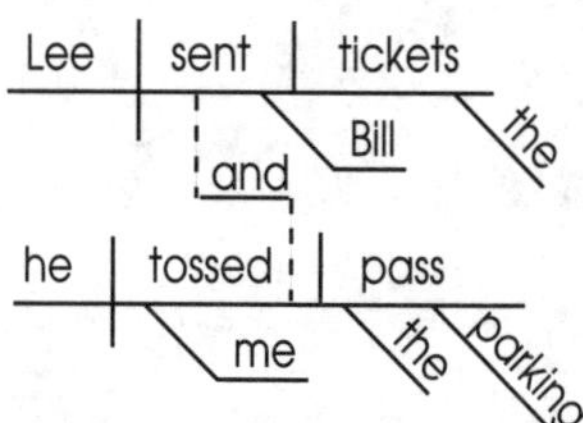

3. Either I will buy you a present, or I will take you to dinner.

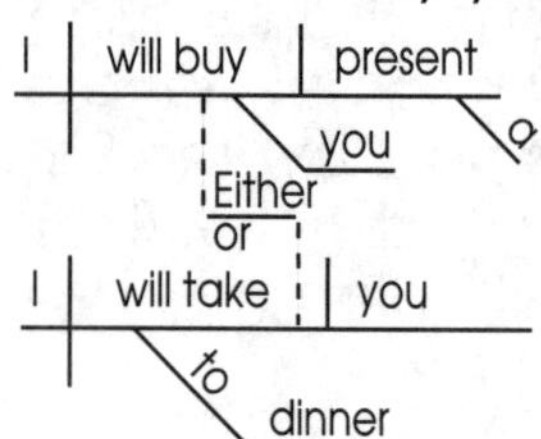

17D Proofreading—page 70.

Correct the mistakes in the sentences below. ***There are nine mistakes.***

I often have the same nightmare. My alarm doesn't go off**,** and it's late when I wake up. I miss the carpool, so I am late for school. I can**'**t get my locker open. Then I am late for a test**,** and I can't find the classroom**,** but more often, I can't get my books and homework out **of** my locker. The bells are ringing **wildly**, and the teachers are yelling at me, and all my classmates **are laughing** at me. If I had known how bad my dreams would be, I would not **have** had that last piece of anchovy, olive, and sausage pizza.

18A Subject and Object Pronouns—page 71.

*Identify the form of pronoun in boldface as subject (**S**) or object (**O**).*

1. __S__ Unfortunately, **I** missed the party.
2. __O__ My brother gave **me** the chicken pox.
3. __O__ My parents let **us** watch videos day and night.
4. __O__ Then we gave **them** the chicken pox too.

Fill in the chart.

Sub. Sing.	Obj.Sing.	Sub.Plur.	Obj.Plur.
I	**me**	we	**us**
you	**you**	you	**you**
he, she, it	**him, her, it**	they	**them**

18B More Subject and Object Pronouns—page 72.

Choose the correct pronoun in the sentences below.

1. Frank likes to play monopoly with Brad, Kayla, and (I, **me**).
2. (**He**, Him) often gives (we, **us**) a run for our money.
3. You and (**I**, me) will be on one team.
4. Frank and I sometimes gang up on (they, **them**).
5. Brad sits next to (he, **him**) and (I, **me**).
6. Please give (I, **me**) and (she, **her**) some cash.
7. When he wants to, Frank always beats (we, **us**).

18C More Practice—page 73.

Diagram the following sentences.

1. John will roll the newspapers and ads and deliver them.

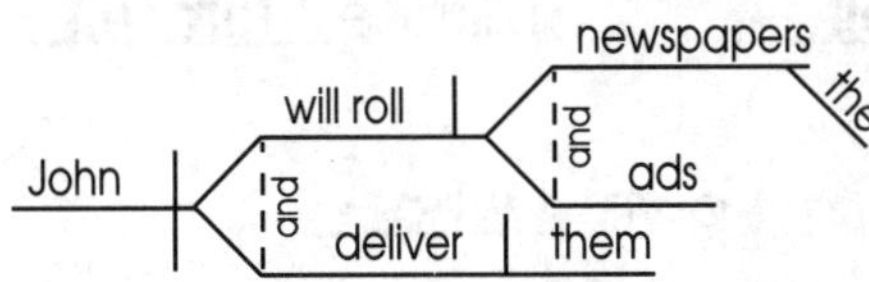

2. Give him and me the best positions on the team.

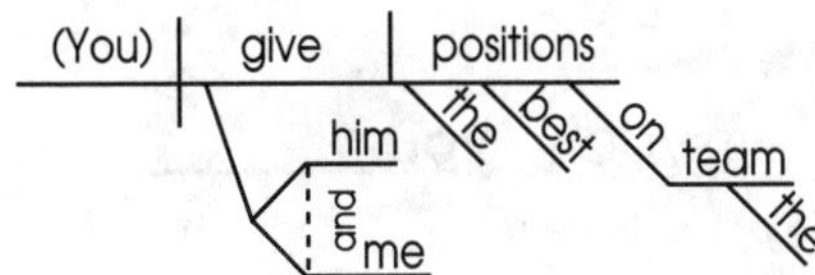

Answer Key, Lessons 11-20, continued

3. Mark baked the pizza and served it to his friends.

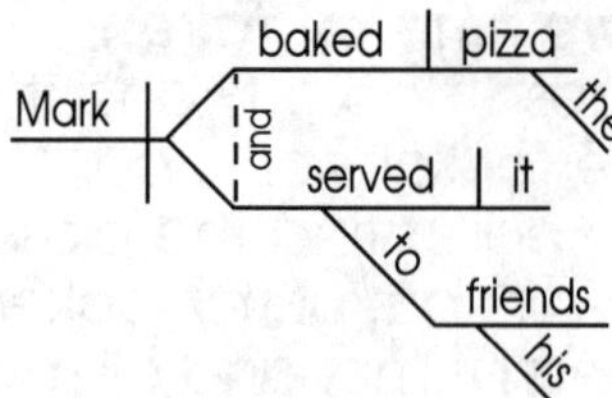

18D Proofreading—page 74.

Correct the mistakes in the sentences below. ***There are eight mistakes.***

Sometimes, you just can't win. The other day, **my friends and I** were at a pizza place. My **buddies** spilled an entire pitcher of soda. I thought, "Either my friends or I **am** going to have to tell the waitress." I knew the **waitress** would be annoyed at the mess**,** but she would be **more angry** if we left without telling her. I wish my friends would not **have fooled** around so much.

19A Who and Whom—page 75.

Choose the correct form of the pronoun in the sentences below.

1. (Who, **Whom**) did he choose?
2. (**Who**, Whom) is going with you?
3. To (who, **whom**) did you send the letter?
4. She is the one (**who**, whom) is blonde.
5. Dave can go with (whoever, **whomever**) he wants.
6. (Who, **Whom**) did you tell the news to?
7. Jack is the unfortunate person (who, **whom**) the car hit.

19B Scrambled Pronouns—page 76.

Someone threw all the pronouns into a pot and the letters were scrambled. See how quickly you can unscramble them.

Subject Pronouns

yeht **they** ouy **you** ew **we**

Object Pronouns

su **us** hetm **them** reh **her**

Reflexive Pronouns

veselmeths **themselves** ylfsme **myself** mlfhise **himself**

Interrogative Pronouns

tawh **what** hiwhc **which** owh **who**

Indefinite Pronouns

smeo **some** neoyna **anyone** bdyoan **anybody**

Possessive Pronouns

nemi **mine** rsou **ours** rsyuo **yours**

19C Who, Whom?—page 77.

Diagram the sentences and choose the correct form of ***who*** *or* ***whom*** *depending on its placement in the diagram.*

1. (Who, **Whom**) did you tell the secret to?

you | did tell | secret
to
Whom
the

2. (**Who**, Whom) will play the lead role?

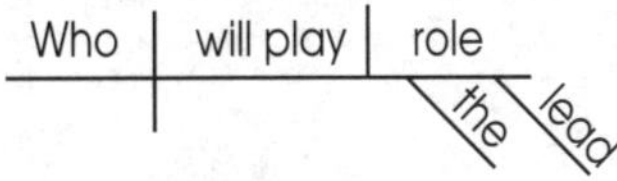

3. With (who, **whom**) did you see the horror movie?

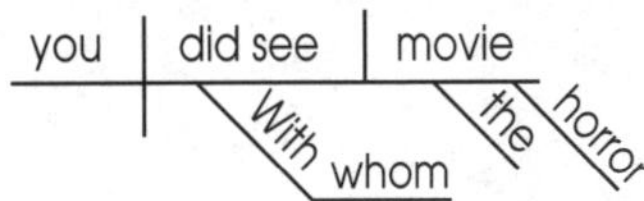

19D Proofreading—page 78.

Correct the mistakes in the sentences below. ***There are nine mistakes.***

A myth is a story that **reflects** the values of a culture. It may or may not be true**.** The importance of the story is based on the lesson and not **on** the history. The story about George **Washington** cutting down the cherry tree and **then** admitting it—"I cannot tell a lie"—is an example of a myth. **Whether** or not George **really** did chop down a tree to try out his new ax **doesn't** matter. What matters is that **Americans** value honesty.

20A Possessive Pronouns—page 79.

*Identify each pronoun as a subject pronoun (**SP**), an object pronoun (**OP**), or a possessive pronoun (**PP**).*

1. Between **you (OP)** and **me (OP)**, **I (SP)** just don't like **her (PP)** attitude.
2. **Her (PP)** chip on **her (PP)** shoulder is bigger than **mine (OP)** is.
3. **Your (PP)** hat is sillier looking than **his (PP)**.
4. Don't make fun of **me (OP)** because of **my (PP)** hat.

Fill in the chart.

Subject Pronoun	Object Pronoun	Possessive Pronoun
I	me	my, mine
you	**you**	**your, yours**
he, she, it	**him, her, it**	**his, her, hers, its**
we	**us**	**our, ours**
you	**you**	**your, yours**
they	**them**	**their, theirs**

Answer Key, Lessons 11-20, continued

20B Pronouns and Antecedents—page 80.

Circle the pronoun and underline its antecedent .

1. The girls lost their homework.
2. The toddler wants to make dinner himself.
3. Barbara is combing her hair.
4. My dog likes to scratch behind his ear.
5. Jack and Joe will be late for their ride.
6. Jack and Joe hope Bob's brother will give them a ride.

20C Be Creative!—page 81

Write sentences to fit the diagrams below and then put the words on the lines.

1. Answers will vary.
2. Answers will vary.
3. Answers will vary.

20D Proofreading—page 82.

Correct the mistakes in the sentences below. ***There are nine mistakes.***

Fashions can be very odd. Why do women **wear** spike-heeled shoes that squash **their** toes and make it impossible to walk **quickly**? **Whose** idea was it to design shoes that can cripple you**?** Do you like the silly fad of wearing **your** baggy pants so far below the waist that **they're** always on the verge of falling **off**? How can that be comfortable? I think **it's** silly!

REVIEW Lessons 11-20—page 83.

Connect each part of speech to its partners

Conjunction	A word that stands for a noun
	"In," "over," "by"
Pronoun	"And," "or," "but"
	"Them" is an object form
Preposition	It is always followed by an object
	It connects two or more sentence parts

Write the plural form:

he **they** you **you** me **us**

Write the object form:

we **us** he **him** you **you**

Fill in the verbs in the correct forms:

Present	Past	Past with helpers
want	**wanted**	have, has wanted
do	**did**	**have, has done**
am, is	was	**have, has been**
know	**knew**	**have, has known**
drive	drove	**have, has driven**

Diagram: I finally sent my mother a long letter from camp.

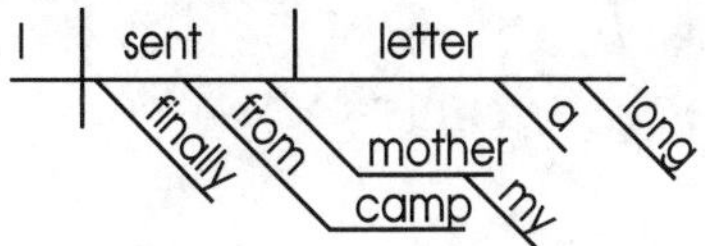

SKILL CHECK Lessons 11-20—page 84.

Identify the part of speech

and	**coordinate conjunction**	am	**verb**
near	**preposition or adverb**	them	**pronoun**
silly	**adjective**	by	**preposition**
but	**coordinate conjunction**	sinfully	**adverb**

Underline the correct answer:

Always use the **subject, object** form of a pronoun following a preposition.
Always use the **subject, object** form of a pronoun as an indirect object.
Always use an **adverb, adjective** to modify a verb.
Always use an **adverb, adjective** to modify an adjective.

Fill in the correct forms:

Subject singular	Subject Plural	Object Singular	Object Plural
I	we	**me**	us
you	you	you	**you**
he, she, it	**they**	**them**	them

Correct the following:

Jack and **I** love to hide from my sister and her friends. They think **they're** so clever and can catch us, but we hide **well**. Sometimes we let them find us, but we could **have gotten** away. I love playing hide an' seek and **celebrating** afterward with ice cream.

Answer Key, Lessons 21-30

21A Barbie's Sleepover—page 85.

Fill in the blanks with the parts of speech. Then enter them into the story below in order. (Hint: To make a silly story, choose outrageous words.)
Answers will vary.

21B Pronoun Agreement—page 86.

Choose the correct pronoun and underline its antecedent.

1. Everyone who is ready will be allowed to choose (**her,** their) new cheerleader uniform.
2. The cheerleaders wanted to choose (her, **their**) new coach.
3. Every guy wanted to have (**his,** their) say in the matter.
4. Nobody will wear plaid socks with (**her,** their) striped skirt.
5. The girls may have (her, **their**) showers first.
6. The locker storing the sweaty practice uniforms is famous for (**its,** their) odor.
7. Each of the players needs to bring (**his,** their) football helmet.
8. If everybody on the team would do (**his,** their) homework ahead of the game, the teachers would complain less about athletics.
9. Anyone who wants to make (**himself**, themselves) eligible for football needs to get his doctor's exam in the spring.

21C Sentence Patterns—page 87.

Identify the sentence pattern: Subject-verb, ***S-V;*** *subject-verb-direct object,* ***S-V-DO;*** *Subject-verb-indirect object-direct object,* ***S-V-IO-DO;*** *Compound subject-verb,* ***S-S-V,*** *Compound sentence with the first clause subject-verb and the second, subject-verb-direct object,* ***Cmpd—S-V; S-V-DO,*** *and so forth.*

1. **S-V** The student studied.
2. **S-V-DO** The ambitious student studied his grammar lesson.
3. **S-S-V-DO-DO** The student and the instructor ate ice cream and fudge sauce.
4. **S-S-V** Either the ice cream or the grammar was tainted.
5. **S-V-V** The student got sick and fainted.
6. **S-V-DO** From then on, no one ever studied grammar again.
7. **Cmpd—S-V-DO; S-V-IO-DO** The student failed the test, but the instructor gave him credit anyway.
8. **Cmpd—S-V; S-V-DO** All the students cheered, and all the instructors lost their jobs.

Adverbs answer the questions **when**, **where**, **how**, **how often**.

21D Proofreading—page 88.

Rewrite the instructions to make each one parallel with the others.

Answers will vary. Each instruction should be either in the form of a command or in the second person form "you."

1. Get approximately six identical envelopes and six plain pieces of white paper.
2. Fold the paper over twice.
3. Inside one piece of paper, write a word.
4. Then refold the paper and insert it in the envelope and seal it.
5. Mark this envelope lightly so you can tell which it is.
6. Next, ask five of your classmates to write a word on one of the squares of paper and refold it and seal it in an envelope.
7. Collect the envelopes and tell your classmates that you have psychic abilities. They must concentrate on the word they wrote, and you will read their thoughts. No talking is allowed during the psychic event because talking upsets the energy.
8. Take the first envelope and after concentrating with great drama, announce the word you wrote originally.
9. Open the envelope and look at the word.
10. Then place it back in the envelope without showing the class.
11. Take the next envelope and announce the word you read from the previous envelope.
12. Continue in this manner, making sure you open your own envelope last.
13. Finally, unfold each word one at a time and show the class how powerful a psychic you are.

22A Subject Complements—page 89.

Circle any linking verbs and draw one line under a predicate nominative and two lines under a predicate adjective. Cross out action verbs and their direct objects.

1. Bethany (looked) embarrassed after the compliment.
2. After the game, the coach (seemed) relieved.
3. My dog (is) an Australian Shepherd.
4. My dog ~~bites~~ ~~men~~ in uniform.
5. During the concert, I (became) enthralled by the music.
6. My parents ~~prefer~~ folk ~~music~~ to heavy metal.
7. The best shortstop on my team (is) I.
8. She (feels) incredibly sad about the incident.

List five linking verbs.

Answers will vary.

Answer Key, Lessons 21-30, continued

22B Subject and Object Pronouns—page 90.

In the following sentences, circle the pronoun(s). In the space, write S if it is a subject pronoun used as a predicate nominative; write D.O. or I.O. if it is an object pronoun used as a direct object or indirect object; write O.P. if it is an object pronoun used as an object of a preposition.

1 **D.O.** The ball hit (him) in the face.
2. **O.P.** The waves washed over (me).
3. **S** The craziest one in the class is (I).
4. **D.O.'s** The teacher sent (him) and (me) to the office.
5. **S's** (It) is (I) (who) did the evil deed.
6. **S** The next lucky person will be (she).
7. **D.O.'s** The dragon will eat (you) and (him) in one gulp.
8. **I.O.** My mother brought me (my) lunch. **(My is called either a possessive pronou possessive adjective)**

22C Diagramming Subject Complements—page 91.

Diagram the following sentences.

1. The error was incredibly foolish.

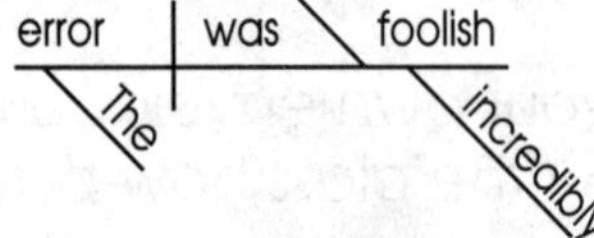

2. My heartthrob looks gorgeous in his new outfit.

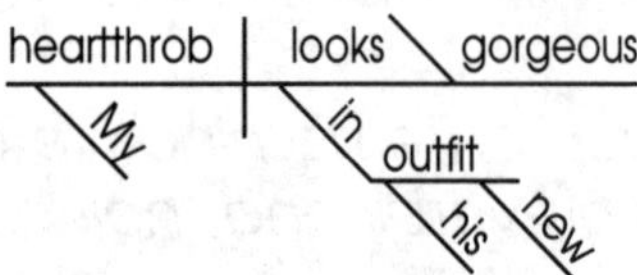

3. This painting is the best example of expressionism in the museum.

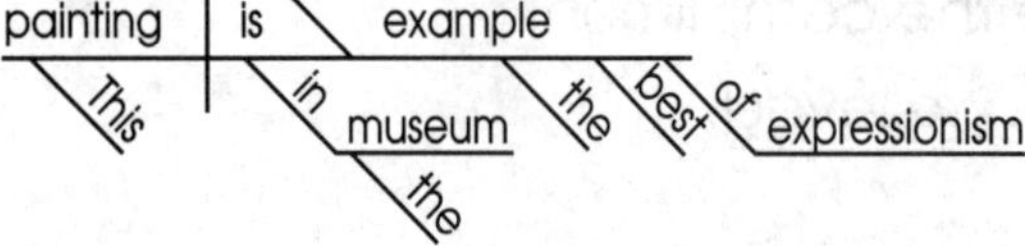

22D Try to Be Politically Correct—page 92.

Rewrite the following to get rid of the awkward expression.
Answers will vary.

23A Linking Verbs and Action Verbs—page 93.

Underline the verb. Write ***A*** *on the line if it is an action verb or* ***L*** *if it is a linking verb.*

1. **L** The floor became sticky.
2. **L** The food tastes repulsive.
3. **A** The monster stared at me with glassy eyes.
4. **L** My sister looks sick.

5. __L__ The locker room <u>smelled</u> bad.
6. __L__ My voice <u>sounded</u> hoarse after all the yelling.
7. __A__ Jack <u>looks</u> at the baseball cards with interest.
8. __A__ The students <u>smelled</u> a wonderful aroma in the kitchen.

23B Subject and Object Pronouns—page 94.

Underline the correct pronoun in the following sentences.

1. The sweetest one is (<u>she</u>, her).
2. The lion crept softly behind (he, <u>him</u>).
3. We found (she, <u>her</u>) behind the sofa.
4. The most skillful in the class was (<u>she</u>, her).
5. The only possible suspect seemed to be (<u>I</u>, me).
6. The first to attack the pizza will be (<u>he</u>, him).
7. With (I, <u>me</u>) in charge, everything will get done.
8. The ones who adore peanut butter are (<u>they</u>, them).
9. Go with (we, <u>us</u>) to the movies tonight!
10. It is (I, me) in that picture.

23C Linking Verbs and Action Verbs—page 95.

Diagram the following, paying special attention to whether the verb is a linking verb or an action verb.

1. Bulldogs with those smashed noses smell badly.

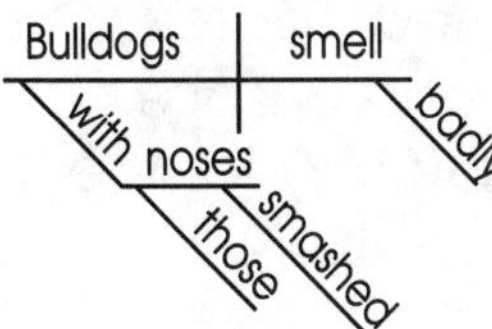

2. After a day in the swamp, my dog smells bad.

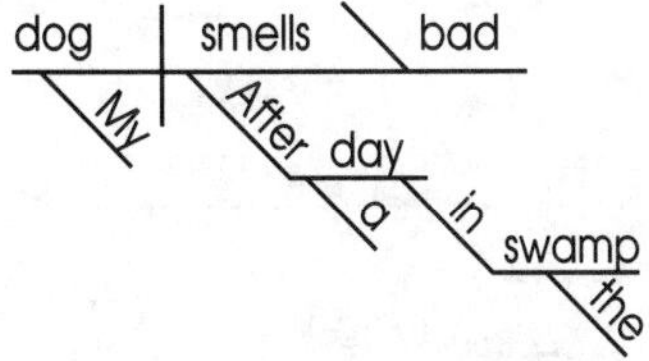

3. My dog hears the can opener and comes quickly to the door.

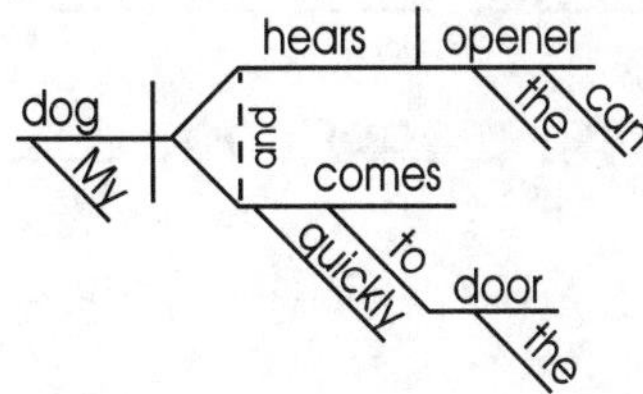

4. My dog may be full, but he still wants more doggy chow.

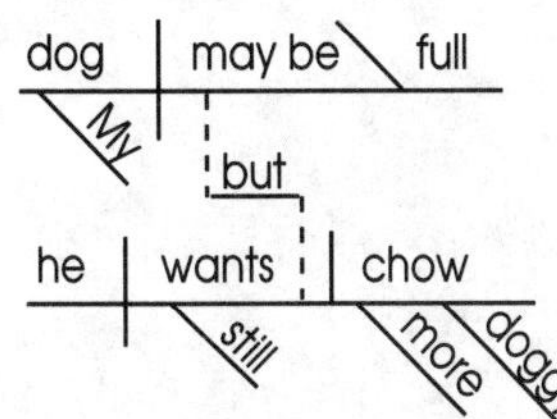

23D Proofreading—page 96.

Correct the mistakes in the sentences below. ***There are eight mistakes.***

If someone offered to sell you the Brooklyn Bridge, would you write **him** a check? Amazingly, the Eiffel Tower, the famous Paris landmark, was sold not once but twice. Soon after World War I, the **Eiffel** Tower was badly in need of **repair** and paint. A con artist saw a news story about the huge cost of upkeep for the tower. Posing as a city official, he invited three businessmen to a secret meeting. He told them that the city had decided to sell the tower for scrap, and that **they** would be allowed to bid for the job. The con artist collected the deposit of a sucker who seemed **really** insecure. The crook then left to live the high life in Switzerland, hoping to avoid arrest. The sucker was so embarrassed about being swindled that **he** never reported the fraud. Two years later, the con man returned to Paris and **sold** the tower again. He then escaped to the U.S. where he was arrested **quickly** for another fraud. He died in Alcatraz. On his death certificate, his profession was listed as "salesman."

24A Predicate Adjectives—page 97.

Choose the correct form.

1. He was hitting the ball (good, **well**).
2. The receiver became (**angry**, angrily) after the late hit.
3. He ran very (quick, **quickly**).
4. My drives were fine, but I putted (bad, **badly**).
5. His attitude seemed (**good**, well), but inside he felt (**sad**, sadly).
6. He ran the bases (good, **well**) until the incident with the umpire.
7. Without any hesitation, the goalie sprinted (quick, **quickly**) for the ball.
8. Ruben runs (good, **well**), but he hits (bad, **badly**).

24B Write the Rules—page 98.

Fill in the blanks.

1. The object form of the pronoun **we** is __**us**__.
2. A pronoun following a linking verb should be in the __**subject**__ form.
3. The subject form of the pronoun **me** is __**I**__.
4. A subject complement follows a __**linking**__ verb.
5. An adjective modifies a __**noun**__ or a __**pronoun**__.
6. An adverb modifies a __**verb**__, an __**adverb**__, or an __**adjective**__.
7. A compound sentence must be punctuated with a __**comma**__ or a __**semicolon**__.
8. If a compound subject is connected with **either, or,** then the verb agrees with the subject __**nearest**__ to the verb.
9. The adverbial form of **good** is __**well**__.

24C Blueprints—page 99.

Reconstruct the sentence from the diagram.

1. My friend looked ill before class, but she was better after the math test.
2. The naughty dog chewed the pillows and the new drapes with gusto.
3. Unfortunately, the professor was an ancient geezer with a constant scowl, and a long, hooked nose.

24D Proofreading—page 100.

Correct the mistakes in the sentences below. ***There are nine mistakes.***

Four brothers**,** I, *Me*, *We*, and *Us*, were camped in front of the refrigerator examining the last remaining **piece** of **an** apple pie.

"Which of us deserves that piece?" mulled *Us*.

"It's **I**!" whined *Me*.

"In your dreams!" answered I **really quickly**. "*We* will split it with me."

"By far the most deserving member of this family is **I**," snarled *We*. "However, I have no plans to share it with ***I*** or anyone else for that matter."

"I was sure you would give me, your adoring younger brother, some of the piece," I simpered, trying to curry the favor of his older sibling.

"That pie smells **bad** and looks worse," suggested *Us*, hoping that the others would lose interest and go away.

While the others argued, *Me* slipped silently behind them, snatched the prize and wolfed it down. "That's **I**, a man of action,**"** gloated *Me* with a mouth full of pie.

25A Phrases and Clauses—page 101.

Cross out any prepositional phrases. Underline once any independent clauses and underline twice any dependent clauses. Circle the comma following an introductory dependent clause.

1. Ripe plums splattered ~~from the tree~~ because no one had picked them.
2. The field smelled ~~like fermented fruit~~, and the cows acted drunk.
3. As the breeze blew brightly, the bees buzzed crazily in circles.
4. ~~Under the spreading oak tree~~, the young man napped.
5. Because he was dreaming happy dreams, he smiled and snored.
6. Unfortunately, he was resting ~~on an anthill~~ that was full ~~of army ants~~.
7. Although the dreamer didn't know it, the ants were upset.
8. They plotted their revenge while they imagined fresh meat for dinner.

25B This an' That and Antecedents—page 102

Rewrite the following sentences clarifying the antecedents to the pronouns.
Answers will vary.

1. My grades are good lately. This **improvement** shows I have become very responsible.

2. Bud did not stick up for his friend. **He** was very disloyal.
3. Koko is a talking gorilla. **Talking makes her** seem very human.
4. If criminals are set free, honest people **will be forced** to live in fear.
5. I worry a lot about finishing tasks on time, but **I don't worry about** homework.
6. Your dog is obese. **Probably,** you are overfeeding him.

25C More Sentence Patterns—page 103.

Identify the sentences as simple, compound, complex, or compound-complex. Underline the dependent clauses, and cross out prepositional phrases.

1. **Complex**________ Because the Chargers have no quarterback, they haven't a chance this year.
2. **Simple**________ Quarterbacks are important ~~to the team~~ ~~in many ways~~.
3. **Compound**________ They direct the plays, and they start off the offense.
4. **Complex**________ The special teams often are responsible ~~for the extra points~~ that mean the difference ~~between winning and losing~~.
5. **Simple**________ ~~During halftime~~, the coach gives the team a peptalk and encourages his players.
6. **Cmpd-Cplx**________ After the players come into the locker room, they shower, and they get dressed.

25D Proofreading—page 104.

Correct the mistakes in the sentences below. ***There are eight mistakes.***

Tidal waves, or tsunamis, make great subjects for horror movies. In reality, they don't occur frequently**,** but they can cause a great deal of damage along low-lying coastlines. Landslides, earthquakes, or **volcanic eruptions** deep beneath the surface of the sea cause tsunamis. The underwater disturbance causes waves to spread out **quickly** in all directions. Although the waves can be up to several hundred miles long, they may be only three feet high. **Their lack of heigth** makes them very difficult to detect. A nearby ship might not notice a tsunami that is only three feet high. When the tsunami reaches shallow water near the **coast**, the height of the wave is amplified. The shape of the sea floor near the coastline determines **its** size. Some tsunamis reach 100 feet tall. Often the front of the wave is vertical, and **it** rushes toward the shore at 30 feet per second. **A wave like that** would be a terrifying sight to see!

26A Subordinate Conjunctions—page 105.

Circle the subordinate conjunction and underline the dependent clause. Cross out the prepositional phrases. Insert commas after introductory dependent clauses.

1. (Until) school starts**,** you can sleep ~~until ten~~.
2. You had better get your work done (before) it is due.
3. You had better get your work done ~~before the day~~ ~~of reckoning~~.
4. (Since) your teacher is heartless**,** you have no chance (unless) you work hard.

5. (Because) you are a hard worker, your friends admire you.
6. (If) you want free time ~~after school~~, you should finish quickly.
7. (Whenever) my teacher is ~~in a foul mood~~, he gives tons ~~of homework~~.

Fill in the blanks.
A clause is a group of words with a __subject__ and a __predicate__.

26B Like and As—page 106.

Choose the correct word or words.

1. His father looked (**like**, as) a clown.
2. His father looked (like, **as if**) he were a clown.
3. Do (like, **as**) I say, not (like, **as**) I do.
4. The thunder crashed (like, as, **as if**) the sky were exploding.
5. The son acts (like, **as**) his father does.
6. Nobody cooks as well as (him, **he does**).
7. Nobody adores hot fudge sundaes like (me, **I do**).
8. Jeff likes you as much as (me, **I do**).

Fill in the blanks.
A clause must have a __subject__ and a __predicate__.

26C Diagramming Adverb Clauses—page 107.

Diagram the following sentences.

1. I love my slippers because they tickle my toes.

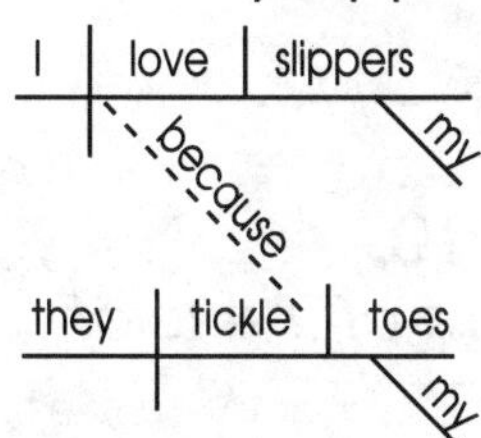

2. When you get a sunburn, you increase your risk of skin cancer.

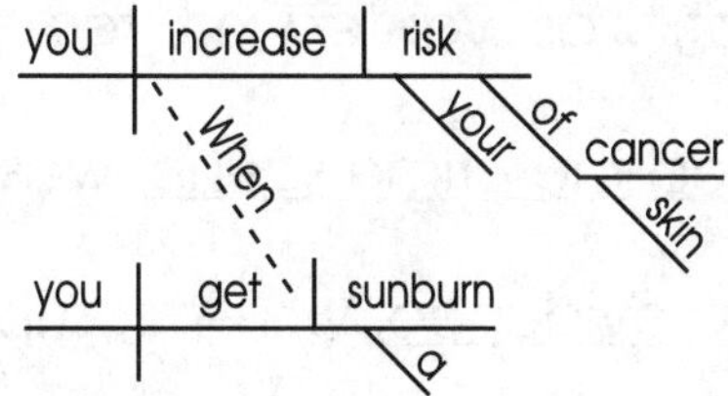

26D Proofreading—page 108.

Correct the mistakes in the sentences below. ***There are nine mistakes.***

The urban myth tells us that 90% of our brain is unused. Of course, that **story** is not true, but most of us do have some extra spots available for a few random facts. I thought you might appreciate **as** I did these items of animal lore gleaned off the Internet. The first amazing fact is that snails can sleep for three years without eating. Around my house, they don't live that long because the garden **snail's** chief archenemy is **I**. The next fascinating fact is that koala **bears'** fingerprints are virtually indistinguishable from human prints, so they could be confused at a crime scene. **Confusion** seems quite likely, considering all the rabid koalas that are running around our inner cities in gangs like Al Capone's buddies. Finally, did you know that **an** ostrich's eyeball is bigger than **its** brain? It is also bigger **than** many people's brains if their actions are any indication of brain size. Lest you complain about the brain size of the author of this piece, I'd better draw it to a hasty conclusion.

27A Relative Pronouns—page 109.

Underline the adjective clause once. Circle the relative pronoun, and underline its antecedent twice.

1. A Mustang is the most exciting car (that) is on the road today.
2. Joel is the only student to (whom) the teacher gave an "A."
3. Ginger was embarrassed by a remark (that) was unkind.
4. The boy, (whose) jacket was lost, was very cold that night.
5. The citizens, over (whom) the helicopters fly, are irate.
6. After the kids (who) were at the football game came home, the family ate.
7. The dust puppies, (which) were under the bed, were as big as Great Danes.
8. The lake in (which) the Loch Ness monster supposedly lives is very deep.

Fill in the blanks.

A clause has both a **subject** and a **predicate**.

27B Who and Whom in Adjective Clauses—page 110.

Underline the adjective clause and choose the correct form of the relative pronoun.

1. The detective (**who**, whom) found the prints was careless with the evidence.
2. The criminal, (who, **whom**) the detective shot, was wanted in three states.
3. The partner, with (who, **whom**) he investigated the crime scene, was crooked.
4. The policeman, to (who, **whom**) he gave the evidence, was incompetent.
5. I believe that the witness (**who**, whom) testified about the gun was lying.
6. He arrested a thief (who, **whom**) he caught red-handed.

27C Diagramming Adjective Clauses—page 111.

Diagram the following sentences.

1. The pitcher who got the two-year contract broke his arm.

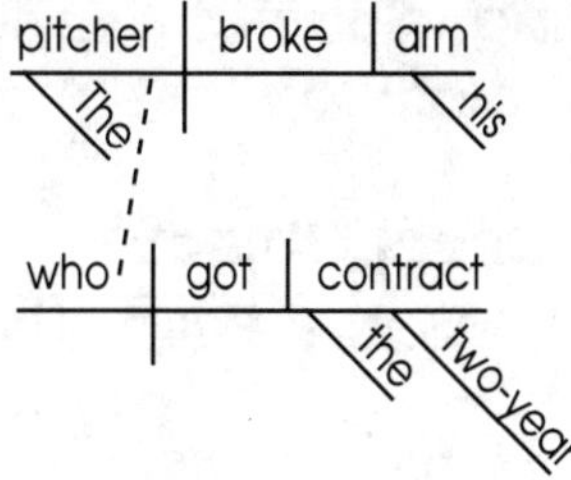

2. My friend, to whom you sent the card, feels better.

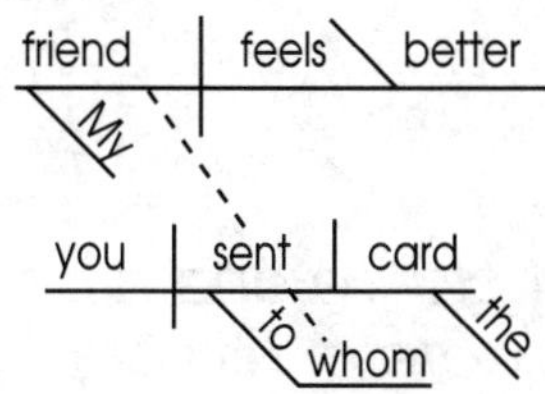

3. I sent a letter that described my situation to the man who overcharged me.

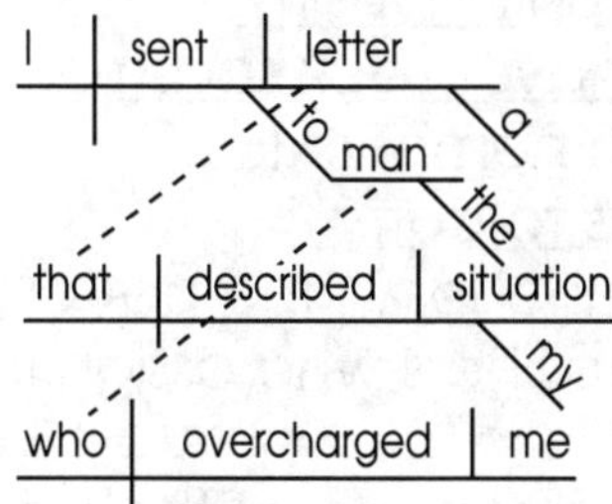

27D Proofreading—page 112.

Correct the mistakes in the sentences below. ***There are seven mistakes.***

Teachers are sometimes more astute **than** students expect. An incident that occurred several years ago at Duke University illustrates **how astute one professor was**. The night before finals, two students decided to go to a party at another college some distance away. **As** college students sometimes do, this fun-loving pair spent the night at the party instead of making the long drive back to their dorm. Unfortunately, the next morning they realized that they had missed **their** exam. To avoid failing, they decided to concoct **an** excuse about how they were returning to campus when they got a flat tire. The professor to **whom** they told their sad tale seemed **really** sympathetic and gave them permission to take the exam the next day. Well rested and right on time, the two students showed up the next day. The professor gave each of them a copy of the exam and sent them into separate rooms to take it. The exam was short—just two questions. The second question was the hard one: "Which tire?"

Answer Key, Lessons 21-30, continued

28A Noun Clauses—page 113.

Underline the noun clause and label the job it does in the sentence: subject, direct object, object of a preposition, and so forth.

1. **What I saw today on Mulberry Street** was astonishing. **Subject**
2. I will give my leftovers to **whoever wants them**. **Obj. of Prep.**
3. **Who you are** makes no difference to me. **Subject**
4. My classmates agree **that Mrs. Fink is obnoxious**. **Direct Object**
5. Young readers think **that the Harry Potter books are the best new series**. **Dir. Obj.**

Underline the noun clause and choose the correct pronoun.

1. I will destroy (**whoever**, whomever) gets in my way.
2. (Whoever, **Whomever**) the teacher likes will get an "A."
3. The prize will go to (who, **whom**) you choose.

28B Sentence Fragments—page 114.

*If the following is a sentence, underline the independent clause and label it sentence (**S**). If the following is missing a subject or predicate or is a dependent clause, label it fragment (**F**).*

1. __**F**__ The individual who owns this backpack.
2. __**S**__ The owner of the backpack who has a runny nose needs a tissue.
3. __**S**__ Students carry backpacks with too much junk in them.
4. __**S**__ Whoever carries a loaded backpack will have back spasms.
5. __**F**__ Whenever he overloads his backpack with homework.
6. __**S**__ This load of books will destroy whoever has to carry it.
7. __**F**__ Old candy bar wrappers and half-eaten lunches in the bottom.
8. __**F**__ Without any thought of student health, teachers who assign loads of homework.
9. __**S**__ Because the students need to develop better posture, they should not carry backpacks over one shoulder.
10. __**S**__ Homework is the root of all evil, and teachers should not assign it.

28C Diagramming Noun Clauses—page 115.

1. We thought that the test was difficult.

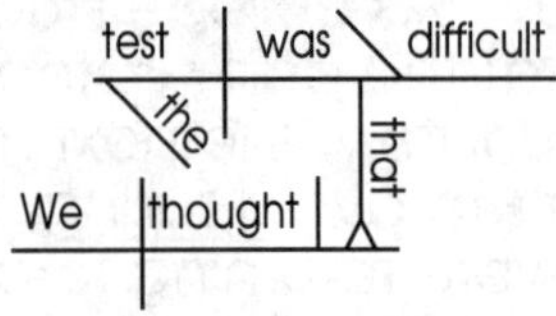

2. What computers can do is unbelievable.

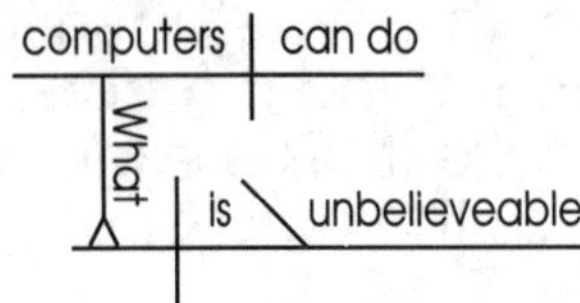

3.We will give passes to whomever the coach chooses.

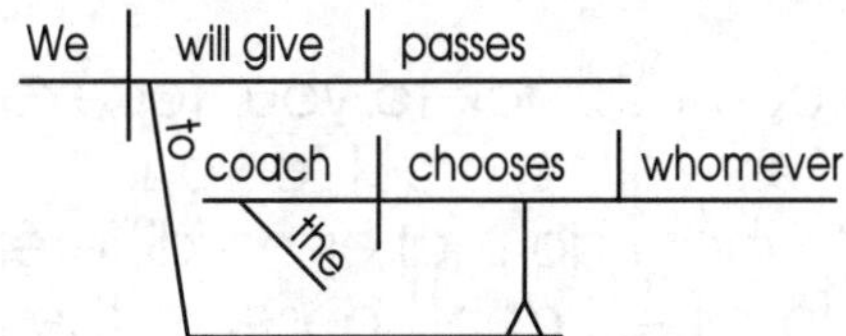

28D Proofreading—page 116.

Correct the mistakes in the sentences below. ***There are eight mistakes.***

"Children should be seen but not heard" is an old saying propounded by an earlier generation. In **Victorian England**, mothers used opium to make their offspring behave **as** mannerly children should. Opium solutions like "Mother's Helper," "Soothing Syrup," and "Infant's Quietness" were sold in large jugs. Children drank it **greedily because** it was often mixed with sweet syrup. Since opium is not readily water soluble, it tended to become concentrated in the bottom of the jug. Thus the child who got the last dose became totally intoxicated. Women of the upper classes as well as the poor sought the relief from their fractious offspring by sedating them. If a child was inconvenient to her social life **or if** she couldn't afford to come home from her sweatshop job to nurse her baby**,** Mom could quiet him with a dollop of syrup. Imagine the long-term effects of drug dependency on a whole generation of children who were "seen but not heard.**"**

29A Conjunctive Adverbs—page 117.

Label the clauses as independent or dependent and punctuate properly. Underline any conjunctive adverbs once and any subordinate conjunctions twice.

1. It is raining (**Ind.**)**.** However I am going to the beach anyway (**Ind.**).
2. The tide is low (**Ind.**)**.** Therefore the waves will be puny (**Ind.**).
3. When I surf (**Dep.**), I get good exercise (**Ind.**).
4. Paddling out through the breakers is tough work (**Ind.**). Still lying on the board waiting for a wave is restful (**Ind.**).
5. Although surfing can be dangerous (**Dep.**), it is worth the risk (**Ind.**).
6. I go to the beach every day (**Ind.**) unless it is stormy (**Dep.**).
7. After a long day at work, a dip in the ocean is refreshing (**Ind.**) because it clears my mind (**Dep.**).
8. I get a rush (**Ind.**) when I see a huge wave bearing down on me and my adrenaline starts to pump (**Dep.**).

29B Run-on Sentences—page 118.

Label the run-on sentences ***r-o*** *and the correct sentences* ***ok.***

1. **r-o** I washed my car yesterday hence it will rain today.
2. **r-o** I think, therefore I am.

Answer Key, Lessons 21-30, continued

3. **ok** Although I don't believe in destiny, I am convinced that we were meant to be together.
4. **r-o** Karma means that what you do comes back to you, for example, if you are cruel to others, others will be cruel to you.
5. **r-o** I am a fatalist, thus I believe that what I do makes no difference.
6. **ok** Unless I was an evil person in my last life, I don't deserve the predicament I am in now.
7. **ok** The pirate's parrot is pecking painfully at my proboscis.
8. **r-o** My nose hurts , moreover I have feathers in my eyes.

29C Clauses and More Clauses—page 119.

Diagram the following sentences. Choose the correct pronoun based on its position in the diagram.

1. Give the raise to (**whoever**, whomever) deserves it.

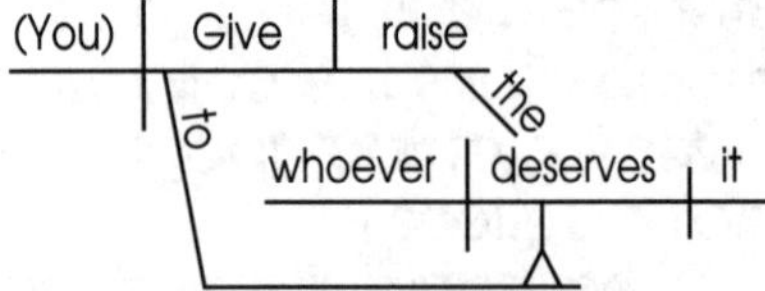

2. The parent (who, **whom**) I detest will chaperone the dance.

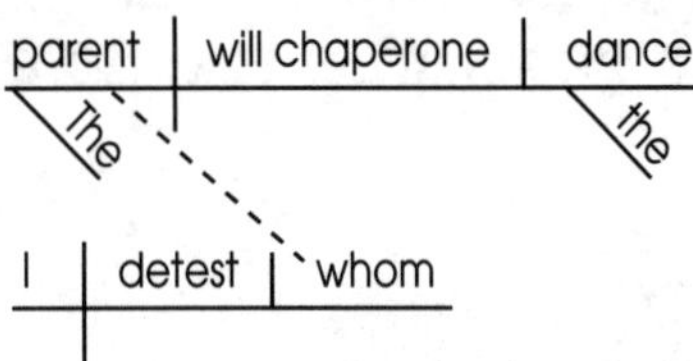

3. Although the treasurer was (**he**, him), George still believed that the money was handled carelessly.

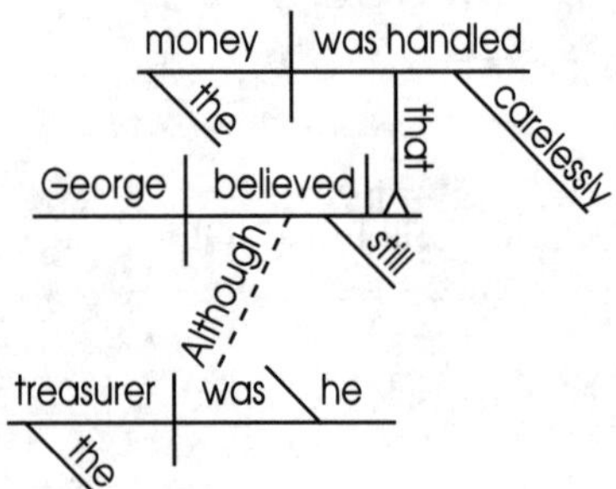

29D Correcting Run-on Sentences—page 120.

Correct each of the following run-ons. Use each method at least once.

Answers will vary.

1. I came**;** I saw**;** I conquered.
2. My heart pounded, **but** still I waited patiently.
3. I fear the future, **because** I don't know how I will support myself.
4. After I graduate from high school, I will start a software company**. Hence** I will become an instant millionaire.
5. I am very good at dealing with financial matters except balancing my checkbook**. Somehow** my totals never seem to add up.

6. Unlike many high school students, I am very responsible financially. **Usually,** I spend within my budget.
7. I wouldn't like to have to pay for all my own expenses, however, **because** living on my salary wouldn't be much fun.

30A Changing Sentence Patterns—page 121.

Rewrite the following sentences changing the sentence patterns to the one indicated.

Answers will vary.

1. After the student finished his homework, he went to the mall.
2. The unfortunate player who made the error sulked, but he was sorry afterward.
3. My parents who still like the Beatles and the Rolling Stones are behind the times.
4. Since I am absolutely addicted to my new computer game. I play it day and night.

30B To Comma Or Not To Comma—page 122.

Correct the punctuation in the following sentences.

1. After the ball game**,** we'll stop for burgers and fries.
2. We'll pick up some pizza after the ball game.
3. Because we stuff ourselves with junk food at the game**,** we rarely are hungry when we get home.
4. Going to the game and stuffing myself with junk food are my favorite activities.
5. When we get home**,** we often have work to do**,** but we don't have the energy to do it.
6. We lie down**;** we watch television and nap.
7. Whatever is most fattening is always most delicious.
8. If you consider all the pain involved in losing weight**,** it probably is better to eat vegetables**,** fruits**,** and whole grain products instead of cotton candy**,** hot dogs**,** and ice cream**,** but it certainly isn't as much fun.

Answer Key, Lessons 21-30, continued

30C The Mother of All Sentences—page 123.

Diagram this monster. ***Hint:*** *Find the independent clause first, and add in the dependent clauses afterwards.*

1. Before the hero who felt no fear and the villain who seethed with unbridled rage could cross their swords, the townspeople rushed to the scene and destroyed whatever was left of the peace in the castle.

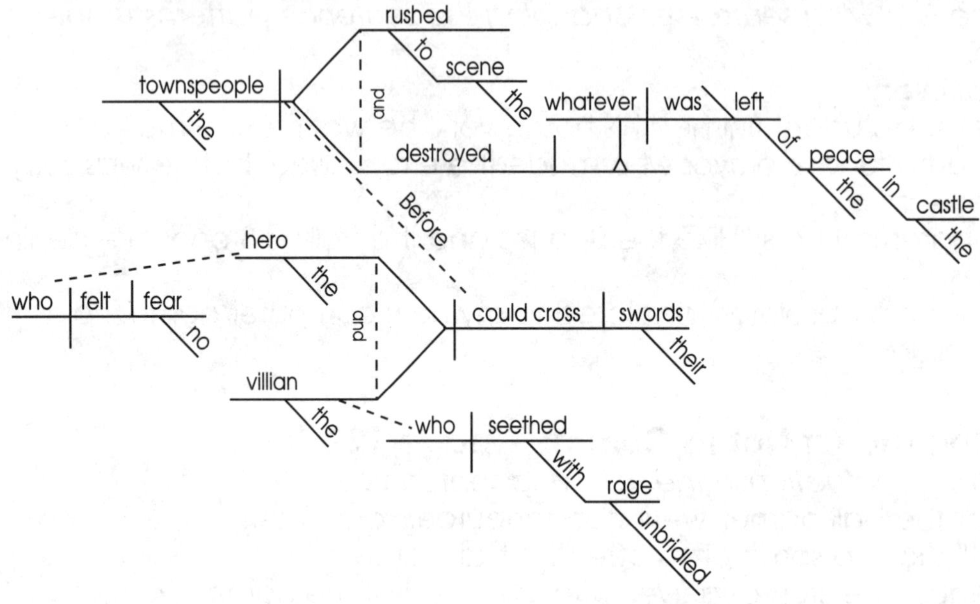

30D Proofreading—page 124.

Correct the mistakes in the sentences below. ***There are six mistakes.***

Pranks that require great engineering skill but cause no damage are legendary at Massachusetts Institute of Technology (MIT). One of the most famous occurred during a Harvard-Yale football game in 1982. Since MIT is located right down the street from Harvard**,** **the** rivalry between the two schools is fierce**.** **Thus** Harvard's big game was the perfect site for an MIT caper. The night before the big game, students smuggled a weather balloon into the stadium and buried it on the 46-yard line. A device to inflate the balloon was attached**,** and wires were run out to an undergraduate **whom** the students had chosen to trigger the spectacle. In the middle of the game**,** a black weather balloon with "MIT" emblazoned on it emerged in a puff of smoke, **inflated** to full size, and floated away. The actual weather balloon now resides in a museum dedicated entirely to MIT's technological pranks.

REVIEW Lessons 21-30—page 125.

Choose the correct pronoun.

1. All of the contestants failed to answer (his, **their**) first question correctly.
2. Nobody trying on the new jackets liked the color of (**his**, their) necktie.
3. The photo of Pia and (I, **me**) is not very flattering.
4. Anyone who tries out for football must bring (**his**, their) permission slip.
5. The bottom man on the totem pole seems to be (**I**, me).
6. Josh is the friend (who, **whom**) I sent the letter to.
7. (Whoever, **Whomever**) the coach most respects is his first choice.

Identify each of the following as a run-on (r-o), a fragment (frag) or a correct sentence (C).

1. __**C**__ The roller coaster dipped and turned ceaselessly, but most of the white-knuckled riders refused to open their eyes.
2. __**r-o**__ The parents down below worried, they hoped the ride would end soon.
3. __**r-o**__ Some happy screeches filled the air, therefore some of the children were enjoying the ride.
4. __**frag**__ Because the track with its excellent safety record was known throughout the world.
5. __**r-o**__ Most carnival rides have the occasional accident for example the brakes on a car might not work.

Rewrite the sentences changing the pattern to the one indicated.
Answers will vary.

1. Many viewers watch the Oscars on television, and the stars attending dress in their most spectacular outfits. (Complex)
   Since many viewers watch the Oscars on television, the attending stars dress in their most spectacular outfits.
2. There are always winners and losers. Some actors are bound to be unhappy. Others, of course, will be ecstatic. (Compound-complex)
   There are always winners and losers, and while some actors are bound to be unhappy, others, of course, will be ecstatic.
3. The actress is half naked. She is wearing a dress slit all the way up to her waist. (Complex with adjective clause)
   The actress who is wearing a dress slit all the way up to her waist is half naked.

Correct the eight errors.

In the theater, popcorn covers the floor**;** bubblegum is stuck to the seats**,** and **pop is spilled on the floor**. While the cleaning crew quickly grabs brooms and sponges**,** the line at the door stretches into the parking lot. Patrons hate to have their feet stick to the floor **as if** they are encased in cement**.** **However** the employees rarely have enough time to clean up after the pigs that watched the previous show. People are often slobs in movie theaters**.** **Spilling on purpose** seems a bit unfair to the cleaning crew. Most employees despise **whomever** they catch spilling and littering in their theater.

Answer Key, Lessons 31-40, continued

Diagram the following:

The long white limousine stopped at the curb while the crowd cheered wildly.

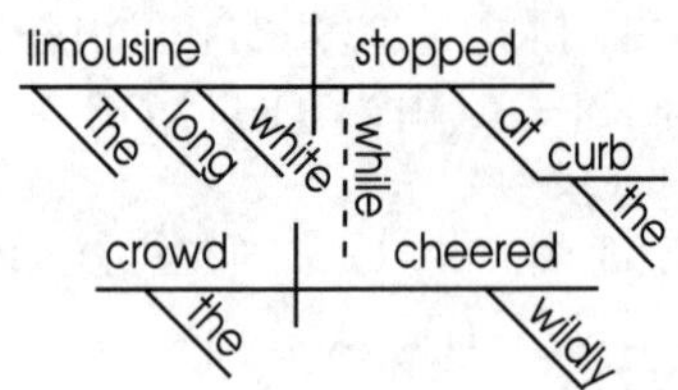

SKILL CHECK Lessons 21-30—page 127.

Choose the correct pronoun.

1. My parents complain that the laziest person in the family is (**I**, me).
2. I want to go with (**whoever**, whomever) is brave enough to climb it.
3. Every cadet will take (**his**, their) turn at peeling potatoes.
4. The crook (who, **whom**) the police caught will get ten years to life.
5. Anyone going to prom should get (**her**, their) dress early.
6. The dope who dented the car seems to be (**I**, me).
7. The prize will be awarded to (**whoever**, whomever) deserves it.

Identify each of the following as a run-on (r-o), a fragment, (frag), or a correct sentence (C).

1. **r-o** Backpacking can be a great adventure however it can be dangerous if the planning isn't done carefully.
2. **C** Remember to bring a water purification system.
3. **C** Ziplock bags are great for keeping clothes dry in your pack during a thunderstorm or heavy dew.
4. **frag** Since wet clothes can be really uncomfortable on a cold morning.
5. **C** Moreover, dry socks are required for keeping your feet healthy.
6. **r-o** Freeze-dried food is convenient, it doesn't taste good though.

Rewrite the sentences, changing the pattern to the one indicated.

1. Hot dogs are not healthy fare. They are usually high in fats. (Complex)
   Hot dogs are not healthy fare because they are usually high in fats.
2. Some brands of ice cream are low in fats. They often have a good flavor but a gummy texture. (Compound-complex)
   Some brands of ice cream that are low in fats have a good flavor, but they have a gummy texture.
3. Vegetarian food should be available in the lunchroom. It should be provided for whoever wants it. (Complex with noun clause)
   Vegetarian food should be available in the lunchroom for whoever wants it.

Correct the seven errors.

For almost fifty years**,** game shows have been popular on television. In the fifties**,** gullible viewers enjoyed rooting for their favorite contestants each week. Shows awarded big money to whoever answered the most questions on *the $64,000 Question* and *Twenty-one***.** **However** the outcome of the contests **was** often rigged. The producers chose the most popular contestants and gave them the answers before the show. **Having the answers** allowed them to practice their acting skills on the air while they agonized over each answer. One contestant who was not given answers complained that the shows were rigged**.** **As** a result, Congress held hearings to expose the fraud. One contestant, **whom** the producers had chosen to fail, instead won the top prize in the category of prize fighting. She was Dr. Joyce Brothers who later became a famous television psychologist.

Diagram the following sentence.

One contestant who was given answers made a mistake unintentionally.

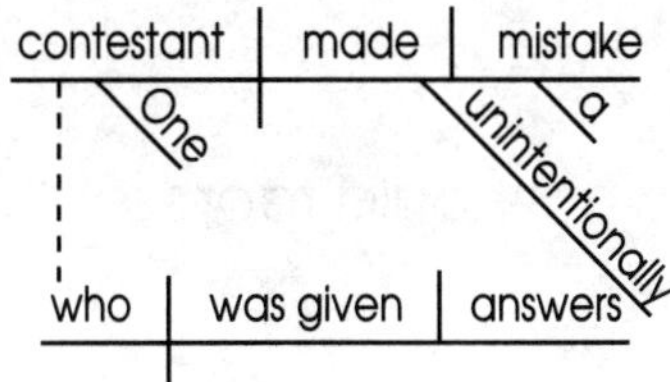

31A Appositives—page 129.

Underline the appositive word or phrase.

1. The cook, <u>my loyal friend</u>, slipped me an extra piece of apple pie.
2. The prize went to Jason, <u>the hardest worker in the class</u>.
3. Charles Dickens, <u>the author of</u> A Tale of Two Cities, was a prolific writer.

Choose the correct word.

1. The Johnson brothers, Jack and (**he**, him) are exceedingly tall.
2. The invitation was addressed to us, Joan and (I, **me**).
3. Two of us, Derek and (**I,** me) are known for our loud voices.

31B Avoid Clichés—page 130.

Underline the clichés and replace them with better word choices.

Answers will vary.

1. My aunt <u>went ballistic</u> when she discovered her car was dented.
2. You had better <u>shake a leg</u> if you expect to get to the game on time.
3. There are many creative ideas <u>out there</u>.
4. He is not the <u>brightest star in the sky</u>, but he works <u>like a dog</u>.
5. I <u>died laughing</u> when Hilary <u>went ape</u> over the student teacher.
6. We have a <u>sneaking suspicion</u> that Charles <u>has a thing</u> for Dana.
7. We can't <u>agree to disagree</u>; we'll fight <u>to the bitter end</u>.

Fill in the blanks.

A clause contains both a **<u>subject</u>** and a **<u>predicate</u>**.

Answer Key, Lessons 31-40, continued

31C Diagramming Appositives—page 131.

1. I felt sorry for my only sibling, Ben.

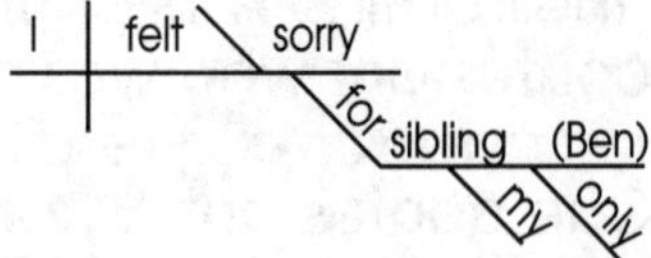

2. Because we won the championship, the local newspaper interviewed Josh, the captain of the team.

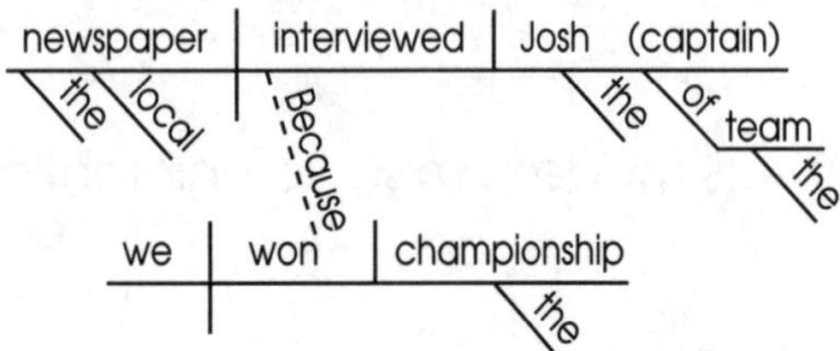

3. The student council president, Laurie, chose who would represent us.

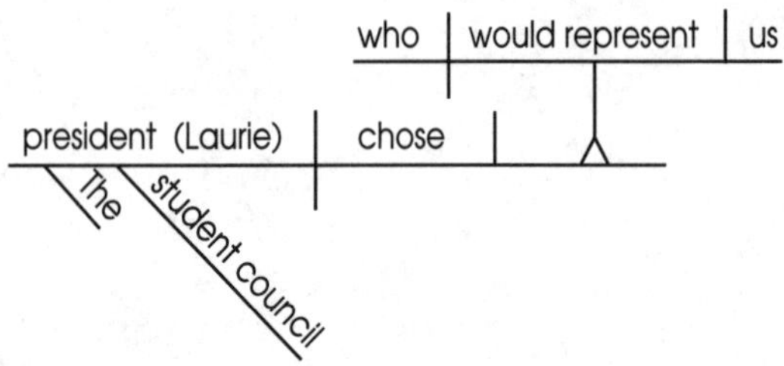

31D A Cliché Casserole—page 132.

Identify the clichés from their literal translation.

1. While you are visiting your grandparents, **pay attention to the 16th and 17th letters of the alphabet.**
   "mind your p's and q's"
2. Jen is such a hard worker that you can always count on her to **travel 5280 feet farther.**
   "go the extra mile"
3. Three-year-old Tim is so active that in a restaurant he behaves as if **his trousers are being invaded by insects of the order *Hymenoptera*.**
   "he has ants in his pants"
4. Surprisingly, during my first speech, I was **the temperature of a common, cylindrical garden vegetable.**
   "cool as a cucumber"
5. My father says he will buy me a new sports car when **Hades reaches a sustained temperature below 32 degrees.**
   "hell freezes over"
6. When you really want something, you need to **use adhesive on yourself and your firearms.**
   "stick to your guns"

32A Participles and Participial Phrases—page 133.

Underline the participles and participial phrases used as adjectives. Cross out participles used as verbs.

1. The dancer, gyrating wildly, was ~~discovered~~ to be insane.
2. My brother, taking a calculus class, has ~~forgotten~~ all his algebra.
3. The crazy dancer was ~~taking~~ a basic basket-weaving class instead of calculus.
4. Pushing aside all his inhibitions, my brother will dance while he is ~~memorizing~~ his geometric formulae.
5. Unfortunately, the Spanish class fulfilling my language requirement includes my brother and the dancer.
6. Usually, a class harboring insane dancers and incompetent brothers is a difficult learning environment.

Name the present participle form of the following verbs:
To be **being**, to go **going**, to find **finding**.

32B Dangling Participles—page 134.

Underline the participles in the following sentences and draw an arrow to the words modified.

1. Ignoring the danger of the searing flames, the fire was contained by the firemen.
2. Hiding in the back room, the babysitter searched for the toddler.
3. The motorist gunned his engine frazzled by the frustrating traffic jam.

Rewrite the following sentences adding words if necessary.
Answers may vary.

1. I found a plastic flower hidden among the fresh daffodils.
2. While fighting off an attack of hay fever, I mowed the grass.
3. Outsmarted by the gophers once again, I set more traps.
4. Running to catch the school bus, I dropped my books in a puddle.
5. I picked up my books lying in the gutter, scummy and dirty, and stuffed them into my backpack.

32C Diagramming Participles—135

1. Running through the fields, my sweetheart stumbled.

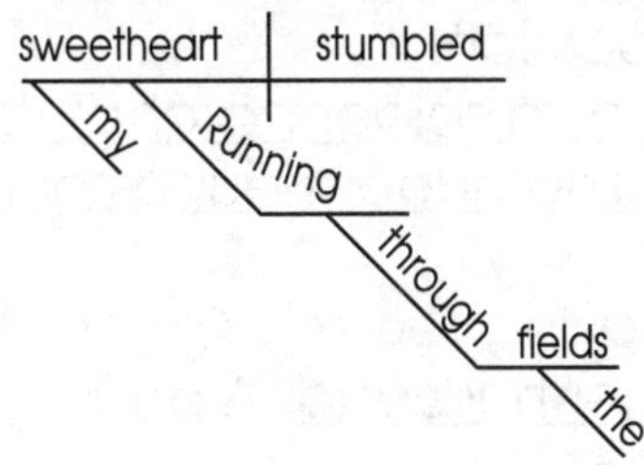

Answer Key, Lessons 31-40, continued

2. Her filmy dress covered with mud clung to her body.

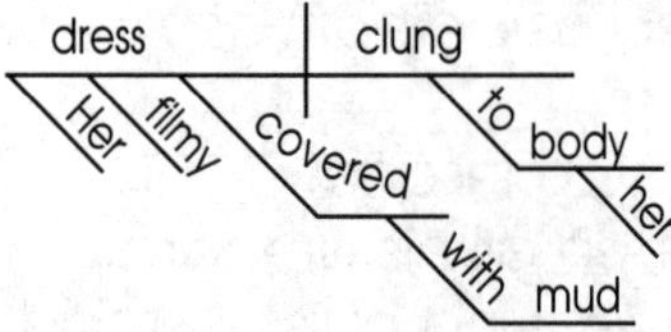

3. She smiled, embracing me fondly while she covered me with muck.

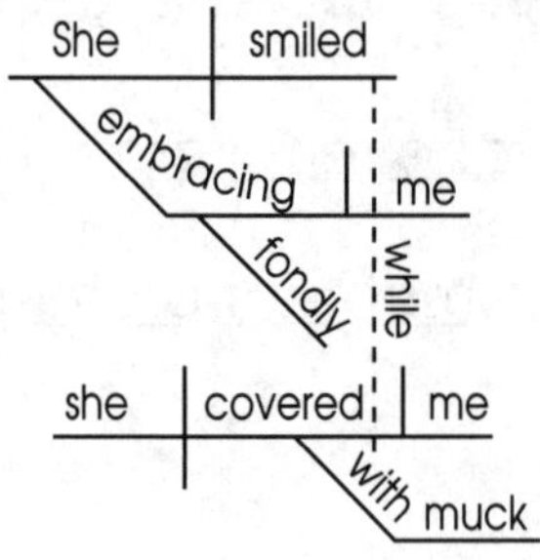

32D Proofreading—page 136.

Eliminate clichés and correct the mistakes in the sentences below. ***Find at least one cliché and more than six mistakes.***

The Soviets, encouraged by the pro-communist Afghan government, invaded Afghanistan in 1979. The United States, **believing that communism was evil, backed the opposition forces.** Obviously, **the US plans backfired.** In 1996, the US-backed Islamic Taliban ousted the pro-communist government. Since then, human rights and the rights of women, in particular, **have** deteriorated **considerably**. Before the Taliban came to power, women worked as schoolteachers and nurses. However, under the Taliban regime, women are not allowed in the workplace. In fact, a woman is not allowed to leave the home **except** when accompanied by **her** husband. Even then, a woman must be fully covered **~~from head to toe~~** so that no male other **than her** husband sees **her**. Thus, a woman is not allowed to go to school or visit a doctor. If a woman is sick, her husband goes to the doctor for her. Clearly, the US had **no idea of** the **effect** of its policy toward Afghanistan.

33A Gerunds and Gerund Phrases—page137.

Underline the gerunds and gerund phrases in the following sentences. Write in the blank the job the gerund does in the sentence (subject, direct object, etc).

1. **<u>subject</u>** <u>Taking photos of insects</u> is Alan's passion.
2. **<u>dir obj</u>** Alan hates <u>running out of film just as a spider catches its prey.</u>
3. **<u>obj of prep</u>** Termites are associated with <u>building huge mounds</u> and <u>making mud tunnels</u>.
4. **<u>subject</u>** <u>Chasing after the perfect shot</u> is taking too much of his time.
5. **<u>obj of prep</u>** After <u>seeing a black widow eat her husband</u>, Alan was ecstatic.

6. **subject** Watching cockroaches scurry into dark corners is fascinating to him.
7. **obj of prep** He gets the perfect shot by waiting patiently and by sitting absolutely still.

33B Gerund and Participle Problems,page 138.

Correct the following gerund and participle errors. If the sentence is correct, mark it OK. If it is a fragment, mark *Frag.*

Answers will vary.

1. Being that I am really tired. **Frag.**
2. **His** staying up late is what made him oversleep.
3. For my roommate, waking up is not difficult. **OK**
4. Seeing as I like to get my work done and to go to bed early. **Frag.**
5. **My sister, getting up at daybreak, usually feeds the dog.**
6. **Jim's** checking my papers has helped me get good grades.
7. Hearing the alarm, **I pulled the blankets** over my head.
8. **My** using a word processor has certainly helped my spelling.
9. Seeing the sunrise while picking up the newspaper at daybreak. **Frag.**

Fill in the blanks

A verb form used as an adjective is called a **participle**. A verb form used as a noun is called a **gerund**.

33C Diagramming Gerunds—page 139.

1. I enjoy munching popcorn at the movies.

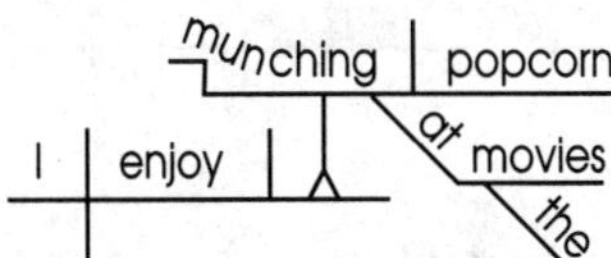

2. I am gaining weight from eating too much candy.

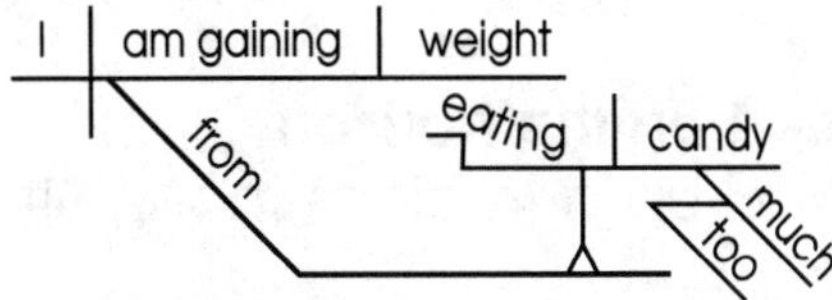

3. After drinking diet pop, my belching is heard statewide.

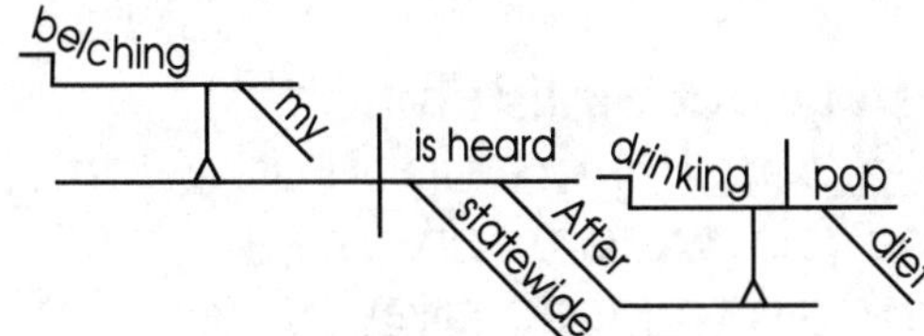

Answer Key, Lessons 31-40, continued

33D Ambiguity—page 140.

Answers will vary.

Correct the ambiguity in the following headlines:

1. WOMAN BEATS UP MAN WITH CLUB **(Who has the club?)**
2. PLAYERS FIGHT BEFORE FANS **(Does "before" mean "in front of" or "first"?)**
3. GERBILS IN TESTING FACILITY SMELL
(Do they stink or do their noses work well?)
4. REVOLTING STUDENTS DEMONSTRATE AGAINST DRESS CODE
(Are the students in revolt or are they disgusting?)

Describe the role of the ambiguity in the following story.

Answers will vary.

34A Infinitives and Infinitive Phrases—page141.

Underline the infinitive or infinitive phrase and write the part of speech it represents.

1. **noun** I love to eat potato chips.
2. **noun** To learn self-control when faced with a bowl of chips is difficult.
3. **adv.** I find it difficult to control myself when I see guacamole.
4. **adj.** The best chips to buy are triangular tortilla chips.
5. **noun** Onion dip tends to make people gorge themselves.
6. **adj.** I made the bean dip to go with the mini tacos.

Fill in the blanks.

An adjective modifies a **noun**. An adverb modifies an **adverb**, an **adjective**, or a **verb**.

34B Too Many Words!—page 142.

Rewrite the underlined portions of the following sentences using the construction indicated.

1. I was terrified while I was seeing the black funnel cloud on the horizon. (Infinitive)
I was terrified to see the black funnel cloud on the horizon.
2. The winds twisted and swirled. They picked up a truck as though it were a toy. (Participle)
The twisting, swirling winds picked up a truck as though it were a toy.
3. It doesn't accomplish much when you run in the other direction. (Gerund)
Running in the other direction doesn't accomplish much.
4. Soon, the winds that roared like wild beasts were upon us. (Participle)
Soon, the winds, roaring like wild beasts, were upon us.
5. It is a wise idea to build a storm cellar in tornado alley. (Gerund)
Building a storm cellar in tornado alley is a wise idea.

Eliminate wordiness in the following sentences.

It is not cowardly when you run away from something that can really hurt you. It is foolhardy to put yourself in danger if you don't need to.
Running away from something that can really hurt you is not cowardly. Putting yourself in danger needlessly is foolhardy.

34C Diagramming Infinitives—page 143.

1. To eat fried chicken with your fingers is acceptable nowadays.

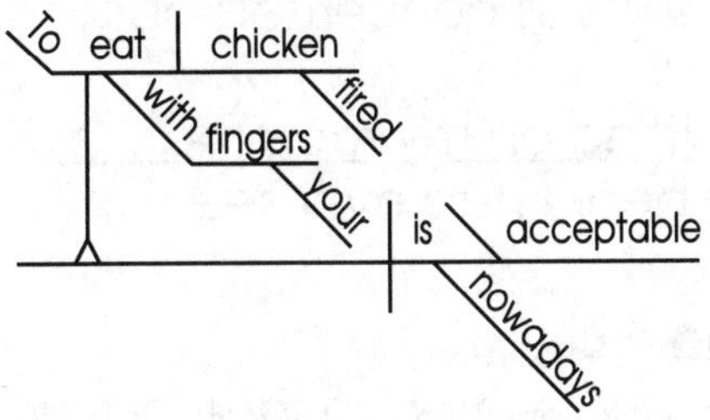

2. Since you want to be polite, you need to put your napkin under your chin.

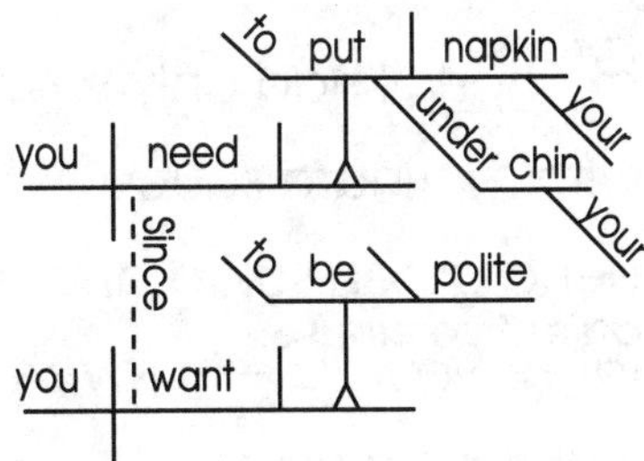

34D Proofreading—page 144.

Correct the mistakes in the sentences below. Eliminate any clichés and ambiguities, and change two adjective clauses into participles. Find at least one cliché, one ambiguity, and more than four other mistakes.

Firewalking gurus claim that your mind can control **matter**. For a not-so-small fee, they can teach you to harness the untapped power of your mind, **allowing** you to walk across a bed of hot coals without being burned. Actually, anyone can walk across a bed of hot coals without harnessing any mental powers. If the coals are **properly** prepared and the participants **having dry feet** walk at a rapid rate, they will emerge unburned**. This fact** has nothing to do with occult forces and everything to do with physics. The ash layer **covering** the hot coals does not conduct heat well**. Instead** it insulates the feet. If you put your hand briefly into a 400-degree oven, it won't burn. If, however, you touch the metal rack that is also 400 degrees, it will burn **you**. Like the ash layer, the air in the oven doesn't conduct heat, whereas the metal rack does. Science is full of amazing facts**,** and if you don't know those facts, charlatans will happily take your money.

Answer Key, Lessons 31-40, continued

35A Phrase and Clause Review—page 145.

Match the number of the phrase or clause with the underlined sentence part.

1. __8__ When I turned two, my father gave me a teddy bear.
2. __6__ He has one cracked glass eye and an ear that I ripped ages ago.
3. __1__ His fur is brown and matted with years of love.
4. __2__ His name is Grizzler, the brave and ferocious guardian.
5. __3__ Sitting on my bed, he listens patiently to all my problems.
6. __7__ My mother always said that Grizzler would go to college with me.
7. __5__ I wanted to take him to college, but I was concerned about what my new roommate would think.
8. __4__ I shouldn't have worried because sitting on my roommate's pillow was the mangiest specimen of a teddy bear I had ever seen.

35B Vary Your Sentence Structure—page 146.

Rewrite the following. Use at least one compound sentence, one adverb clause, one adjective clause, one appositive, one participial phrase, one gerund, and one infinitive.

Answers will vary.

It is six o'clock, and I am starving [**compound sentence**]. Eating at my desk [**participial phrase**], I had only a small lunch, a Cobb salad [**appositve**]. I'll make some pasta with marinara sauce since that always fills me up [**adverb clause**]. I'll throw together a green salad and some garlic bread to subdue the hunger pangs [**infinitive**] that are gurgling in my stomach [**adjective clause**]. If that isn't enough [**adverb clause**], going out for pizza later [**gerund**] will do the trick.

35C More Infinitives

1. The chapters to read are lengthy.

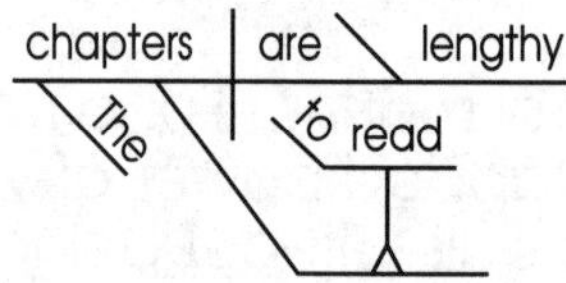

2. After you have learned to hum the melody, the lyrics are easy to memorize.

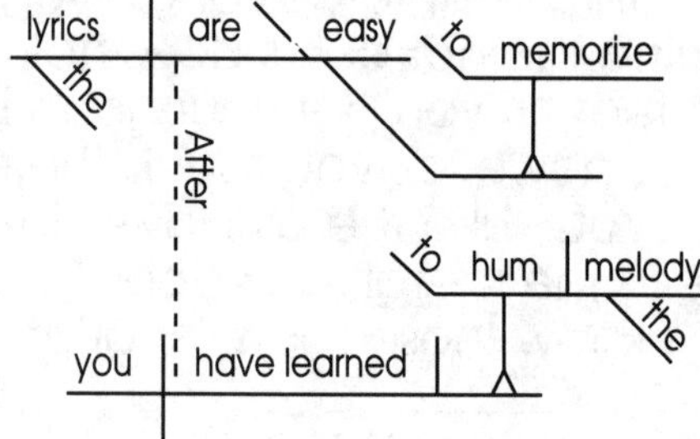

35D Grade the Essays—page 148.

Read the two essays below and determine which received the higher grade.
Answers will vary.

What makes one essay better than the other? Evaluate the essays for content, organization, grammar, spelling, and expression.
Organization, spelling of technical terms (Locke), expression, and grammar are problems in the second essay.

36A Active and Passive Verbs—page 149.

*Underline the verb and identify if it is active **(A)** or passive **(P)**.*

1. **A** The carpenter **struck** the nail on the head.
2. **P** Then, a thumb holding the nail **was struck** by the unfortunate carpenter.
3. **P** Several disgusting but colorful words **were uttered** by the workman.
4. **A, A** "I **will never hammer** another nail," **screamed** the enraged carpenter.
5. **P** However, nails **would be pounded** tomorrow by this man.
6. **P** The next day, his thumb **was bandaged** by yards of gauze.
7. **P** His pride **was** also **wounded**.
8. **A** Carpenters **should not mash** their digits.
9. **A** This carpenter **decided** to switch to plumbing.

36B Active and Passive Verbs—page 150.

Rewrite the sentences below changing passive verbs to active verbs wherever possible.
Answers will vary.

1. The aria was sung by the entire choir.
   The entire choir sung the aria.
2. An off-key note was struck by the tenor with the cold in the back row.
   In the back row, the tenor with the cold struck an off-key note.
3. The discordant sound was noticed.
   (Since we don't know who noticed the sound, we cannot change this verb to active.)
4. The tenor was embarrassed by his mistake.
   The mistake embarrassed the tenor.
5. Suddenly, sneezing was heard throughout the concert hall.
   Suddenly everyone in the concert hall heard the sneezing.
6. The tenor was hidden by the singers next to him.
   The singers next to the tenor hid him.
7. He was dragged off the stage into the wings by an irate stage manager.
   An irate stage manager dragged him off the stage into the wings.

Answer Key, Lessons 31-40, continued

36C Too Many Fragments!—page 151.

Correct the fragments and diagram the corrected sentence.

Answers will vary.

1. The first baseman hitting the ball into left field.

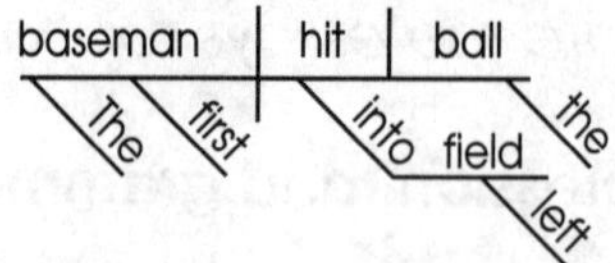

2. Making loud noises in a movie theater.

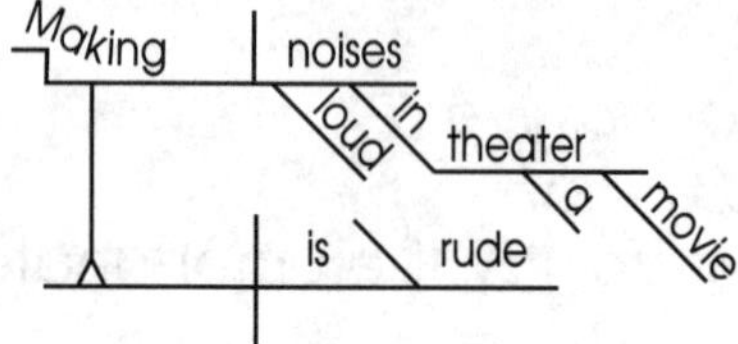

3. My friend, the kid with the freckles on his nose.

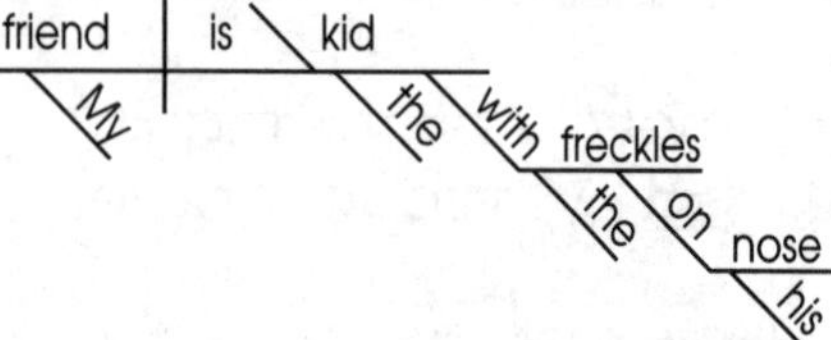

36D Proofreading—page 152.

Eliminate wordy expressions and correct the mistakes in the sentences below. Change passive verbs to active verbs if possible.

Answers will vary.

The Black Death (the bubonic plague) swept through medieval Europe in deadly waves. Though usually associated with Europe, **the plague was apparently born in China in the first century A.D.** After **traveling** slowly through Asia, it arrived in Eastern Europe in an extremely virulent form. During the worst of its reign, **between two-thirds and three-quarters of the population in parts of Europe died.** The death toll was **highest** in cities, since the flea **spreading** the plague lived on rats in densely populated city centers. Death was quick**.** **Most** people died within two or three days of noticing the first symptoms. The nursery rhyme "Ring around the Rosy" dates from the plague years. The "rosy" is the fleabite, and the "ring" is the inflamed circle around it. The posies are either the black swellings near the lymph nodes, or the flowers **brought by mourners** to ward off the smell of the dead bodies.

37A Verb Tenses—page 153.

Fill in the blank with the tense of the verb indicated.

1. You jump. (Future) **You will (shall) jump.**
2. We choose. (Present perfect) **We have chosen.**
3. I am. (Past perfect) **I had been.**
4. I drive. (Future perfect) **I will (shall) have driven.**
5. He finds. (Present progressive) **He is finding.**
6. They fly. (Future perfect progressive) **They will (shall) have been flying.**

7. You buy. (Past perfect progressive) **You had been buying.**
8. We take. (Present perfect progressive) **We have been taking.**
9. They rise. (Present perfect) **They have risen.**

37B Tense Ambiguity—page 154.

Choose the correct verb form to express the meaning indicated.

1. I (arrive) **arrived** at school when the bell (ring) **had rung**. (I got there after the bell.)
2. I (arrive) **arrived** at school when the bell (ring) **was ringing**. (I got there while the bell was going off.)
3. When I (arrive) **arrived**, I (miss) **had missed** half an hour of class. (I was half an hour late.)
4. At the end of the term, I (finish) **will finish** three years of Spanish. (The term ends soon, and my Spanish class ends at the same time.)
5. By the end of the term, I (finish) **will have finished** seven essays. (The term ends soon, and my essays are due a week earlier.)

37C Grab Bag—page 155.

From the words listed, create a sentence that fits the diagram.

1. **He slipped and fell, but fortunately, he avoided hurting himself seriously.**

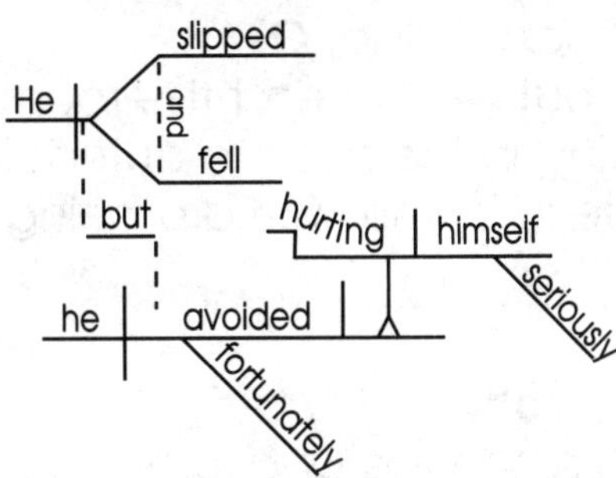

2. **By the light of the silvery moon, we danced the funky chicken while we made faces at each other.**

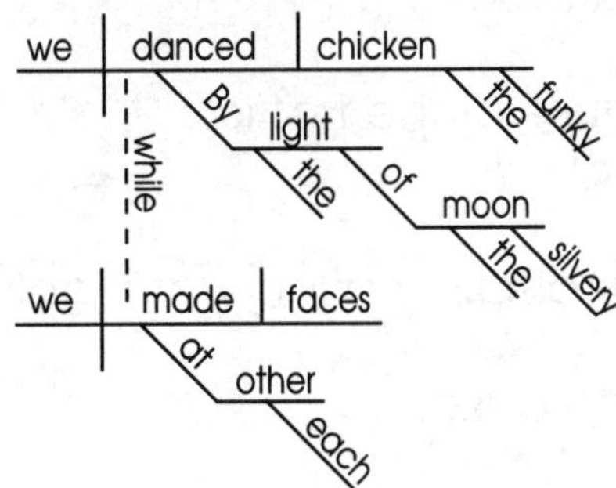

Answer Key, Lessons 31-40, continued

37D Correct the Tenses—page 156.

Correct the tenses in the following passage.

In the Hornblower saga written by C. S. Forester, the author **depicts** the difficult and often dangerous life of the young sailor during the early 19th century. He **describes** how boys as young as 10 years old **are** sent to sea during that period. Horatio Hornblower, at seventeen, **is** older than most midshipmen when he **signs** on to his first berth. He **is** the son of a poor clergyman who **has** died leaving Horatio with no inheritance. Life on shipboard **is** brutal. Singled out for hazing by an older midshipman, Mr. Simpson, Horatio **is** teased and tortured. To add to his problems, he **is** continually seasick. When other younger midshipmen **object** to Simpson's tyrannical rule, the bully **beats** them until they **are** unconscious.

38A Subjunctive Verbs—page 157.

Change the boldfaced verbs to the subjunctive.

1. If I **were** an expert, I would show you how to do it.
2. I wish I **were** climbing Mt. Everest.
3. If my father **were** king, then my mother **would be** queen.

*Correct the following sentences. Write **OK** after the ones that need no corrections.*

1. If the sun **were** out, we could have a picnic.
2. Since it is raining, we can stay warm and cozy inside. **OK**
3. I wish it **were** practical to build a hot tub, but we haven't the room.
4. If it **were** a warm rain, we could enjoy sitting in the hot tub outside.
5. After we build the hot tub, we will luxuriate in it while we are being tickled with peacock feathers. **OK**

38B Redundancy and Oxymorons—page 158.

*Underline the redundancy or oxymoron in each sentence and label it either **R** or **O**.*

1. **O** We need an **exact estimate** of the cost.
2. **R** This budget cut is **absolutely essential**.
3. **O** They are **alone together** in the back room.
4. **O** **Anarchy rules!**
5. **R** **The reason why** we are late **is because** of the traffic.
6. **R** Be ready at 8:00 **a.m. in the morning**!
7. **O** The ghost **appeared to be invisible**.
8. **R** The worker was fired **at a time when** discrimination was legal.
9. **O** **Save up to 50% and more.**
10. **O** This recipe makes a **12-ounce pound** cake.

38C Choose the Correct Form—page 159.

Diagram the sentence and then choose the correct word form.

1. If I (was, **were**) a hero, I would rush into that burning building.

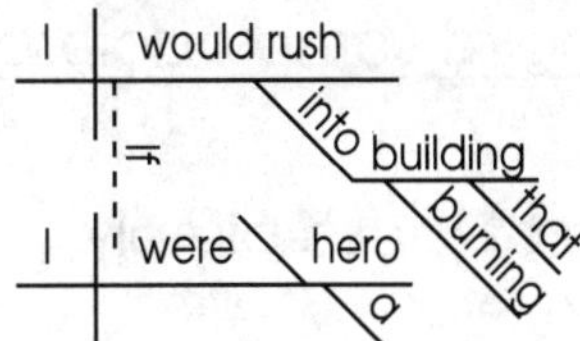

2. The firefighter hands the ax to (**whoever**, whomever) looks strong.

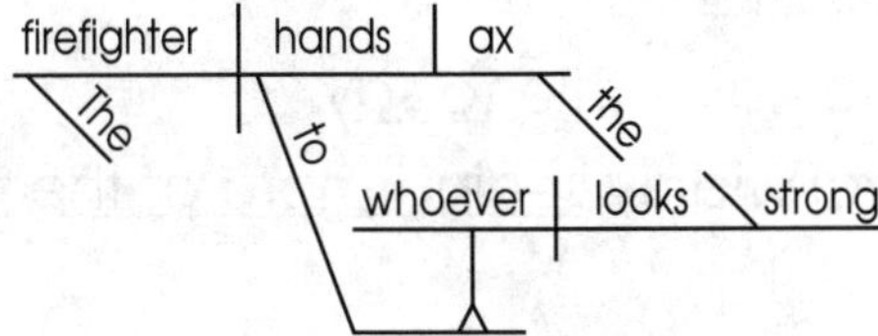

3. Because of our insistence, the firefighter gave us, Meg and (I, **me**), the kitten.

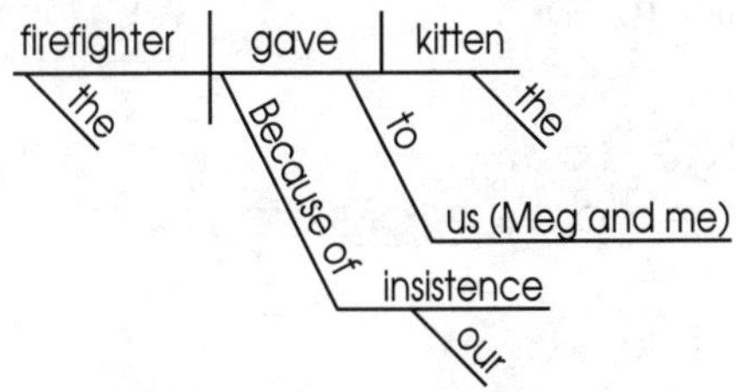

38D Proofreading—page 160.

Correct errors and rewrite wordy or ambiguous passages.

Answers will vary.

Consider the plight of the poor mermaid**.** **How** does she care for her skin? Her upper torso **is** bathed in salt water a good portion of the day. What kind of moisturizer can handle that abuse? **While she sits on the rocks, the sun scalds her bottom half.** Does sun screen work on fish scales? What SPF **provides sunburn protection? Combing out that long hair filled with salt water must be excruciating. Since shampooing** sever-al times a day is out of the question, if I **were** a mermaid I'd chop off my long locks right away. **Sitting out on the rocks in the sun day after day sounds boring.** For entertainment, a mermaid can sing **with a beckoning voice to attract sailors,** but suppose **she catches** a handsome one. What would **she** do with **him**? Perhaps mermaids like to toast sailors in the sun and eat them with tartar sauce.

Answer Key, Lessons 31-40, continued

39A Verbs and More Verbs—page 161.

Underline the verbals (infinitives, gerunds, participles), cross out the passive verbs and circle the subjunctive verbs (contrary to fact).

1. I ~~am disturbed~~ to see a lot of preteens screaming at some adolescent rock star.
2. Suppose you (were) a preteen, and you met one of these pimply millionaires.
3. What (would you say) to someone that rich?
4. Rock stars ~~are not known~~ for their intellectual prowess.
5. They may well be very dull people who have little to say.
6. On the other hand, perhaps they travel widely seeing more of the world than most ordinary people.
7. Most likely, they are just ordinary people fascinated by music.
8. The music ~~produced~~ by such people can be very creative.
9. Still, swooning over performers seems silly to me.

39B Words...Words...Words...Snore—page 162.

Rewrite the following sentences eliminating the wordy expressions.

Answers will vary.

1. There were fireworks dancing across the sky.
   Fireworks danced across the sky.
2. The dogs that were barking made a racket.
   The barking dogs made a racket.
3. On Independence Day, July 4th, there is barbeque smoke in the air.
   On July 4th, barbeque smoke fills the air.
4. Nothing beats a hot dog that is slathered with mustard and sauerkraut.
   Nothing beats a hot dog slathered with mustard and sauerkraut.
5. The grill is manned by my brother while the lemonade is stirred by my sister.
   My brother mans the grill while my sister stirs the lemonade.
6. There is always a pool party that is fun at my neighbor's house.
   My neighbor always throws a fun pool party.
7. The teens at the party were ogling the opposite sex, but little conversation was taking place.
   The teens at the party ogled but didn't talk to the opposite sex.

39C Misplaced Modifiers—page 163.

Rewrite the following sentences removing the ambiguity and then diagram.

Answers will vary.

1. The pre-school needs a 3-year old teacher.

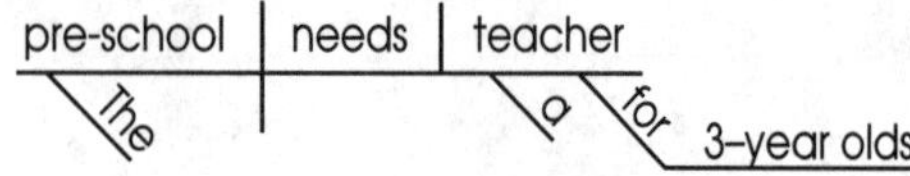

2. After driving for 50 years, Mr. Smith ran into a telephone pole.

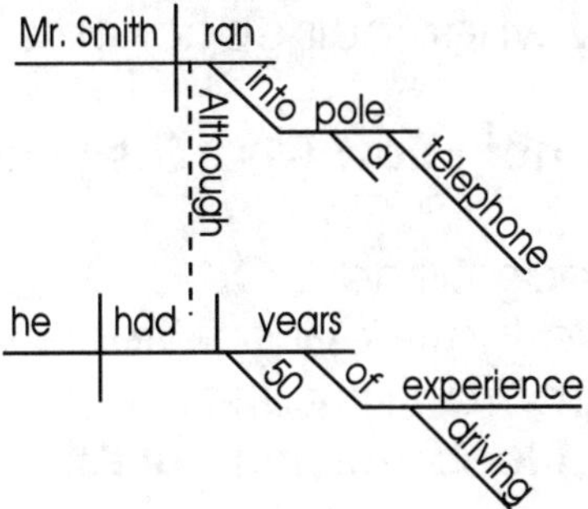

3. We need someone to care for Bessie, our cow, who does not smoke or drink.

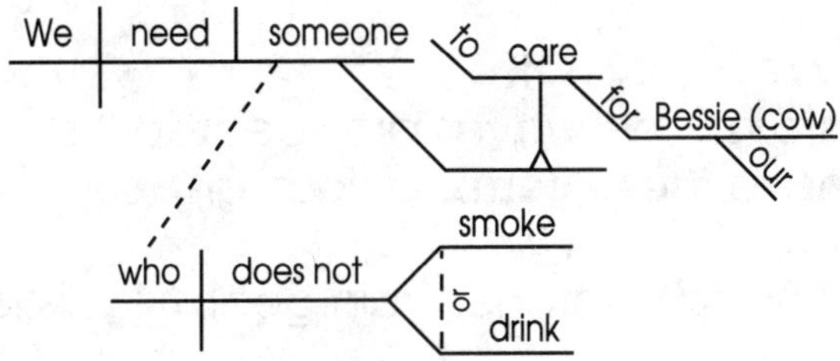

39D More Wordiness and Redundancy—page 164.

Rewrite the following passage eliminating the wordiness and redundancy.

Answers will vary.

The passage is a wordy rewrite of Abraham Lincoln's Gettysburg Address. Lincoln's address is a model of forceful, concise writing. Here is the start of the original.

> Four score and seven years ago, our fathers brought forth on this continent a new nation, conceived in Liberty, and dedicated to the proposition that all men are created equal.
>
> Now we are engaged in a great civil war, testing whether that nation, or any nation so conceived and so dedicated, can long endure. We are met on a great battle-field of that war.

40A Sentence Fragments—page 165.

Rewrite the sentence fragments below to make complete sentences. Write OK after any complete sentences.

Answers will vary.

1. Television wrestling is nothing like high school wrestling. **OK**
2. Seeing as wrestling on television is fixed.
   Wrestling on television is fixed.
3. High school wrestlers who train as rigorously as any school athlete.
   High school wrestlers train as rigorously as any school athlete.
4. In addition, high school wrestlers to watch their weight.
   In addition, high school wrestlers watch their weight.
5. Being that it is better to be in a lower weight division.
   It is better to be in a lower weight division.

Answer Key, Lessons 31-40, continued

6. However, television wrestlers are performers and acrobats. **OK**
7. Unlike high school wrestlers who do not know what their opponents are going to do.
   They are unlike high school wrestlers who do not know what their opponents are going to do.
8. Television wrestlers have all their moves choreographed. **OK**
9. I wish high school wrestlers had silly monikers like the television wrestlers. **OK**
10. High school wrestlers wearing those great leopard skin outfits.
    High school wrestlers should wear those great leopard skin outfits.

40B Commas, Semicolons, and Colons—page 166.

*Correct the punctuation and the sentence structure in the following sentences. If a sentence is correct, mark it **OK.***

1. Hurricanes frighten me and terrify my dog. **OK**
2. I like to go to the beach after a storm**;** the waves are spectacular.
3. If a storm threatens, you should have **these items:** a flashlight, some bottled water, and a first aid kit.
4. The complete list includes the following: matches, rain gear, a whistle, and Granola bars. **OK**
5. Hurricanes rarely hit Southern California**;** in fact**,** they usually miss the entire West Coast.
6. The states that have been extensively damaged by hurricanes in recent years **are the following:** North Carolina, Texas, South Carolina, Georgia, and Florida.

40C Mixed Practice—page 167.

Diagram the following. Use your imagination.

1. Although the Braves tried to slip into first place, the Mets were unstoppable.

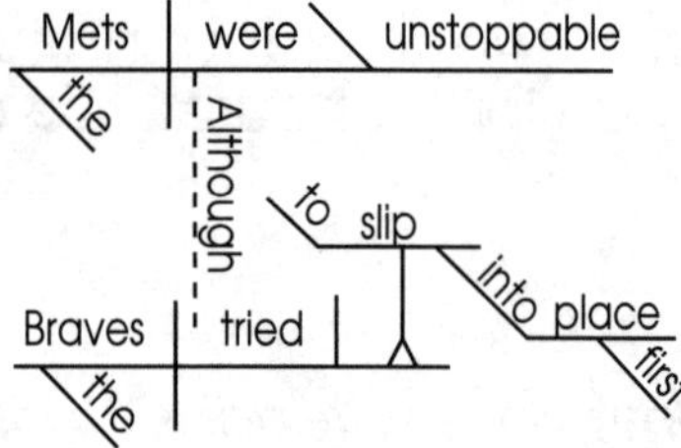

2. The constant dribbling and shooting of basketball are exciting; in comparison, baseball is boring.

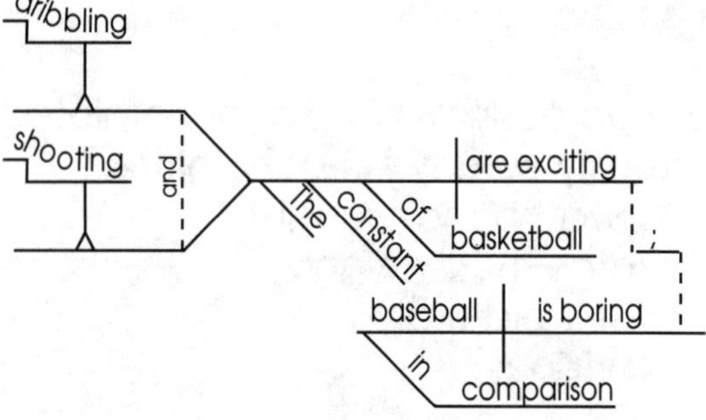

40D Spell-check Goofs—page 168.

The spell-check says the following poem has no errors. What does it say?

I'd never win a spelling bee,
But anything I write
Is spell-checked by my new PC,
So everything is right.

The teachers working at this school
Hate spelling words confused,
So spell-check is a useful tool
Which always should be used.

You can see how well I write
With my spell-checker's aid.
I do my work with confidence
And no mistakes are made.

REVIEW Lessons 31-40—page 169.

Rewrite the sentences using the parts of speech indicated.

1. To run on the beach is good exercise. Gerund
   Running on the beach is good exercise.
2. You should stretch your muscles before you exercise because it is important. Gerund
   Stretching your muscles before you exercise is important.
3. The runner who is panting is out of shape. Participle
   The panting runner is out of shape.
4. Personally, I prefer sleeping. Infinitive
   Personally, I prefer to sleep.

Choose the best sentence in each group. Explain what is wrong with each of the others.

A. <u>Displaying them on the blackboard</u>, the teacher encouraged the students to create original paintings. **Misplaced Modifer**
B. <u>There are paintings</u> displayed on the blackboard that encourage students to be original. **Wordy**
C. **The teacher encouraged the students to create original paintings by displaying them on the blackboard.**
D. The teacher displayed the students' art on the blackboard, as a result the students created original paintings. **Run-On**
E. Paintings <u>were displayed</u> on the blackboard by the teacher to encourage the students to create original art. **Wordy, Passive**

A. Children enjoy a variety of media; painting, sculpting, and <u>collages</u>. **Semicolon, Parallelism**
B. Children enjoy a variety of media <u>such as:</u> painting, sculpting, and making collages. **Colon Error**

Answer Key, Lessons 31-40, continued

C. **Children enjoy a variety of media: painting, sculpting, and making collages.**
D. Children enjoy a variety of media: painting, sculpting, and collages. **Parallelism**

Choose the correct word.

1. The leads in the play, Jason and (**she**, her), were unconvincing.
2. If I (was, **were**) the lead, I'd take a different approach.
3. The villain (who, **whom**) I detest is quite handsome.
4. (Whoever, **Whomever**) the director chooses will get the lead.

Correct the errors and eliminate clichés and wordiness in the following passage.
Answers will vary.

In each deck of standard playing cards **every king, queen, and jack represents an historical character. The king of hearts represents Charlemagne, the Emperor of Rome who oddly enough is not wellknown for his love life.** The king of clubs is Alexander the Great. **The king of diamonds sporting a wicked mustache is** supposed to be Julius Caesar**. However, a** Roman with a mustache seems unlikely. The king of spades **is** supposed to be King David of the **Bible.** Do you wonder who chose such a bizarre collection of **heroes**?

SKILL CHECK Lessons 31-40—page 171.

Rewrite the sentences using the parts of speech indicated.

1. I like to cook, but mostly I love to eat. Infinitives
2. Measuring ingredients carefully is important when cooking. Gerund
3. The Soup simmering on the stove smells fragrant. Participle

Choose the best sentence in each group. Explain what is wrong with each of the others.

A. **Wrapped in an old shawl, the elderly man carried a smelly fish he had caught in the river.**
B. The elderly man carried a smelly fish wrapped in an old shawl he caught in the river. **Ambiguity, Tense**
C. The elderly man carried a smelly fish he caught in the river wrapped in an old shawl. **Dangling Participle, Ambiguity, Tense**
D. The elderly man carried a smelly fish that he caught in the river, it was wrapped in an old shawl. **Tense, Run-on**

A. There are old boots, tires, and dead fish floating in the rivers of most major cities which shows how polluted they are. **Wordy, Antecedent, Ambiguity**
B. The old boots, tires, and dead fish floating in the rivers of most major cities show how polluted they are. **Ambiguity**
C. The old boots, tires, and dead fish floating in the rivers of most major cities. This garbage demonstrates how polluted our waterways are. **Fragment**

D. **Floating in the rivers of most major cities, the old boots, tires, and dead fish show how polluted our waterways are.**

Choose the correct word.

1. (Me, **My**) dancing is a sight to see.
2. Either the boys or I (**am**, are) responsible.
3. I washed my hair after I (finished, **had finished**) my homework.
4. I would feel more relaxed if my science project (was, **were**) finished.
5. Elect the two candidates best for the job, Jason and (I, **me**).

Correct the errors and eliminate clichés and wordiness in the following passage.

Answers will vary.

A dead whale that had washed up on the beach caused a nuisance in a small Oregon town. The highway department asked to clean up the odiferous object, decided to dispose of it **as they disposed of old highways: blow it up.** They stacked dynamite underneath the beached behemoth and sent the onlookers well back into the dunes. When they pushed the plunger, the whale exploded, raining rancid whale parts all over news crews and onlookers. **The falling whale guts crushed a car parked more than a quarter mile away. Unfortunately,** the whale didn't disintegrate sufficiently for the sea gulls and crabs to finish the clean-up job. Instead, the highway crew was forced to bury the remains.